A Fire Within

Someone Set the Fire and Left Us for Dead

By Sherry Graves

Copyright © 2012 Sherry Graves

Copyright © 2012 Lady Knight Enterprises Publishing

Lawrenceville, Georgia www.ladyknightenterprisespublishing.com

All rights reserved. Contents and/or cover may not be reproduced in whole or in part in any form without the express written consent of the Author or Publisher. This includes stored in a retrieval system, or transmitted in any form or means, for example but not limited to; photocopying, recording, electronic copying etc., other than purchased as an e-book.

Printed in the United States of America.

A Fire Within

Someone Set the Fire and Left Us for Dead

ISBN-10: 0615671756
ISBN-13: 978-0615671758 (Lady Knight Enterprises Publishing)
LCCN- 2012944792

Cover Design inspired by Sherry Graves and created by Rhonda Knight

All quoted biblical scriptures are from the King James Version-Liberty University, 1988

To N
La'Trese,
Michala, Achaunte

Love
Sherry

DEDICATION

I wish to dedicate this book to my loving grandparents, Austin & Indiana Malone for leaving their legacy of "family first" behind for generations to come, and to the love of my life (besides Dee,) my handsome father "Lis" Graves,

And, especially to Josh who remains in that sacred place in my heart.....

RIP Forever....

ACKNOWLEDGEMENTS

First of all, thank you Lord, for giving me the vision to give birth to this spiritual assignment. I would also like to give a very special thanks to Ms. Laura Pagano, for without her the divine connection with my brilliant Publisher, Ms. Lady Rhonda Knight, an awesome woman of God, would never have happened. Thanks, to both of you ladies for believing in my vision and helping me to make it a reality.

And to my beautiful cousin, Denise and her amazingly handsome husband, Kev, thank you for giving birth to the title of my book, "A Fire Within".

CONTENTS

	DEDICATION	
	ACKNOWLEDGEMENT	v
	FOREWORD	x
	INTRODUCTION	xi
CHAPTER 1	FAMILY FIRST	1
CHAPTER 2	FUN TIMES	7
CHAPTER 3	THE FAST TRACK	13
CHAPTER 4	THE CRACK EPIDEMIC	23
CHAPTER 5	NO WAY OUT	35
CHAPTER 6	THE FIRE	38
CHAPTER 7	BUT FOR THE "GRACE OF GOD"	43
CHAPTER 8	I WILL CREATE A NEW SPIRIT IN YOU	48
CHAPTER 9	BOND FOR LIFE	50
CHAPTER 10	BEHIND MY SCARS	55
CHAPTER 11	THE RELAPSE	64
CHAPTER 12	IN TREATMENT	72
CHAPTER 13	HE MET ME IN MY LOWEST PLACE AND HE PULLED ME OUT	84
CHAPTER 14	MY JOURNEY BACK	89
CHAPTER 15	BABY STEPS	95
CHAPTER 16	GONE BUT NEVER FORGOTTEN	98

CHAPTER 17	THE "BIG" WEDDING	103
CHAPTER 18	ROCKED OUR WORLD	106
CHAPTER 19	BETTER AND BETTER	109
CHAPTER 20	HEART BROKEN	111
CHAPTER 21	9/11	114
CHAPTER 22	LIFE CHANGING	118
CHAPTER 23	JUST GETTING STARTED	120
CHAPTER 24	MY SHINING STAR	128
CHAPTER 25	A POWER MOVE	131
CHAPTER 26	LIFE AFTER	143
CHAPTER 27	BEYOND MY SCARS	148
CHAPTER 28	A FIRE WITHIN	156
	LOVE THOUGHTS TO THE LORD AND THANK YOU'S...	165
	LOVE LETTERS FROM MY FAMILY	172
	TEN JEWELS FOR MY READERS	179
CHAPTER 29	THE STRAIGHT FACTS ABOUT DRUGS	184
	ABOUT THE AUTHOR-BIOGRAPHY	239
	COLETTE, DORIAN & LAURA'S BUSINESS INFORMATION	242

FOREWORD

"A Fire Within" is brilliantly written! Sherry Graves writes from the heart, allowing God to lead her as she pens her work. Therefore, her readers are sure to be blessed and benefit from the excellent literature displayed in this book that depicts Ms. Graves' story. She is open and honest as she retells her life's plight, the good, the bad and yes, even the ugly. She brings hope to those who may struggle from various forms of addiction and to the family members of those addicted or recovering. This book that recounts her journey, proves that when you trust in God, He will deliver you from all things and set you on a path to a blessed life full of purpose. Sometimes we think God has left us because of our making unhealthy decisions in our lives, but know this, that when you give your life to Christ, the Lord will never leave you nor forsake you. God knows that you will come back to Him eventually and He is waiting for you. He has that much love for each of us. Remember, we all fall short and must come before God daily and ask for forgiveness, and He is so faithful to forgive each of us. As you read this book, allow the Lord to minister to you, because there is a wealth of knowledge and love poured into "A Fire Within". Now it's time for your flame to burn brightly and for you to shine as an example for others, just as Sherry does…

Yours in Love,

International Author, Motivational Speaker and Talk Show Host, Evangelist Rhonda Knight

INTRODUCTION

Millions of people in the world either have a drug problem or know and love someone that is addicted to drugs. In my book "A Fire Within" what I'm sharing with my readers is an honest depiction of the life of a former drug addict. But what's more important is that it's also my testimony about being a victorious over comer. So to all of you out there who are addicted to drugs, what I really want you to know is that if I did it so can you. In "A Fire Within" I am especially willing to share my "Rock Bottom" experiences with my readers to let you see the truth about drugs. I'm giving it to you raw just like it happened to me. I'm not "sugar coating" any of it. This is done intentionally because I want my readers to know the real deal. This is my story of how God saved my life in more ways than one. Come with me as I take you on this journey from drug addiction to a Spiritual healing. But be sure to buckle up because we're going on one heck of a ride. I'm sharing my testimony with you in hopes of saving you or someone you know and love. The bad choices I made almost cost me my life, more than once.

Honestly, by the time I saw the real trouble coming it was already too late. My life has never been the same. If I could turn back the hands of time I would but since I can't, I choose to share my testimony with you. As you read about my life you will see that the picture wasn't always pretty. As a matter of fact it's going to get really ugly. But if you ask anyone addicted to drugs what their lifestyle is like and if they tell the truth, what they will share is that it's ugly. In "A Fire Within" I'm giving you a look inside that lifestyle. And for those of you that have ever wondered what a person addicted to drugs' life really looks like, don't worry; after reading this book you will know. The drug lifestyle is real, it's dirty, and it's grimy. Many of my family members and friends know my story, but they don't really know my "story" and for some of them they will be hearing parts of my life for the first time ever, that is sure to blow them away (love you all, LOL). But what was most profound to me throughout my Journey was finding out that God will meet you even in your lowest places, he will pick you up, bring you out and set you on "Higher Ground". To all of you reading my story if you have a substance abuse problem, and for all of you who are even thinking about using drugs, but especially to my young people that have never used drugs, I want you to know that you don't have to try to take care of a bill that's already been paid for by me and so many others. Of course anyone can make the decision to use drugs and it may or may not take you to the places that it took me to. But the question I have for you is "Are you willing to take that chance"? It breaks my heart every time I think about my close friends that were killed as a result of their drug addiction and the lifestyle. They are not here to tell their story today. I will share their lives with my readers so as not to let their deaths' be in vain. Each of "my girls" that I lost were good people but just like me and so many other people out there they just got caught up and unfortunately they never made it out. But if you don't get anything else out of hearing my story, I want you to make sure that the choices you make in your life are taking you on the Journey you really want to be on. Yes, I have regrets but through it all I never lost my faith in God. I am alive today sharing my testimony with you "But For the Grace of God". God saved me and he uses me as a vessel to encourage, motivate and support others and lift them up in their spirits. And so I graciously give Him myself. My life is not my own it belongs to God. And my scars are my "Gifts from God". So grab some munchies, sit back chill and read on!!

CHAPTER 1

"FAMILY FIRST"

Hello Ms. Malone, I'm Dr. Meyer. Ma'am I am so sorry to inform you all that we have done everything in our power to save your granddaughter. I'd like to suggest to everyone that if your family believes in a Higher-Power, Sherry needs all the prayers she can get right now, unfortunately her condition is critical. She has a fifty-fifty chance of living or dying. Sherry sustained 3rd degree burns, covering twenty percent of her body in the fire. We are watching her closely. We have her on a treatment protocol that will help in preventing infections from setting in, however her will to survive is crucial at this point. Someone cried, oh no, no! As the news spread from one family member to the next, they started showing up to the hospital. Oh my God, it's not looking good, the doctor's said they don't know if she's going to make it. Oh God please let her be ok! Crying and holding each other trying to comfort one another, one by one my family started to breakdown after hearing the news. My aunt and cousins that arrived at the hospital first were so distraught when they realized that I really was in a fire. My aunt Glo was so overwhelmed, she passed out in the waiting area. There were other family members who had to be escorted out of the waiting area and into other areas of the hospital because it was too much for them to deal with. Is she going to be ok?, where is she? Doctor can we see her? How badly burned is she?

Laying in my hospital bed all alone I was so broken. I had been unconscious the past several weeks. I was in so much pain. The pain I was feeling wasn't physical, it was emotional and every time I looked at my badly burned body, I wanted to disappear. Will those horrible images of being in a fire ever get out of my head? Why would someone want to kill me? Kill us? I knew I would never be the same Sherry again. I didn't know how I was ever going to accept what happened. It hurt so bad that tears were in my eyes, yet I couldn't even cry. I laid there thinking about the drugs and how much fun I had in the beginning smoking cigarettes and marijuana, hanging out. No one could have told me back then that the weed would turn into crack cocaine and that the drug lifestyle would nearly cost me my life. And after all of the things that I've been through, I never dreamed that I would be telling my story about a journey from drug addiction to a total Spiritual healing.

Reminiscing about my life and my family, I began thinking about all of the good times. It was the only thing that helped me feel better. We were so happy growing up. My parents Mina and Lis had three children, Ramel, Colia and of course me. Unfortunately, they divorced and the funny thing is I can't ever remember a time when we were all together as a family. That's because I was still a baby when mommy and daddy separated. Ramel is the oldest, he's our brother and our protector, the only person who could bother any of us was him. Having Ramel for a big brother is like laying on the beach, with an ice cold beverage and huge palm trees hanging all around, he is so refreshing. Ramel is that dude, you know the one everyone enjoys being around, he is so lively, upbeat and exhilarating. When you are in his company, he has the gift to make you feel like a king or queen. I always count on him being there. Ramel would do anything for family and friends. I never have to worry about anything because my big brother always makes sure we are good. Growing up, no boys could talk to my sisters and I when he was around. I could just hear him now, man you better get out of here. Dude would be laughing because they all knew what time it was. I know for sure Ramel missed his calling, he should have been a comedian. Sometimes he has my stomach aching from laughing so hard. He would definitely make lots of money! I love my brother so much. Then there is my sis Colia, AKA Cocoa, she is one year younger than Ramel and the second oldest child. Cocoa is my next breath. She is beautiful; we call her Cocoa because that's what her complexion looks like. Cocoa, she's like fine wine, she just gets better with age. But I try not to tell her that too often, we have a hard enough time trying to keep her away from cameras as it is. I love my sis so much. She and I have always been like twin sisters, we are inseparable. She is only two years older than I and I guess that's why we are so close. Growing up we did everything together, we slept together and took baths together. We played together and got beatings together. We laughed together and cried together. I can't imagine my life without her. Cocoa is a Champion, she has always been that girl, you know that go-to-girl that everyone wants around, because you know she will get the job done. Even at a young age she was the responsible one. When Ramel and I did something stupid, she would be the one to say, if ya'll do it I'm telling ma or if ya'll don't do it I'm telling ma. Cocoa had her first job at around thirteen years old. She gives me strength when I don't even know I have it. I was always the baby of the family that is, until mommy got pregnant eleven years later, that's when she gave birth to Shainne, our little sister. Shainne is our Diamond. When Mina got pregnant she told us she was having a girl. Even though we were in New York and she was living in St. Thomas V.I. at the time, we went through the whole pregnancy with her. She would call and ask us what names we had for our baby sister, I wanted Tiffany, Cocoa had chosen a few names and Ramel, well he really didn't care one way or another, all he knew was that he just wanted her to be healthy. The funny thing was nine months later and twenty-five different names from each of us, our lil sis was born and mommy named her Shainne, and we all loved Shainne. I remember it so clearly, the day finally came, we were all standing in Kennedy Airport, Cocoa, ma and daddy, (which are our grandparents), Ramel and I. We were searching the faces of everyone in the baggage area, looking for our mother whom we had not seen for a few years. She was coming to New York to stay for a while this time, and she was bringing our little sister with her. This was the first time we would meet her. We were all so excited then finally, we spotted her and the first thing I saw in her arms was this beautiful little girl and from that day, she stole our heart. Mina had Shainne's hair in a thousand colorful barrettes. She was wearing the prettiest pink dress with sandals that matched her outfit and her tiny little toes were so pretty. She even had some little gold bangles on Shainne's arms. For all of my life it had only been me, my brother and sis, now we had a little sister and she was our prize. We were all trying to grab her out of mommy's hands, we held little Shainne so tight. All the while she was just smiling and looking at each of us. Poor child must have been wondering who are these fools? All of us just cheezin and smiling, basically we were looking stupid. We all took turns grabbing her out of each other's hands. All of us felt the same way, Shainne is our baby sis and no one better not ever dream about hurting her because they would get beat down by all three of us. Shainne was born in St. Thomas Virgin Islands. In fact, my family is of West Indian descent from the Caribbean. I am blessed to have a family who has always loved me unconditionally.

One day I was Sherry, a beautiful little girl with chubby cheeks and with caramel skin tone as brown as honey. My piercing brown eyes and juicy lips all complimented my round face. I was blessed with beautiful shiny jet black hair (although now I have a head full of naturally dyed red hair, LOL) that caressed my shoulders, which everyone loves. My mother Mina always says I got my beautiful hair from my grandmother on my father's side, her name was Darling (rest in peace Darling, love you). She was Cherokee Indian and the joke is I really do have Indian in my family. By the way every time Cocoa heard mommy telling someone about my hair it made her sick to her stomach because unfortunately for Cocoa she did not benefit from that same gene. Growing up Cocoa's hair was short and kinky. Well I might as well just put it out there, the child's hair was just plain nappy, not even a super perm could straighten out those naps back then, (sorry sis). But thank God for jheri curls in the late seventies because when my sis first got her curls, you couldn't tell that poor child a thing.

I remember when Cocoa was about ten years old and I was eight, we were in our front yard playing together as we did every day however, Ramel was not outside with us at the time. At first she and I were playing dress up, (this is where we would act like our favorite characters that we watched on

TV). This one day in particular, I don't know what we was thinking but we got to talking real stupid and the next thing I knew we got into a major fist fight over some scissors we were playing with. Then after that, it was on. We were in our yard throwing down, pulling, screaming and cursing like crazy, fighting for the scissors. The craziest thing was that the person who won would get the scissors but they also had to cut their own hair off. Stupid right, well we realize that now but back then we was going at it, clearly we were both delirious. I'm still thanking God to this day, that was one fight I was so glad my sis won. When our grandmother came home from work that evening and saw Cocoa with her head almost bald and we told her what happened, both of us got a behind whipping so bad, we still regret it even today. I can't believe we played such a stupid game. Nowadays when we talk about that fight, I start cracking up and Cocoa gets pissed off. So that's why she was so happy when jheri curls came out because her nappy hair never grew back after she cut it off. Cocoa loved her curls so much, I think she was the last person on earth who wore her jheri curls. Oh my bad! There was only one more person even happier than Cocoa, her husband Quan. Truth be told his happiest time was when she finally got rid of her curls in the "nineties" and by that time Quan wasn't the only one sick of jheri Curls, everyone was. But even I have to admit it now, my sis has beautiful hair almost as long as mine, key word is "almost".

 I've been complimented so many times about my curvaceous bowlegs and told that my legs are runway material, of course I agree. But enough about me (crazy, child). We were raised by our grandparents' ma and daddy (pops), they moved to New York in the 1950's and bought a two family home in East New York, in Brooklyn. Growing up, I never considered our area the ghetto or anything because compared to the other neighborhoods in Brooklyn, we were chillin. The teenagers in the community had these slangs that they used to identify the different neighborhoods. There was Bed-Stuy "do-or-die", Brownsville "never-ran-never-will," which was funny to me because at the time I was living in Brownsville, all I ever did was run and most of the time it was from gunshots. There are projects all over Brooklyn including Cypress Hills, Pink Houses, Linden Plaza, Vandyke Houses, Tilden Projects, and Marcy Projects. Back in the day Sutter Avenue was the place to be. Anybody in East New York knew about Milford and Sutter. They especially knew about those sista's that lived in the house right on the corner of Milford Street, the house with the balcony. Ma and daddy lived downstairs and Ramel, Cocoa and I lived upstairs. Their house is warm and inviting, their living room has all the comforts of home. Ma has pictures of all six of their children, and their thirty-something grandchildren and great grand's, covering the walls and sitting on tables. The beautiful burgundy and white velour living room set (with the plastic slip covers still on them, lol), and matching burgundy carpet made the room look so cozy. At home I always felt safe and loved. My grandparents purchased the home when I was just a baby and after living there for over forty years, thank God the house is paid for and it's ours. Being born and raised in that house, I can honestly say we had it going on. Growing up we had the run of the whole house, it was every kid's dream.

After three children together my parents weren't getting along. I think it had something to do with the fact that my father realized that my mother was crazy as, "you know what" and she wasn't having anymore of his drama. But even with their separation, we loved both of our parents equally. When we were small mommy traveled back and forth from New York to the Virgin Islands. After their divorce my father always remained a constant part of our lives. My father was a tall big man. He had to be at least 6"4 and I'm guessing he weighed about 290-300 pounds. He was chocolate brown and he had curly hair, that is before it started balding on top. I would always crack up about his bald head. He was a big man, so sweet and gentle, but as sweet as he was, you definitely didn't want to catch him on a bad day. We all looked forward to seeing him holidays and birthdays and we always talked to him on the telephone. My father was the love of my life, in my eyes, he could do no wrong. He instilled in me values and taught me how to be a lady. My father adored each of us equally. He was a family man, he loved his family very much. He was so giving of himself and he loved cooking and listening to Calypso music. He would come pick us up for the weekend and take us back home with him to spend time together. Whenever we were at his house, my father would have his music blasting so loud and he would cook us all kinds of Caribbean food. He showered all of us with so much love. When I was a little girl, he bought me a red tricycle. Whenever we stayed at his apartment, I loved riding my bike. My father called me Minna-Soda-Fats, (I think he was a pool shark or something like that). I got into trouble at daddy's house too. One day he left us at home and went out somewhere. Ramel, Cocoa and I were running around playing all crazy in the house. All of a sudden I ran and jumped on top of his glass table. The next thing I knew, I went crashing in through the middle of the table. I found myself sitting on the floor inside the table. The only thing left was the round frame. The glass shattered all over the place, but I did not have a scratch on my body and then the funniest thing happened after that. I started crying immediately, because Ramel and Cocoa started scaring me. Ooh! You are going to be in so much trouble. Daddy is gonna get you! I was so scared, I was crying hours before my father even came home. So by the time he got home, he saw the glass all over the place and his broken table. All he said was, what happened? And just like two birds, Cocoa and Ramel started singing. Sherry did it, we were playing and she jumped on the table and broke it. I yelled and screamed, I became hysterical saying they're lying daddy. I did not break your table, they both broke it. Crying my eyes out. My father did not say anything. I guess he knew I was lying, after all I was the only one crying like a crazy person. He just checked me to make sure I was not cut or bleeding and he actually laughed then cleaned up the mess and never said another word about it. Later on that night Ramel and Cocoa both double teamed me, cursing me out for lying about what really happened.

When we became teenagers we loved staying with our father because we could chill at his place. He'd let us hang outside at night with the other crazy people who were outside. He lived in River Park Towers a sort of Co-op, but basically it was a really nice building in the projects. On the ride to the Bronx. Daddy always said the same thing, ya'll want to go eat now? And every time I was the first one to shout, we want McDonalds and he would crack up laughing. I could eat two Big Macs, fries and a soda. Nowadays I can only eat one Big Mac.

As for my mother Mina, she is my heart, she is the reason I am. She taught me how to be free and to be myself. When I am in my mother's comfort, I know that I am protected always and she will never let anything happen to any of us. Mommy is so loving and caring, however she had an issue. She never really liked living in N.Y. because she was born and raised in St. Thomas V.I., so she needs to be home in the beautiful island beaches, eating mangos and coconuts. Growing up mommy would come to New York, spend time with us and then before it started getting cold, she was gone again. She would go back and forth every year. Mommy left us with ma and daddy because she knew that we were well taken care of.

Ma, my grandmother is mommy's mother. She's not just ma, she is my ma. Now here is a woman who gave her heart to taking care of her family and not only her family but her friends too. Ma is where we all got our beauty from, her honey brown skin tone is so pretty. Even in her late 80's she didn't look a day over 70. She still had all of her teeth and the most beautiful smile and she had blue eyes, go figure. When ma laughed, heaven smiled. She had a head full of straight jet black hair. I remember putting her rollers in her hair many, many nights. Ma is my "Shining Star" when I need her I know exactly where to look. She has always been there for all of us.

And daddy, my grandfather he is the kindest and the most gentlest man that I have ever known in my life. daddy and ma were married over fifty years and if we saw them argue five times, that was a lot. I always knew he put his family first and when I needed him the most, he showed me what love really means. He was there for me in a way that I will never, ever forget.

CHAPTER 2

"FUN TIMES"

As a child growing up, I was full of life. I loved playing games with Cocoa and Ramel. Our lil sis Shainne was not born during this time. Every night after we finished our homework, the three of us would dash downstairs in our basement and play a game called skelly for hours or sometimes we played double-dutch, even though Ramel would never admit it today, but yes, truth be told, he played jump rope with his sister's and he had just as much fun as we did (sorry R.). When we weren't playing skelly, we played school. We even had a blackboard, chalk, and all the paper and books we needed to make school real. One of us would be the teacher while the rest played as students.

The only thing that could compare to this fun was playing with my baby dolls. Every Christmas Cocoa and I got dolls for presents from our aunts. But none of those dolls could hold a candle to my two best baby dolls ever. I'll never forget that I got Baby-that-Away for Christmas, then I got Baby Alive for my birthday. Now Baby Alive was a trip, I know ya'll Diva's from the old school remember that doll. All ya'll girls who had that doll know we had the bomb baby doll, she really ate her baby food. I mean her mouth moved and she sucked her bottle and everything. And my other baby was Baby-That-Away, this doll actually walked around. Boy, you could not tell me I wasn't the bomb mommy. I had a ball feeding my babies and changing their clothes every two seconds. Most of all I loved telling my babies what to do.

But nothing, and I mean absolutely nothing in this world could out do my biggest pleasure, yep, sucking my thumbs. Notice I said thumbs because it did not matter which one, left or right when I got tired of one, I would just stick the other one right in my mouth. I started sucking my thumbs at about age two and by five years old I was completely hooked. My family tried everything to get me to stop. They would put all kinds of things on my fingers like hot sauce, spit, dirt anything they could think of. But they really thought they had got me good when my aunt Lee (she's mommy's sister), was so tired of me sucking my thumbs that one day she tackled me threw me on the ground and put some of my little cousin's doo-doo on my thumb. You can bet when my aunt saw me get up off the ground and run to wash my hands off and I stuck my thumb right back in my mouth, they knew then this child is serious. My mother spoiled me with that because she would tell all of them, leave the girl alone. I guess since mommy sucked her finger when she was a little girl that sure did help me out. As far as I was concerned I was never going to stop sucking my thumbs. As grown as I thought I was, I sucked my thumbs morning, noon and night, yep for breakfast, lunch and dinner. I suppose that was a sign that I was really that little girl lost. No one was more surprised than I when I finally did stop. But of course that didn't happen until I turned thirty years old and even then I went through major trauma having to give my thumbs up. Oh I might as well get this out now too, I did not stop playing with my baby dolls until I was fifteen and by then it was just way too emotional for me.

For years Ma had Cocoa and I on lockdown, so forced to play in the house, we made the best of it. Our basement became our playground. But as we started getting a little older, Ma took the ropes and chains off, little by little. She started letting us play outside, but of course it had to be on the porch or in the yard. We had a ball playing in our gate and instead of jumping rope in the basement, now we could chill on the stoop. so that's when we were playing hop scotch, jacks, skelly, hide and seek, hot peas and butter, we loved all of those games. The older we got Ma would give us a little more room to breathe but we definitely couldn't go off the block. Eventually we could go out the gate, but we better not be too far. Now mind you Ramel had it good, because even though he is only one year older than Cocoa and two years older than me, he was able to hang out wherever he wanted. He could even leave from in front the house. Of course Cocoa and I would be pissed, how come he gets to leave from in front the house Ma? And every time she would say the same thing, because he is a boy. We must have heard that a million times and every time we heard it, the madder Cocoa and I got. That was cool, because soon we were able to go outside the gate too. We began hanging out around the corner on Milford Street between Sutter and Blake, roller skating our behinds off. We would be skating up and down the block, sometimes on just one skate each, we loved skating and Ramel did too. I was never really able to skate backwards, but you couldn't tell me that.

Hanging out around the corner is where we met all of our childhood friends. Cee-Cee and Kat, they were sisters just a couple years older than me and my sis. They lived with their mom and brother (RIP/poppa) on the second floor at 310 Milford Street, back in the day that was the place to be. Ms. Ann was a grown woman she had daughters Karen, Natrina and her son (Rest in Peace, Meme), and her husband Mr. Jess, they lived on the first floor. They were down to earth and if anyone knew the happenings and the "goings-on" 24/7, they did. Then there was Zay, lil mama, and their mother Gerry, they all lived on the second floor too, right next door to Cee-Cee and Kat. They all lived in the same building and we were like family. So everyone would be running either upstairs or downstairs, depending on where the drama was "going on". The drama didn't stop there, because directly across the street at 307 Milford Street was our other best girlfriends, Shakia and Toni girl. They were sisters the same age as Cocoa and I. They lived with their parents, Ms. Miriam (RIP/love you), Buzz their father and their younger brother. We hung out at their house every day too. And right next door to them were the Gregs. They had a son, everyone called him Fat Tony. As funny as it sounds, Fat Tony thought he was the ghetto Casanova because every girl who walked past his house or any house on the block, he had to holla at her. His little sister was Laura. Their parents, Mr. and Mrs. Gregs were kinda like our ghetto Huxtables. Basically we knew everyone on the whole block, but there are too many names to include here.

Cocoa and I loved hanging around the corner. Every day after school we ran around the block and everyday was a party. I will never forget our block parties, they were the bomb, we had so much fun. Everybody pitched in and made the day something so special. Some of the best times of my life was hanging on Milford street in the Summertime. It was a trip, because during the summer, we didn't have to worry about the street lights. We could hang out until late playing cards or whatever. Spades was our favorite game or Pit-a-pack. We would play for hours and depending on who was playing, things could get very critical. You spade players out there know we take our spades game very seriously. I actually saw people get into fights over a game of cards. Talk about having fun, I remember our punch ball tournaments, this is where the whole block would get down to play and it could easily end up being 10 people on each team. Both sides of the block would be getting down.

Cocoa and I never stayed home. Once we met our friends, we practically lived on Milford Street. Ramel, he had his own crew, Crazy Kindu, Hakeem, David, Sha-Bu, Supreme, Jimmy (RIP) and his home boy, Shamel (RIP). They always looked out for me and my sis. So Ramel didn't really hang out on the block that much.

It's getting dark, when are ya'll coming inside? That's Ma calling us in the house. Ma it's not even dark outside yet, the street lights is not even on. Can we stay a little while longer, please? OK, but get inside when the lights come on. Cocoa, Ma said we gotta get ready to come inside. Ok, I'm coming, but Cocoa and I both knew we did not want to go inside, we were just starting to have fun. Year after year we got closer and closer to everyone around the corner.

Cee-Cee eventually became my second big sis. I love her so much, and to this day we are still close. Cee-Cee is a beautiful, tall, light-skinned sista. She had two daughters Tisha and Kita, they are so pretty. Cee-Cee had long wavy hair all the way past her back. Hanging out together, we got so close. I used to love to go around the corner and visit her. I would sit down and watch her all day. We would be laughing and talking all kinds of "smack". Cee-Cee ended up being Ramel's girlfriend later on and I was so happy, especially when she moved in with us. After that we were inseparable. Whenever she wasn't with Ramel, she and I were hanging out. She protected me like I was really her lil sis. One night Cee-Cee and I were sitting on her stoop, hanging out just chillin. Look who's coming. I see her. It was Shakia, she was on her way coming across the street. Let her mess around today if she wants too. Now Shakia is our girl, we all loved each other but every once in a while she liked to go there. Sure enough, I don't even remember what me and that child got into it about that day, but the next thing I knew we were going at it. Somehow while we were throwing down, we both fell down in the yard right in the dirt and it was on. My sis Cocoa was there, that's right Sherry get her, you got her Sherry, that's right. And then all I could hear was Cee-Cee's mouth, she jumped in too, yelling that's right sis, turn her over, do this and do that, punch her in the face and nobody better not even try to jump in! Cee-Cee was talking to Shakia's family. We fought for a good ten to fifteen minutes and when we got up I said, now take yo behind back across the street, don't come back over here. The funny thing was a day after the fight, we were all best friends again. Shakia just knew, don't mess with me, I ain't the one. Shakia's lil sis, Toni girl, well she and I ended up becoming best girls, because we went to the same junior high school. Every day we hung out together. Toni was a chocolate complexion, slim girl and so pretty. She and I would walk back and forth to the store a million times a day. Anytime we played punch ball, we made sure we were on the same team. We had gotten so close. I will tell you more about Toni girl a little later on. I had some of the best times of my life on Milford Street.

Cocoa and I had started hanging out around the corner when we were teens and we remained lifelong friends with everyone. But that's how life is, everyone grows up and goes their separate ways. True friends, although few and far between, remain lifelong friends. Not surprisingly, some of the old crew moved away, but believe it or not, thirty years later, some of them still live on the old block. So a big "SHOUT-OUT" to the Milford Street Crew, I love ya'll.

Looking back now, things started happening so fast in my life. I went from this pretty little girl to a fast beautiful young woman. But, I guess I should have known I was headed for trouble after all, I had started playing hookie from school in the six grade.

As a little girl growing up people especially men constantly told me how pretty I was. Eventually I became a pretty girl to grown up for my age. I wore high heel shoes to my sixth grade graduation. By the age of fifteen, I wasn't hanging around the corner as much any longer. I would pass through to check out the old crew, but by now I had started hanging out with grown women who were raising daughters my own age. Right across the street from our house, I met two ladies who had a huge influence on me. Jenny and Gina, they were sisters. I found out later on that they were not blood sister's but best friends who were as close as two sisters could be. I can remember those hot summer nights sitting on our balcony, watching them as they strutted back and forth to the grocery store, which was basically like watching that television show Rip-the-Runway. It was definitely Show-n-Tell with all eyes on our two ghetto fabulous stars. The men and young guys driving by were honking, whistling and yelling all kinds of crazy things. It was my way of having fun, especially since ma had us on lockdown before it got dark outside.

The balcony became the entertainment spot for me and my sister and we got to see all kinds of drama sitting right in the comfort of our home. The only things missing was some popcorn and soda, but our chips and juice was good enough. You could not tell us we weren't chillin.

Jenny had four daughters all teenagers a couple years younger than I was. She had twin girls, another daughter and her son. He was a couple years younger than his sisters. A few years later, she had another baby boy, so needless to say she had her hands full. Living right across the street from them, our friendship began with me playing with her girls. Jennifer and Gina had cousins who also lived on the block. My family was friends with their family, because our grandparents established friendships when each became homeowners in the neighborhood. So we played with their grandchildren for years before I ever met Jenny and Gina. Neecie was a little older than we were and she had brothers the same age as Ramel and that's how I first met Jenny and Gina. We were all hanging out on the steps at Neecie's grandma's house. Before long I found myself at Jenny's apartment babysitting her kids but really I had so much fun just chillin, watching and listening to all their beezwax. A couple weeks later, I was part of their family. So it was easy for me to jet across the street to their house, hang for a while and get back home, without too much drama from my ma. I'd hang with Jenny and Gina for hours, just listening to them talking about their men. I loved watching Gina, she was so sexy. I watched how she put herself together. The clothes she wore seemed like she poured herself into them and the heels on her shoes were so high. Many a day I wondered how she never fell and broke her neck. She wore long, thick, hair weaves bushy and wild just like Chaka-Kahn. Whenever I was outside with Jenny and Gina, I saw how traffic stopped just to let them walk across the street. I may have only been fifteen at the time, but I realized right then and there, I wanted that attention (never realized at the time that it was negative attention). I was young and naïve and all I knew was that I was hot even for my age, so my thing was "what's the problem". Back then I didn't really think about it, I was just having fun, but fast girls usually find themselves in situations they should never be involved in and unfortunately for me, I would soon find that out. I knew I was young but I did not care and by then I was already smoking cigarettes and everything. My bottom line was that I was ready or at least I thought I was. Ready for what? For whatever, enough said. I realize now it was those experiences that I had learned as a teenager that caused me to develop into the young woman that I was to become. Tragically several years later, one of Jenny's little girls passed away while giving birth to her own child. So if by chance ya'll (yes, ya'll), but seriously Jenny, if you or any of the girls get the opportunity to read this book, I want you all to know when I heard about your girl, it broke my heart and although I have not seen any of you in 30 years, just know that I never forgot the special times we all shared (RIP-Red).

CHAPTER 3
"THE FAST TRACK"

In public school my best girlfriend TaShawn and I attended the same school P.S 345. I had always gotten very good grades in school. I was the first person to raise my hand to go up to the board to do a math problem or write the days assignments. Believe it or not, I actually liked school. I was an excellent reader and I never had a problem with other classmates. My teachers loved me and always called on me for different things. So when I started playing hookie from school, I was in the 6th grade and guess what, it was a shock for me too. One day TaShawn and I decided we were going to play hookie. For all of my young teens who might not know what hookie is, let me tell you. Hookie is when you skip school without your parents' knowledge or consent. Anyway we would make arrangements the night before to meet up at the local park the following day. All of the smallest details were taken care of in advance. I would sneak and pack all of my stuff that night. So I would make sure that Cocoa or Ramel wouldn't catch me, because if either one of them ever found out what I was up to, I wouldn't be writing this book right now, I'd be dead. During these little escapades of ours of course I would have one of my baby dolls, her food and clothes, my lunch and a blanket for us to sit on, all stuffed inside my book bag. The next morning I was in the clear. Since Cocoa and Ramel were in junior high, they both had to be in school earlier than I did. Every morning they left about a half hour before I did. While I was getting ready, all I had to worry about was making sure I smelled the aroma of my breakfast cooking. Of course all I was really concerned about was that my Ma had made my favorite, "cocoa". I just loved to sit there in her kitchen, looking at her with her flowered house dress on with a thousand tissues stuffed in her dress pocket. I never knew what she needed all those tissues for, but one sneeze from any of us and she was prepared. I would watch her with her hair net on top of her hair rollers and her brown slippers that she wore for years. While she added all her special ingredients to make me what I considered the best cocoa in the whole world. The more I thought about it, I realized that I loved her cocoa so much and drank so much of it, that to this very day I can't stand the smell of coffee or cocoa. No one but Ma could make my cocoa just the way I liked it. Every night before I went to bed and every morning I looked forward to having some ready for me.

After breakfast I'd kiss her goodbye. When she was finished asking me a thousand questions, I'd grab my bag then I would be off to school. But, instead of going to school, I met TaShawn "by the school" and we went to chill at the park. One day while at Hiland Park we met four girls, I was so impressed with them. Here we go for a ride so buckle up. They were older than we were and in junior high school. They befriended us, when the day first started out. We were having so much fun with them; well at least I thought we were. We ended up spending most of the day with them. While we were riding on the swings, they gave us cigarettes and everything. They treated us like everything was cool. Tashawn and I were laughing and joking, having a ball, funny how things changed after that. Hours later one of the girls said let's go up the hill to the other side of the park so we can throw rocks and stones at the animals. So I'm like alright let's go, now mind you I had not a clue there was another side of the park. As many times that I had been to that park before on family trips, I had never known there was another side of the park. Silly me, should always follow that inner voice. So we went with them anyway. Instantly, while we were on our way over there, I felt in my spirit that something was wrong, but you know me I never listen, right. We walked up this long hill and crossed some highway far to the other side of the park. I had no idea where we were, but we walked side by side with the girls, some in front and some in back of us. Right away you know what I'm thinking, I'm like umh huh, ok! I know something is up and by now that funny feeling is back, and not a ha ha funny feeling either. The next thing I knew, I started feeling rocks hitting me. At first it was soft hits, then the rocks started hitting us harder and harder.

Now mind you, every time I turned around to see where the rocks were coming from, the girls would be laughing their behinds off and acting like they did not know what was going on. Yo, you saw that, where are those rocks coming from? I'm looking at TaShawn like yea, ok. I guess by now you figured it out ha. Yep, Shawn and I were the animals they were talking about. Next they started pushing us and cursing and everything. Now I'm scared because I really didn't know my way back to the park. But I knew this was going to be a problem so I whispered to TaShawn, yo, we outta here and of course she was like I know that's right let's go. If it was just two of them and Shawn and I we would of kicked those girls "you know what's" because Shawn definitely was one of those girls that will throw down and ya'll already know what time it was with me. I wasn't that girl that was ok with just taking a behind whipping, you know what I mean, but remember we were outnumbered four to two. The way I saw it, the only logical option was to jet. Shawn we have to make a run for it and get back to the swings, which by the way is where we had stashed our school bags earlier that morning, you know when we were "chillin". So Shawn and I knew we had to go back there to get our stuff, correction, at least I knew I did because if I ever went home without my book bag it was a sure-nuff whipping from Ma. So I told TaShawn when I count to three we are gonna take off running. The only problem with that was we never said what direction we was gonna run in, so as we continued walking again, correction as we continued being pushed around, we tried to stay as close as possible to each other given the situation. I whispered one, two and on three, me and TaShawn took off running as fast as we could with the girls all yelling and chasing us cursing us out. Eventually TaShawn and I got separated from each other. By now I'm thinking here we go miss know-it-all. So I ran as fast as I could, my heart was pumping so fast but what those heffas excuse me "those girls" didn't know was that I was a track star in school. I had run in plenty of competitions and actually won first place in several events. Every team I ever played on, we won. As I was jetting across a street, I'm saying which way Sherry, this way, no it's that way I was definitely lost so I just kept running. Did I forget to tell ya'll I'm what I like to refer to as "directionally challenged" even to this day I can get lost going around the corner. But thank God the road led me back to the highway. But of course there were cars speeding back and forth and by now I could care less about any of that, all I knew was that I had to keep running because one of those "girls" was right on my behind. I ran and ran and ran until I was out of breath. Eventually I lost the girl who was on my tail. I don't know how I ended up back by the swings but I found my book bag and by now I was crying, not because I was scared no, I was crying because I was pissed about what they did. I trusted those "girls" and they betrayed us. And the worst thing was I didn't know what to do especially since I didn't know what happened to my girl. A little while later as I was walking, crying and cursing all of those "girls" out, their mama's and everybody else I could think of, I finally saw TaShawn walking in the park. We ran to each other and hugged. Apparently, she was pissed too and crying, so we went back to the swings. Thank God our stuff was still right there where we put it and we left the park. I mean we cursed those "girls" out so bad. We learned a lesson that day, unfortunately it wasn't that we needed to stop playing hookie, but rather, do not hang out with crazy behind "heffas". Oh! By the way our paths did cross again, and it was a very different story but that's another tale for another day.

As I said already, back then my head was hard as nails because on another time TaShawn and I played hookie from school, we was in a park inside this projects called Linden Plaza, about a half hour walk from both of our houses. This day was so crazy and again we had our baby dolls with us, our blankets spread out on the grass, just TaShawn and I. We were bugging out feeding our babies, minding our business as usual, ain't that a trip, minding our own business, our butts were supposed to be in school. When here comes this security guard talking about, "what are you girls doing here? don't you belong in school?". I was like, oh! Lord here we go, everyone buckle up! We couldn't think of a good enough lie quick enough, so we said nothing. That did not help us at all. So the guard made us get our stuff but not before scaring the mess out of both of us,, telling us we were going to jail. I never forgot it because he was actually cracking up while he waited and watched us putting all our baby stuff away. He escorted us to some little police station within the project, which if the situation wasn't so serious, I would have been pissed because I didn't even know that they had police stations in the projects. Probably because in all the years I had hung out in the area and when anything jumped off with people fighting or worse shooting, everybody knows you had to wait at least five hours for a police officer to show up if you lived in the projects. On the way to the station we were still trying to think of a good lie to tell, but we both knew it was useless and our behinds were in big trouble. At the station we made one last attempt to get our lies together but we were cold busted. He made us give him our telephone numbers and everything. Now here's another joke, I just knew I was over like a fat rat, because Ma was at work and she was not getting home until after 8:00 pm.

But I found out real quick, I wasn't as slick as I thought I was. Because when the officers called TaShawn's mother guess what, she was at home. TaShawn had the type of mother who was cool, you know what I mean, for her age and everything. I guess she had to be in her thirties back then, but she looked young and beautiful. She smoked her Newports, which by the way, those just happened to be our favorites too, so of course we borrowed some of her cigarettes out of her pack every chance we got. Ms. Delores knew all the latest slang, so we used to bug out with her all the time when I visited TaShawn. Even though they lived in the projects, her mother's apartment was tight. They're living room was all white, I mean the carpet and the furniture. Everything was so pretty. I loved to sit in there and bug out with TaShawn and Ms. Dee. But when Ms. Dee got that phone call from the police officer that day, she flipped out. She made that officer put TaShawn on the phone and all I heard was her mom yelling, screaming and cursing. TaShawn was holding the phone away from her ear looking stupidly at me, all of a sudden I felt like I had to doo-doo. All I heard from TaShawn was yes, yes, and yes. Then it was my turn. Her mother said, and put miss fast behind on the phone, so she handed me the phone.

I looked at Tashawn like she had seven heads or something. I wasn't trying to hear her mother curse me out too, but TaShawn wasn't playing. She informed me that her mother said I better get on that phone before she come down there and kick both our you know what's. And for some reason I knew Ms. Dee wasn't playing, she was pissed. Funny enough I bet she didn't sound so cool to me then. I was seriously scared she was going to come kick both of our behinds.

When I got on the phone she said let me tell you something, both of you got five minutes to get ya'lls "you know what's" to my house, and she slammed the phone down. Now if you remember I already said that it was at least a half hour walk from Linden Plaza to Cypress Hills projects where TaShawn lived. So I don't have to tell you how fast we had to run to get to Shawn's house in five minutes right? By the time we reached TaShawn's apartment, Ms. Dee already had the door wide open. Her music was blasting and her belt was ready. All she said to her daughter was get your "you know what" in that room and TaShawn took off running to her room, already crying. Then she looked at me and said now you got five more minutes to get your behind home and then her next words made my stomach drop. And your grandfather is waiting for you and you know I already told him everything. And I am calling him back in five minutes and you better be there, now get moving. As I walked out the door, I starting thinking fast, now look what you got yourself into. So the only thing I could think of was, well I have to run away from home now, because I knew if daddy knew, he surely called ma at work and told her blow by blow of Sherry's latest news flash. I didn't even want to think about the whipping I was going to get the second she got home from work that night. So as soon as I got home I called Ms. Dee to let her know I was there. Next, I wanted to see what daddy knew, so I went into the living room. We all called him daddy because he was like our second father. All I heard him say was young lady, I don't know what you was thinking but your ma is going to tear your "you know what up" when she gets home tonight, you hear me? I said to myself, oh no she ain't cause I'm getting the "you know what" outta here right now. As soon as he went into their bedroom to take his nap I jetted to my bedroom. I grabbed my book bag and started packing. This time I forgot about my baby dolls and all that other nonsense, I had to get outta there with the quickness. Almost tripping over myself, all I had the time to grab was a few of my clothes, toothbrush, mirror, hair rollers, comb, brush and just in case, I put on three pairs of pants and some more blouses and I hid everything else in my bag. Then I just waited. The later it got, the more the butterflies started jumping around in my stomach. Every night my grandfather drove to the train station at Shepherd Avenue to pick up ma at 8:00 pm sharp. Usually, Cocoa and I would ride with him and hide in the back seat of the car and when ma would open the car door to get in we would jump out and scare the living mess out of her and she would be cracking up laughing. But this night was very different and not so funny at all. I was outside on the stoop just waiting until I saw the car pull up to our house 8:10 pm sharp, just like clockwork and out of the car came Ma. One look at her face and I almost peed on myself. All she had the chance to say to me in her West Indian accent was "you get yourself in the house"., before I took off running out the gate and around the corner. Now if you think I ran fast when those "girls" was chasing me in the park that day, was nothing compared to the speed I ran with now. I was gone, because I knew that Cocoa and Ramel were coming after me. While I was flying around corners, I did not have a clue where I was going but I ended up two blocks away at our other best friends' house which by the way was the stupidest place to go. I should have known that would be the second place they were going to look for me. Glenda and Sharon were sisters, the same age as Cocoa and I. We've known them for years and we are all very close. Cocoa and I hung out at their house mostly every day and when we weren't at their house, they came to our house. They were good girls, responsible, smart and very respectful. Although Sharon was right behind me when it came down to being fast. They were from down South and Cocoa and I just loved their accent. I would always say what you say Sharon? just so I could hear her talk. We loved their mother Ms. Linda, she used to make the best pound cake in the world. And every time we went to their house and I saw that cake pan on the table, I begged for some of her cake. And I sure could eat some of her mac-n-cheese right now too um, um delicious. Glenda are you there, ring, ring I'm ringing their door bell and knocking on their front window, so scared because I know Ramel and Cocoa are coming. Sharon opened the door. Girl what is wrong with you ringing the bell like you are crazy or something? I pushed right past her and ran inside. Lock the door Sharon. So as quickly as I could I told them everything that I had did. I begged them not to tell anyone that I was there. Five minutes later I heard the banging on the door I begged Glenda please, please don't tell them I'm here. Please, my Ma is going to kill me! The next thing I knew, I heard Glenda and I heard Ramel and Cocoa talking outside. Of course my sis, "the best CIA Agent in town", was interrogating Glenda I know she's in there just tell her to come on out, she shoulda took her behind to school. For real Glenda, ma is so mad at Sherry, she is in so much trouble. Two seconds later all I heard Glenda saying was, Sherry come on they know you here. I couldn't believe my ears, didn't I just beg and plead for them not to tell on me. So of course I'm thinking what the "you know what". And right as I was walking past them both in their hallway going outside where Ramel and Cocoa was, I promised to kick both Glenda and Sharon's behind the first chance I got. I still loved them, but at that point they were still snitches better yet, "sell-outs" (just kidding, love ya'll). So as we were headed back home, I tried one more time begging and pleading to Cocoa and Ramel for my life, but they weren't having it and all they said to me was, you might as well start crying now, and of course, I did.

So by the time we got back home my Indie was outside waiting, of course with her belt in hand. And what's even funnier is that back then we did not have any cell phones, so I guess ma would have just waited all night long to tear my behind up, because she did not know how long it would take for them to find me. So as soon as I walked in the gate, she did not say one word, she just grabbed me and dragged me inside, of course kicking and screaming. You see where I come from we don't know nothing about no child abuse or Department of Family And Children's Services (DFACS). All we knew was, you did something stupid, you got your behind whipped. So Ma said you won't run from me this time and get in there and take off some of those clothes. After that she shoved me into her bedroom, she must have only hit me about three times before my grandfather came in and he saved me. I guess he knew that ma was so mad at me that she probably really would have killed me that night. He said Indie stop, don't hit her no more. He looked at me with a look I have never seen on him before and he made me promise never to do anything like that again so I promised. And although my little hookie playing days had come to an abrupt end at least temporarily, I was so glad because at least I was still alive. I never ran away again. I did stop playing hookie at least, until I got to junior high school. Oh, did I forget to tell ya'll that I was extremely hard-headed too? By the end of the school year surprisingly, I graduated from public school and made it to junior high. By the time I got to Jr. High School, I had hooked up with some of the baddest girls in the school. I.S 218 was the bomb school.

And this is the beginning of the end of the fun games I played as a little girl. I quickly went into playing with the "Big Dogs". It wasn't until years later that I found out, if you want to play with big dogs you gotta know that you just might get bit. I loved my Jr. HS because it was right around the corner from ma's house and it was only a fifteen minute walk to Minas' house. During this time mommy had come to N.Y. to live for a while so Cocoa, Shainne and I lived with her and Ramel never left ma and daddy's house. He said, ya'll go ahead with mommy, I'm chillin right here. I loved getting out of school at 1:00 in the afternoon because it gave me plenty of time to do whatever I wanted the rest of the day. My first semester in the 7th grade I met this girl, her name was Ochie. She was so pretty. A light skinned girl, she was beautiful and she had beautiful wavy hair. I knew right away that she was mixed with something, Puerto Rican or Indian or something. I almost fell out when I found out that Ochie already had a baby. I never knew anyone that had a baby so young and in some ways, I was fascinated by her. I could not believe that she had a child because she was only 13 years old herself. Her baby was so beautiful. She had a head full of curly jet black hair and the prettiest piercing black eyes that I had ever seen in my life. She had the chubbiest cheeks. I fell in love with that baby. But I also remember Ochie telling me how hard it was on her raising her child as a single mother. The boy who had gotten Ochie pregnant was long gone. I thought what kind of guy would get a twelve year old girl pregnant and then leave her and the baby. Of course Ochie's mother ended up having to care for the child financially as well as emotionally because Ochie was too young to understand the importance of raising a child. When I think back now, I can't believe that I ended up having my first sexual experience and I was not even in High School yet. So what I always do now is to encourage you young girls to "WAIT". At least wait until you finish high school and hopefully college.

I can tell you from my own experiences of starting out so early in life and having sexual relationships, it's "Not" all that. Looking back now, I realize I have always been curious, impulsive and a risk taker. These characteristics have one by one gotten me into more trouble throughout my life than it was worth. Young ladies you can learn a lot by listening to someone who has "been there, and done that". Take it from me, there is nothing better than finishing school, going to college, working and being independent, when you're young. Because if you don't learn the lesson the first go around, some time later on in life, you will have to repeat it. One of the best feelings in the world is when you can take care of yourself and be responsible for the choices you make in your life. Then you can enjoy life and have fun doing things you enjoy, without having to worry about taking care of a child (you can't afford) because you dropped out of high school. Also you won't have such a hard time finding a job, as you would as a high school drop-out. And you won't have to get involved in unhealthy relationships with men who only want one thing from you (and I know you all know what that is). And usually after they get what they want, you end up pregnant and he leaves you for another girl (who does not have any children). So many young girls had to find out how hard it is taking care of a child with no help. It wasn't until womanhood when I understood that one of our most precious gifts from God is what I like to call our "Cherries". As I have matured now, I understand how precious our cherries are. We should cherish our "cherries" and then when we find the man we love and we get married, he will also know how precious our cherries are.

One of my favorite Scriptures in the Bible talks about
"A Virtuous Woman".

PROVERBS 31: 10-31

10 Who can find a virtuous woman? for her price is far above rubies.

11 The heart of her husband doth safely trust in her, so that he shall have no need of spoil.

12 She will do him good and not evil all the days of her life.

13 She seeketh wool, and flax, and worketh willingly with her hands.

14 She is like the merchants' ships; she bringeth her food from afar.

15 She riseth also while it is yet night, and giveth meat to her household, and a portion to her maidens.

16 She considereth a field, and buyeth it: with the fruit of her hands she planteth a vineyard.

17 She girdeth her loins with strength, and strengtheneth her arms.

18 She perceiveth that her merchandise is good: her candle goeth not out by night.

19 She layeth her hands to the spindle, and her hands hold the distaff.

20 She stretcheth out her hand to the poor; yea, she reacheth forth her hands to the needy.

21 She is not afraid of the snow for her household: for all her household are clothed with scarlet.

22 She maketh herself coverings of tapestry; her clothing is silk and purple.

23 Her husband is known in the gates, when he sitteth among the elders of the land.

24 She maketh fine linen, and selleth it; and delivereth girdles unto the merchant.

25 Strength and honour are her clothing; and she shall rejoice in time to come.

26 She openeth her mouth with wisdom and in her tongue is the law of kindness.

27 She looketh well to the ways of her household, and eateth not the bread of idleness.

28 Her children arise up, and call her blessed; her husband also, and he praiseth her.

29 Many daughters have done virtuously, but thou excellest them all.

30 Favour is deceitful, and beauty is vain: but a woman that feareth the Lord, she shall be praised.

31 Give her of the fruit of her hands; and let her own works praise her in the gates.

CHAPTER 4
"THE CRACK EPIDEMIC"

Junior high is when I first got involved with drugs. I had already experimented with cigarettes. Then I was introduced to marijuana (weed, as it is called today) by my friends at school. I used to love smoking weed, it made me feel so mellow. I would roll a joint take a couple of puffs and just chill. And over a couple of months, it went from me sharing my weed with friends hanging out, to me selling joints. And by my last year in junior high school, I was addicted not so much to the drugs, but to the lifestyle. I would roll about fifty joints and sell them after school. I was making money and very soon I was able to buy what I needed. Somehow, I made it through junior high and graduated but according to the principle I made it by the skin of my nose. One day he saw me in the hallway, he pulled me to the side and told me I am very lucky. But all I could think of when I was staring at Mr. Tricarrico was that he is one of the finest white men I have ever saw. I think he was Italian or something. And by the time I got into high school, I was out of control. I wasn't listening to anyone, not my grandparents, mother, father, sisters or brother, nobody could tell me anything. I did what I wanted to do. I guess by now you can tell that that was another one of my biggest problems.

It was in high school where I met my best girlfriend. Roxanne is as crazy as they come. We would take a deck of cards with us to school and every time we got a chance to leave out of class and jet to the girls bathroom, we would be in there playing cards gambling, by the end of the day, we were paid. Ramel and Cocoa was in Lane but by the time I got there, both of them were on their way out in the 11th and 12th grades. This is how bad I was, even though my sis was on me like bees on honey because she knew me so well, every day she would come to my classroom to check up on me and make sure I was in class. I can't tell you how many times she caught me and Roxy in the bathroom gambling. Let's go, before I have to hurt you. My sis would take me back to my class and sometimes she took Roxy back to her class too.

I'm not playing with ya'll don't let me come back in this bathroom and see ya'll in here. Of course we just laughed our behinds off. The classroom door didn't even close good after she left before I was gone again. That's my sis and I love her but she shoulda asked somebody. One of my biggest regrets in life was when I eventually dropped out of high school altogether. I was in the 11th grade. By that time I was way out of control. And what started out as fun, you know smoking a little weed here and there, eventually became my worst nightmare. Over the next several years the drugs went from weed to cocaine and the cocaine eventually went to crack. I had gotten so strung out on crack, to the point that I never even saw my own death sentence come, until it was way too late. My life changed in ways that I never could have imagined.

There was nothing glamorous about the drug lifestyle. Looking back at the life of a drug addict from the inside now, I see how it all started and ended with me. I used to watch TV and read books about the gangsta lifestyle and it always looked like they were having fun. Seeing them in their beautiful cars and fly houses... everyone wants to have nice things too. But what I didn't really understand was that there was another side of the glamour. The side when they ended up in jail or dead. I kept thinking everyone knows someone who is using drugs and even the people who are just thinking about experimenting with drugs. I just want everyone to know that it ain't all fun and games. I'm living proof of that and what happened to me can happen to anyone. My heart still breaks every time I think about my friends that never made it out of the drug war (RIP, Toni girl, Zay and Vee). Good girls, they just got caught up like the rest of us. But sadly they never made it out, they didn't have a second chance. Remember I talked about Toni girl earlier on? She was my home girl from around the corner on Milford Street, Shakia's sister. Well Toni girl was one of my best friend's, my sista-girl. We knew each other for over ten years. She was shot and killed in the 90's due to the crack lifestyle. I knew that she had been using the drugs but you just never know how bad off a person is really. Back then everyone knew the signs of a person addicted to crack, they were extremely skinny, usually their cheeks were sunken in, and you could usually find them outside late at night on the streets, doing what we called "feigning" for a hit. I guess Toni girl got desperate one night and stole drugs from a drug dealer and he found her and put a gunshot into her neck that killed her. Toni girl died alone. I'm sure she was scared to death, seeing that gun pointed at her and I know she begged for her life right before he shot her, but he killed her anyway. Toni girl wasn't even 25 years old at the time of her death. She didn't deserve to die in such a horrible way. I'd like you to know who she was before she started using crack. Toni was a vibrant, smart, beautiful girl. She loved to dress fly. I can remember all the times that we would be in her bedroom getting ready to go outside. It didn't even have to be anywhere special, just outside but she would spend at least two hours ironing the crease in her pants until she felt they were just right. She always took pride in herself. Her hair always looked good. She was also well respected by everyone around the way. Toni girl and I went to I.S 218 together and she was an A student. She would be the last person that you would think would have ended up using crack. Toni girl already had a daughter and shortly before she was killed, she had just given birth to a baby boy. Toni loved her children so much and one of the saddest parts of losing her is that she never got to see her children grow up, and she won't get to see them graduate from school. She won't be there when they get married and she will never get to see any of her grandchildren. Her children never got a chance to know their mother because they were still so young when she died. The drugs robbed her of the chance to raise her children. The drugs robbed her of her future. And ultimately the drugs caused her to lose her life way, way too young. Toni girl I love you, I'm so sorry that you lost your life so senselessly. I know that had you not gotten caught up in the drug war you could have made such a positive contribution in society. Rest in Peace my sista. Thankfully, Toni girl's brother ended up raising her two children, who I have not seen in many years. But I heard from family members that her children who are now young adults, are doing well. Toni's brother took very good care of them for her and so the good news in all of this is that her legacy will live on.

And then there was Zay she didn't die using drugs and she didn't get killed like Toni girl, but she ended up contracting AIDS due to the drug lifestyle. Remember Zay she was our home-girl she lived at 310 Milford Street with her mother and sister's on the second floor. Zay was our life of the party girl. She was at least 6'4; she was always a skinny kinda girl. She had a chocolate complexion and was crazy as "you know what". Whenever there was any drama going on, all you had to do was look around because Zay was somewhere near. She would give you her heart. She would give you her last. But one of her problems was that she was also a heavy beer drinker, long before she ever started smoking crack. She loved Ole Gold beer and whenever she drank that beer, you better watch out. She had this dance that she would do if she was drunk or sober, because she knew it would have all of us cracking up on the floor laughing. It was sort-of-a-slow shake your shimmey. Just picture this a jolly-green-giant who was drunk and doing the shimmey dance, and there you have Zay. I'm cracking up laughing right now just remembering her. Zay was born crazy, even when she was sober she was a mess, but honey after a 40-ounce of that Ole English, all I can say is, watch out. The funniest thing about her was that even in a regular conversation, she would be all in your face screaming so loud, and because she was so tall, either you had to look up, up, up or she would stoop down all up in your face. Can you imagine what that conversation was like after those 40's? We loved Zay so much and whenever we needed her to beat anybody up male or female, she was down, anytime, day or night. And please don't tell her somebody was trying to start some trouble with any of the Milford Street crew because Zay was definitely gonna go off on them, yep all up in their face. She always had our backs, always. It was so sad to see all of her fire die after she got addicted to crack. It changed her so much just like it changed every one of us. I knew that Zay was out there saying yes when she really wanted to say no, because by then the crack had taken complete control of her. The last time I saw her, she looked so sad and her spirit was broken. And then one day I heard the news, Zay had died. I had seen her just a couple of weeks before. Brokenhearted, I cried. I cried for her, I cried for her family, and I cried for me. It was such a huge loss to her family. So Zay, Rest in Peace, girl I love you and miss your fire. I have never met anyone since that can light a candle to her fire.

And then there was Vee, she was murdered because of drugs. Vee was Roxy's older sister. I was friends with Vee for a couple of years. The Vee I knew when she was sober, was a loving mother. Her kids were her life. But she was addicted to crack too and eventually it took control of her. I didn't know Vee all that well, but she was Roxy's sister and I loved her. Vee died a horrible, horrible death, she was murdered. I never really got a full understanding of her murder, but I just want to say that just like the rest of us that got strung out in the crack epidemic of the 80's, Vee was not a criminal or a killer, she was someone's daughter, sister, aunt, wife and mother. Her life meant a lot to many people and it was taken so senselessly. But her legacy lives on forever in her children and grandchildren. And I trust that God has forgiven her for her sins too. Love you Vee, Rest in Peace.

There have been many people who have lost their life to drugs or you may have lost a loved one due to drugs. This is my "Tribute" to every one of those people especially my girlfriends and even the people that I never knew. Finally you don't have to live life suffering any longer, Rest in Peace. You didn't die in vain because I live to tell people the truth about the drugs, about the lifestyle. I shared those personal experiences simply to let everyone know that these girls never thought they would end up dead either. I learned that "drugs don't discriminate". I was young, curious, impulsive and fine. I was also a risk taker. Throughout my life these qualities have gotten me into more trouble than I could ever have imagined. I never thought about how the drugs would impact my life, my family, my future.

> "The little white rocks looked so innocent on the table"

It was a hot summer day, I was all grownup now an adult living with my boyfriend at the time. We had a really nice apartment in the Flatbush section of Brooklyn. We lived in a Co-op building with a doorman and everything. I really liked our apartment. I had it hooked up. I was home just relaxing, when all of a sudden my intercom rings. Who is it? It's Roxy, open the dang on door. Roxy and I had been best friends now for over five years, she was my hang out partner. What's up girl, I'm good girl what you doing here this early. Of course she was all hyped up, yo, I got a little something, something you want some. Now ya'll remember I already told you that back then I was fast right. So of course I said, girl what are you talking about and what do you have.

The little white rocks looked so innocent on the table. I never dreamed that those little pebbles could cause so much destruction, but I was definitely about to find out. I watched as Roxy crushed up some of the rock and put it inside the weed, rolled it up and lit the joint. After taking a couple of hits, you want some more. Immediately after taking a puff, I began to feel the effect of the drug, it didn't taste like anything I had ever used before.

Crack is a derivative of cocaine freebasing. Crack smoking ripped through American ghettos in the late 1980's and Roxy, Toni girl, Zay, Vee and I certainly were affected during that epidemic. I had been smoking weed and cigarettes as well as an occasional drink, when we went clubbing, since we were teenagers. I had even tried cocaine before, but it never did anything for me except make me feel like I wanted to pull my nose off. I did not like to sniff cocaine but sometimes we would put some in our cigarettes. We were chilling out doing our thing but after a while all the crack was finished and we both wanted some more. I told Roxanne that the guys around the corner that I used to buy weed from probably knew where we could get some more of the white rocks from, so we went outside. Sure enough by the time we came back in the house, we had some more of the crack. While we were at the spot, I saw when Roxy bought some glass thing too. I did not know what the "you know what" that was either so I just looked at her like she had seven heads or something. We got back into doing the do. This time instead of her rolling it in the weed, she put a pebble into what looked to me like a glass pipe. I watched as Roxy used a lighter, she put it at the end of the glass and all of a sudden I saw the glass fill up with thick cloudy white smoke. What are you doing? What do it look like I'm doing? If I had only known that smoking that pipe with Roxy that day would be the beginning of the end of the Sherry that I had known and loved my whole life, I would never have taken any. But of course that impulsive part of me, the one that always gets me into trouble, couldn't wait for my turn. I did not think twice about what I was doing because if I had I would have understood that I was about to make one of the biggest mistakes of my life. The drug started to take effect immediately within a few minutes. One thing about crack is that the method of smoking crack in a crack pipe produces a high in a matter of seconds. I quickly found out that "one hit of crack is too much and a thousand hits are never enough". A little while later it was time to go, both of us needed another hit because ours was finished. Before I realized what I was doing, I had taken a shower and got dressed. I wore my heels, a tee-shirt and jeans, my hair was wild and crazy just like I like it. Roxy is light skinned and beautiful, and like I said before she is crazy as all get up. Roxy has the gift of gab. She knew all of the latest slang, she knew where to go to have fun and everybody knew her wherever we went. She was only 100 pounds soaking wet. The two of us together were unstoppable. Roxy is like my sister. Back in high school when I met her, we just clicked. I soon learned that Roxy is one of those girls that either you liked her or you hated her and trust me when I tell you we have met many females who just hated her. I know the poor child is crazy as all get up, but I have learned so much from her about life and we have always been there for each other. By that evening when all of our drugs were gone, we were both off and running. Let's go! Roxy said, so we jumped in a cab and of course Roxy said she knew exactly where we were heading to get more drugs. Roxy was the one who traveled, even though it was only in the five boroughs in N.Y., but she could find any place. On the other hand the only place I knew was right around the corner from our house, because that's as far as Ma was letting me go. So when I hooked up with Roxy, it was a whole new world for me. In the beginning I had so much fun. A half hour later we pulled up on this block and when I looked out the window, I was like, "what the you know what.". It was the weekend and it was summer time, it was dark outside and people were all over the place. As we got out of the cab I heard yo, Roxy what's up? Who's that? how you doing tonight miss lady? I was like, oh no. I remember looking at her like I always do whenever we would find ourselves in a situation. But this time I'm thinking for sure Roxy has lost her mind. I'm like these fools look crazy. I saw heads sticking out of windows. People were whistling and just acting like they never saw a woman in their life. We were in the Bushwick section of Brooklyn. I was very familiar with the area but I had never been on this particular block before. Years earlier I had lived about 10 blocks away. The only thing I have to say now is buckle up!! If I had known then what I know now, I would never have gotten out of that cab that day, instead I should have run for my life. That was the day that my life changed forever. I paid a price getting out of the cab on that block, that day and when I look back now, it just was not worth it. We entered this huge building directly across the street from where those fools were peeping out the window. Right away you know what I'm thinking right, "what the you know what". Roxy knocks on the door, then I hear her say, "house in". Someone says from the other side of the door, which by the way is still closed, yo who that Roxy? Move to the side, who that with you? So she says, stop playing open the door, she with , that's my sis. She looks at me, of course I'm thinking there goes those seven heads again. She says, wait until you see who lives here. The moment the door opens, I hear yo, what's up. Sherry is that you? I look down this long hallway, I see this guy named Tee. I couldn't believe it. We have known Tee for years but I had not seen him in a long time. Remember when I said that I lived in that area a few years earlier? Well, Tee and his baby's mother and me and my boyfriend all shared an apartment together.

Tee is this little Jamaican dude, soaking wet he couldn't weigh no more than Roxy did, which was probably somewhere around 105 pounds. Tee is that you? oh no, what's up. There were people all around just chillin, hanging out right there on the 1st floor in the hallway. Me and Roxy just walked passed all of them, all eyes on us like we were on the Red Carpet. It was a creepy feeling but I knew if anything jumped off Tee had our backs. You look good girl, what you doing in my neighborhood? Tee says to me. I'm just chillin with Roxy, you know what's up. So Tee takes us into this apartment. My first impression was, yup, you guessed it, "what the you know what". I see junk and garbage all around. At least where we were in the kitchen there was a table, chairs, refrigerator and stove, you know regular kitchen stuff. But then there are these people popping in and out of the woodworks, from different rooms in the apartment and to make matters worse it was dark in there. People coming in and going out, it was like an indoor expressway or something. Everybody who came in talked to Tee and checked me and Roxy out. We might as well have been on a display shelf. Believe me, I felt like when I walked through that door I walked into a whole different world. I thought for sure I was in the "Twilight Zone". Of course, Roxy knew them all and I'm just looking around like they all got seven heads, especially Roxy. When Tee and us lived together, he was only using marijuana. So when I see him pull out the same glass pipe thing that Roxy and I had used earlier, I was shocked. I watched as he did the same thing Roxy had showed me earlier. The only difference was that the piece of white rock that he put into his pipe, was ten times the size as the one's Roxy and I was smoking. Once the rock was inside the pipe, Tee raised his lighter to the end and ignited the fire to it and instantly I saw the pipe fill with the white cloud of smoke. He gave some to Roxy, she smoked and then passed it back to him. He looked at me, you smoking. I was so embarrassed so of course I played it off I said no, I don't get down with that. After watching all kinds of scary looking people come in the kitchen, give Tee some money and then go into the other rooms, I knew what time it was, Tee was hustling drugs there. So I was like oh, ok. That night I held out, I did not smoke any of Tee's white rock because I had the feeling all night that he was just waiting to get me. I just pretty much watched everyone else acting like some dang fools. What really amazed me was how the white rock made everyone act after smoking it. In case you never saw anyone smoke crack, it is considered one of the most dangerous and addicting drugs around because it reaches the pleasure centers of the brain in eight to ten seconds. Once in the brain, crack produces a short, intense, electrifying feeling of euphoria as it causes a sudden release of neurotransmitters, especially dopamine, in the brain. Its effects are much more intense and pleasurable than snorting or IV use of cocaine. The high generally lasts three to five minutes, followed by crushing depression which may persist for ten to forty minutes longer. Crack is relatively cheap, costing as little as $5, up to $20.00 dollars. Large doses create the feeling of enhanced sexuality, particularly in males. The "rush" that is experienced is generally compared to a sexual orgasm. The physical effect of the drug with high doses, create more intense euphoria and creates some adverse reactions, including bizarre and violent behavior, extreme anxiety and restlessness, twitches, tremors and loss of coordination, hallucinations and delusions, chest pain and nausea. I said Tee, where is your bathroom? He pointed to another room toward the back. As I started walking away, I felt his eyes burning a hole in my behind. I looked back and sure enough there was a hole in my jeans. As I walked through the apartment, I came across a room where I saw a frail looking elderly lady sitting on a bed. I assumed it was her bedroom. When I looked around the room, I could not believe my eyes. There were all kinds of junk all around her, on the bed on the floor everywhere I looked. I cleared my throat and I heard myself say, hello ma'am. She did not respond to me. So I said it again. She was just staring ahead. When I came out of the bathroom I asked Tee about the old lady. He just shrugged me off, he said that's Ms. Holmes. Later on I found out that she owned the 4 story building. The apartment that we were hanging out in that night belonged to her. I also found out by Tee that Ms. Holmes is blind. I guess that's why she did not respond to me because even though she heard me, she could not see me. Evidently to her, I was just another crack head using her apartment to get high. I have never felt so sorry for anyone in all my life. I mean, this old blind lady was unable to see anything. All she did was sit in her bed all day with the T.V playing. Every day she was forced to wait for her crack head son to finish smoking his pipe and then maybe she could get something to eat or someone would have mercy long enough to clean her up. She had no control over her situation. She was old, her appearance was deplorable, her hair was a mess, her clothes were dirty and she just looked so pitiful. She appeared to be at least in her late 70's. She seemed completely vulnerable and defenseless. Her son was old himself, he appeared to be in his fifties. His name was Ras, at least that is what everyone called him. His appearance was unkempt and the clothes he wore were dirty. He had the longest beard I had ever seen. He wore a sort of afro with very nappy hair. Basically he was just a plain mess to look at. He definitely scared me all night long. By the end of the night, I realized that Ras was like the gatekeeper or something. He monitored everyone who came into the apartment. He knew who was copping, when and how much. That was the way he supported his habit. He was Tee's lookout man. I soon found out that Tee was running the whole show. He controlled the apartment and he controlled Ras and Ms. Holmes. Ras depended on Tee for money and drugs, so he did whatever Tee said. We ended up staying there the whole night, it was daybreak when we left. Once outside I said to Roxy, that was the craziest thing I ever seen in my life. It was an experience I was not accustomed to and even though I did not realize it then, that reality very soon became my very existence. All of the crazy people I saw coming in and out of the building that night to buy and use the white rock, I would soon become very familiar with these same people. As a matter of fact, not soon after, I became one of them. It was not too long after that I found myself hanging out at Tee's on a regular basis, even without Roxy. I would call him and he would say jump in a cab and come over here. Eventually I was hanging out there and not only spending the night, but I could end up being there for a whole week straight. Over a period of months, I realized that the only time I went home was to get clothes or when I really needed to get some rest. By the way, it was not long after that first night that I quickly got over my embarrassment of getting high in front of Tee. One day while we were chillin, Tee offered me some of the drug like he had done on many other occasions, but this time I did not refuse. He put a big rock inside the glass pipe and passed it to me. I took a long drag from the pipe and inhaled the drug, that was it I was hooked. After that I was Tee's girl and everyone knew it. He flaunted me around like his prize possession. The word was out that none of the other guys that hustled drugs in the building better not even try to push up on me because I belonged to Tee. The only problem was that I forgot one little thing about Tee. I had lived with Tee years earlier, it was him and his baby's mother, Leney and me and my boyfriend Mikale. On several occasions I had witnessed firsthand how Tee physically abused his baby's mother daily. They were constantly fighting and Mikale had to intervene to break them up. I should not have been surprised when he started doing the same thing to me.

Shortly after I began hanging out at Tee's, I met his best friend, his name was J. J was a tall slim Jamaican brother. He was brown skinned and he always kept himself looking good. But along with J came his woman Gee. Not long after meeting her I figured it out. The G was for G-building, because the girl's elevator definitely didn't go all the way to the top. Don't get me wrong she was ok, but when it came down to J, she was what I considered a tad bit unstable. This child had serious issues, seriously. I mean she never left J's side and I mean that literally. But I really knew she was trippin when one day we were all hanging out in our favorite spot, the kitchen. Her and J came in and he made a mad dash for the bathroom, he closed the door behind him. Here she comes running in behind him, trying to go in the bathroom with him. She was banging on the door, yelling and screaming for him to open the bathroom door. We all looked at each other and all I heard Nay-Nay say is, now that's a dang shame the man can't even go to the bathroom by himself. The next thing we all knew she stood guard in front of the bathroom door until J was finished. When he opened the door and came out the bathroom, we all laughed our behinds off.

Then there was the notorious Nay-Nay. Now it did not take but a minute to figure out that she could have utilized a bed in the room next to Gee at the psychiatric hospital because she was another trip. Nay-Nay was Tee's ex-girlfriend but I soon found out that she was also three other guys' girlfriend that lived in the building including J. She continued to live in the apartment even though she was not going out with Tee anymore. The thing was that she came here from Jamaica and Nay-Nay did not want to leave because she didn't have any family in N.Y. and she did not have anywhere to go. More importantly Nay-Nay was in the same boat just like the rest of us who chose not to leave the "Twilight Zone", because we had all the access we needed to get drugs on a daily basis. After all, the drugs were sold right there in the building. Tee supported her habit along with the other guys that she was seeing and each one of the guys Nay-Nay had a relationship with was hustling drugs in the building. It was one big happy crazy family. After a couple of months, Tee came up with a bright idea instead of staying downstairs in Ms. Holmes apartment, why not take the empty apartment on the 4th floor and occupy it. So we all went upstairs to check out the apartment. When I first walked in the door I could not believe my eyes. The apartment was huge, there were four bedrooms, enough space for all of us to have our own room, however the apartment was a disaster. It's no wonder no one lived in there. I certainly was not trying to stay in there let alone sleep in there. But funny enough, after everyone started pitching in and cleaning up the hellhole, it didn't look so bad after all. It took us days to get the place clean enough to live in.

CHAPTER 5

"NO WAY OUT"

Tee had never approached me for sexual favors in the beginning but that was about to change. One night it was just the two of us upstairs hanging out. The next thing I know Tee says to me I have to have you tonight. I thought he was playing or you know just trippin on the drugs, but when he started ripping my stockings and panties off of me and pinned me down on the couch, I quickly realized that he was very serious. As bony as he was, Tee still overpowered me and when I looked into his eyes and asked him, are you just going to rape me like this? He simply said I have too, and he did. I felt disgusted because I wasn't feeling Tee on a sexual level, but as crazy as it sounds I couldn't shake the feeling that I had co-signed the rape because after all, I could have left, right. It was a violation that I live with to this day, but even worse than the violation I felt like I deserved it because I had put myself in that situation. Overtime, I blocked it out of my mind, but the truth is it never really leaves you, it's always there. I was not shocked when we started getting into little arguments, which quickly turned into big fights. I already knew that Tee had anger issues and that he could be physically abusive. I had witnessed Tee's anger outbursts several times, years earlier between him and his baby's mother. So when it started happening to me, it wasn't a surprise. I was hurt but not surprised. One night we were hanging out upstairs, we started arguing. Tee pulled out his loaded gun and put it to my face, say something, you think me playing he said. I just looked him straight in his eyes and I did not say a word. Another time we were in Ms. Holmes kitchen arguing, he grabbed a knife and put it to my throat, gently sticking it in my neck, all the while he was laughing at me. Another time Tee took scissors, held me down on the bed with my arms behind my back and he cut about 2 inches of my hair off yet, I still would not leave him. Now when I look back at all the physical abuse I endured from Tee, I know that I didn't stay because I was afraid of Tee and it sure wasn't because I loved Tee. I stayed for the same stupid reasons Nay-Nay and the other girls did. I stayed because I was addicted to drugs. J saved me so many times. Whenever Tee and I would fight, J would get Tee off of me and tell him you stupid man, you got a beautiful woman, you gonna end up losing her. I had so much respect for J because he was the opposite of Tee, J was a peacemaker. I used to love to sit and listen to him sing. J could sing his behind off. Whenever you saw J he was smoking and singing something. A few months later Nay-Nay was pregnant and it was a mystery baby because she was sleeping with three men in the building so none of us, including Nay-Nay knew who's baby it was. We all had to wait until the baby was born to find out who was the baby's daddy. We all lived upstairs together me and Tee, J and Gee and Nay-Nay.

As time went on a lady moved in with us her name was P. After a couple of weeks, P became a part of our crazy family. The days turned into weeks and the weeks into months. One day Tee went across the street to the other building where he hustled. The next thing I knew, we heard police sirens blearing. I ran to go look out the front window, what I saw scared me so bad. It looked like the S.W.A.T team outside, there were at least five to ten police cars all circling the building across the street and on our side of the block. There were police everywhere. One by one the officers brought someone out the "spot" across the street in handcuffs. And as I am watching and waiting, sure enough there he was, they brought Tee out in handcuffs. He was walking in front of an officer. Of course cursing loud and arguing with the officer, right up until they shoved him in a police car and closed the door. Word on the street spread quickly. The spot was raided and Tee got caught, he was cold busted. This is it Sherry, Tee went to jail. You can leave now, can't you? But instead of me going home where I belonged, I stayed. The choice to stay is what caused me to almost lose my life. I never saw Tee again after he went to jail. So many days and nights, I hated him because I wished I could have left him. But I couldn't because I was addicted to his drugs. I knew Tee before we started smoking crack and even though he was crazy back then, it was a different kind of crazy now. Before the drugs Tee was not really a bad brother, he just made some wrong choices in his life, just like the thousands of us who got caught up in the crack war. For all of the hurt and misery we caused each other, I ended up despising him. It was sad because there was a point in my life when we really had love for each other (as friends), before the drugs. But because of the drugs the love turned into hate. As crazy as it sounds, I understand, because Tee played the game and eventually he lost. Just like I did and so many others.

    After Tee was gone I found myself using the skills that I had learned from watching him. I started hustling drugs to support my habit and whenever I needed help J was right there to assist me. The more time J and I spent together, the closer we got. A couple of months after Tee was gone, Gee made a mistake that pretty much caused the end of her relationship with J. Gee became obsessed by her fears that she was losing her man and she started doing crazy things, completely out of the ordinary. One afternoon she left the building which was unheard of, and she was gone for the whole day. The only time Gee left the "Twilight Zone" was to go across the street to our other spot to hang out with J while he hustled, or to the corner store. After J checked across the street to make sure she was not there, he was so angry at her. No one saw her until later that night. We found out that Gee had cheated on J. That day when she got back she was acting very weird. She went into the bathroom and stayed in there for a long time. When she came back out she appeared very self-conscious. Gee admitted to J right in front of me that she slept with some man and he gave her a couple of dollars. She used the money to buy some crack and she offered J the drug, but he told her he don't want anything from her. I never saw him so mad at her. I mean I had seen them argue before but he never flat out disrespected her the way he did after that night. He told her that he did not want anything to do with her anymore and in fact he told her it was over. Gee was devastated and confused. I felt sorry for Gee because I could see it, J had broken her heart. He started to ignore her after that night and before I knew it, he and I got really close. All of the things he used to do with her, he only wanted to do with me now. And just like with Nay-Nay and me, although she and J's relationship was over, Gee could not leave, not because she didn't want to leave, the drugs kept her there. It wasn't until a few weeks later I guess, when it became too unbearable for Gee as she watched the closeness that developed between her man and me. One day she finally couldn't take it anymore, she packed her things and left "strike one". I never saw Gee again after that day but if I had the chance to, I would tell her I'm so sorry for the pain I caused her. I realize that it was different for her and that is why she was so possessive of J. She was not with J just because he supported her habit, she really loved her man, unlike me and Tee. I understand that it wasn't that she really needed to be in a psyche hospital, but like the rest of us the drugs had taken control of her mind. Ok maybe she probably could have benefited from some Outpatient Therapy (only kidding). But now with both Gee and Tee gone J and I began hustling together. Over the next several weeks I learned all the tricks of the game. What happened between J and I definitely was not planned, it really did just happen. J had been my protector all along. He took care of me even before Tee went to jail. Now with Tee and Gee gone, it was J and me. He made sure I ate, had the clothes I needed, he made sure I was safe and we had all the drugs we wanted. J was there for me in every way he could be, right up until the day we almost died together.

CHAPTER 6

"THE FIRE"

She "warned" me that day, you better not be here when I come home from work tonight and then she left "strike two". That was Jamaican Cynthia, she is Tee's ex-mother-in-law. Cynthia moved in downstairs months ago to help out Ms. Holmes. From the first day that she came to the "building", Cynthia wanted to take over control of everything and everyone. The first time she saw me in the "building", it had been years since the last time we saw each other, what you doing in here? I don't want to see you in here no more Sherry?. At first I thought ok, I know she is just tripping because she was upset that Tee and I had hooked up. Tee was her ex son-in-law so I thought maybe she was angry because her daughter and I were friends years ago and she did not like the idea that I was seeing Tee. But over the next couple weeks she made her feelings about me perfectly clear. We had gotten into several arguments. I never wanted to get into anything with Ms. Cynthia because number one she was old enough to be my mother and I respected her. But after she started threatening me, it became a major problem. I felt something much deeper was going on, it was as if she hated me and back then I really couldn't understand why, and I definitely did not care. Looking back, I wish I would have taken her threats a lot more serious. J was asleep so he didn't know Cynthia and I had just had an argument. J wake up, J wake up Cynthia and I just got into it again. J I'm leaving, it's something about her. I don't trust her. She is crazy and before we get into something serious, I'm leaving. She threatened me. She wants me outta here by the time she gets home tonight. She can't put you outta of nowhere, mon you crazy. Come mon and get some rest. Later for Cynthia, J said and then he pulled me to lay down with him, J held me close and he went back to sleep. That small voice in my spirit was talking to me again and I got a really weird, scary feeling. I laid down, I figured I would get a little rest. I knew things were getting critical, too much had happened and I knew it was time for me to leave. I had finally made up my mind when I wake up I'm going home. Shantel, Shantel (that is the name I went by in the streets) wake up! When I opened my eyes it was Nay-Nay who by the way had a baby girl. But of course when the doctors found drugs in the baby's system, DFACS got involved and took the baby. All I kept thinking was that I hope she has a better life than the one Nay-Nay would have given her. This was Nay-Nay's fifth child born addicted to drugs and put into the system. Maybe now the baby will have a decent life. We never saw the baby girl again. I remember as if it were yesterday, Nay-Nay waking me up, Sherry give me your pipe, I'm going to get some rock, I'll bring you some back. I was so sleepy, girl leave me alone. Shantel, wake up, come on let me hold your pipe. Here, I just gave it to her so she would leave me alone and I went back to sleep. I don't' know how long it was after that but she left and the next thing I heard, Shantel here, wake up, here take some she handed me the pipe as she put a rock in it. I smoked some of the drug and that is the last thing I remember (strike-three).

> **This is the actual reenactment of what it was like being in a house fire:**

    Oh, my God! Oh my God I repeated over and over as I pleaded with God for my life. Looking back now that day definitely didn't start out good at all. I had gotten in a very bad argument with Cynthia earlier remember, and she threatened me that I better be gone by the time she got home that night, so I was upset about that. I wanted to take a nap because I finally decided that I was going home. I wasn't comfortable with what went down between me and Cynthia. But I thought I could catch a nap and then be gone by the time she got home. Then Nay-Nay came woke me up and gave me the drugs. I remember lying down to sleep that afternoon with J. All of a sudden I began choking uncontrollably, for some reason I couldn't breathe. As I tried my best to focus my eyes to what was happening, the only thing I could see was black smoke. It was as if my eyes were closed but I knew they were open. Everything was black and red. I panicked! I could not recall where I was and then I realized that something was horribly wrong. All the while the room I was in was quickly filling with thick deadly smoke making it even harder for me to see anything, as my eyes began burning. I tried stretching my eyes as wide as I could, trying to see my surroundings. I felt like I was in a room with psychedelic lighting. Everything seemed so surreal as if I were dreaming. At first I was thinking this can't be happening to me. But it only took a second for me to understand what was really going down. At the same time there was this unbearable heat illuminating from everywhere. I just remember being in the darkest, scariest place of my entire life. I began to lose touch as the reality sunk in. I could no longer function. At first I couldn't even comprehend how to get to safety. I was overwhelmed by my fear. It really hit me like a ton of bricks. My God I'm in a fire. Unfortunately, I never had a chance. Especially since I never saw actual flames or fire burning anywhere in the whole apartment, just pitch black dark therefore, any chance of us escaping within those first few seconds were gone. I had been caught out there in my most vulnerable state, I was asleep. My chances to get to safety were hindered because precious moments were wasted just trying to focus my mind to what was happening to me and figuring out where I was. Had I been awake I could have reacted differently but as you know, it takes a few seconds to adjust when we wake from a sound sleep normally, so just try to imagine that you can't see anything and to make matters worse you can't breathe either. I was drugged, the room I was in was set afire, and they left us there to die.

In my attempt to comprehend what was happening, I'm thinking this can't be happening to me! Is this for real? It was so dark in there and I had nothing that I could use as a guide to help me see which direction the fire was coming from, that only made it worse. There was nothing to warn me which direction I should be going to. Go to your left Sherry, no Sherry go right. Oh God, it's so dark in here, I can't see anything! I didn't know with each step I took, if I were going deeper into danger or if I were going in the opposite direction to safety. It was impossible to tell where to run, I'm crying. At first I was, you know, just panicky but that quickly turned into horror, when I understood that this was not some dream or any joke. I understood that I had to get out of there real fast. I only knew one thing and that was I didn't want to die in there, not like that. And that is what brought me back to reality. I must be in hell! I'm suffocating to death! it's too dark in here… God I can't find a light. At first I was just scared, but within a matter of seconds the terror of not being able to get out of there for real, almost made me lose my mind. By now I was getting very dizzy from the smoke inhalation. I completely lost it, I was actually giving up, I tried everything I could think of and I couldn't get out. I saw death in that place. "If not for the Grace of God", he sent his Angel to come to me and willed me to fight for my life. Each time I tried to breathe, my mouth and nose was quickly filling with the deadly thick black smoke and carbon monoxide, I'm going to choke to death! The taste of burning fuel in my mouth and nostrils alone was enough to kill me. I became paralyzed with an unknown fear from the depths of my soul… My mind racing and my time running out, an unimaginable feeling of panic like nothing I've ever experienced before, overtook me. I'm screaming inside trying to think how I could get out of here. Desperately, I began reaching out in the dark trying to touch something, anything familiar, everything was black and red. Find a door Sherry, you've got to find a door! Is it over here? where I am? or is it over there somewhere? Please God, help me, help me get out of here! By now I was screaming for help at the top of my lungs. Knocking objects over trying to escape. I heard things crashing on the floor as I was bumping into tables, stumbling into things. I kept hearing all kinds of things falling and breaking. Some things I touched felt soft, other things were hard but everything I came into contact with was burning hot. It was the creepiest feeling not knowing what to do next. I became petrified in the darkness… I never stopped praying, God please show me some light. But the light never came. What was very weird to me was that I never saw any flames or fire while this whole thing was happening, just black and red heat waves. After a while I became too afraid to touch anything. I was scared to death standing still because that would mean I'd suffocate and die standing right there. But then I was even more terrified to take a step, for fear of walking into something or someone. Sherry, think, think, you gotta go now! Come on please get to a door or window. I became completely desperate; I thought I would go insane. I guess this is when I started going into shock. All I knew was that I needed to find the door or a window to jump out of or else I would die. I made up my mind I'd rather keep fighting than suffocate to death. So again I started taking baby steps, feeling around, not caring about getting burned or anything at this point. I just needed to get to someplace where I could breathe. By now I actually felt my hands burning when I came into contact with objects, so I had to touch things and squeeze whatever I came into contact with and release very quickly. I did not even know what I was feeling. When that did not work I thought to myself, ok you have to find a window and jump out, I kept telling myself. So I began stretching out my hands trying to feel for a wall. I knew that if I could find a wall it would lead me to the door or window and I would surely jump out. It never dawned on me that I was on the fourth floor. By now my only concern was to get out of the room, because the heat in there was so intense. It had to have been burning my skin and I now have the scars on my body that proves I was being burned, but for the life of me, I can't explain how this happened other than "But For The Grace Of God", I was not really feeling pain as I was being burned alive. I was more scared than I was feeling pain. Shantel, I keep hearing my name. J where are you? I can't see you. J, Oh my God help me! I can't breathe! When I could no longer inhale or exhale or scream any longer because the smoke would go in my mouth, I began reaching in the air stretching my arms out in front of me feeling out my surroundings and trying to mentally picture where I could be at in the room. For some reason, I thought I was in the front bedroom and I knew there were windows towards the front of the room. I frantically searched the dark looking around, all the while trying to scream and then close my mouth, scream and close my mouth. Who is that? I see someone running away. Help us! I'm screaming. But whoever it was, went running away in the opposite direction. I couldn't see the person but as sure as I was burning alive, I saw the reflection of someone going through the other rooms. For a second I just stood there watching the shadow running away, thinking what is that. In my desperation, I continued to search for an exit like a blind man walking with my hands stretched out, wildly walking or spinning around in the dark. I probably was just going in circles. When I actually began to feel myself slipping away, my body swaying back and forth for a few seconds, I just folded my arms standing still, I held myself crying and praying to God and screaming for my mommy, please help me! Still gasping with each breath I took, I stopped running around and I knew I was not going to get out. I was going to die. Before I passed out, I kept hearing J's voice screaming out my name over and over again. But every time I tried to open my mouth to answer him, I had to close it quickly because the smoke kept coming inside my mouth, choking the very life out of me. I felt myself falling down, it was like the floor jumped up and slapped me in my face. After collapsing, I don't know how long I laid there before the fire department showed up, but the next thing I heard was the familiar voice of Nay-Nay. She was responding to the Emergency Medical Technician's question. "What is her name? He yelled" the sound of her voice sounded urgent and very panicky when she screamed, "her name is Sherry, Sherry Graves". They saved me I don't know how, when or why. But God, and who ever finally called the fire department. All of the Firemen, the EMT's and the Doctors, surely saved my life that night. I regained consciousness for a minute and I knew I was safe. I'm laying down on something but I can't see, oh my God I'm blind! I can't see you, please help me. What I did not know was that I was in the ambulance. Then I heard a man's voice again, this time it was a different voice. He was speaking to me but it sounded like he was a million miles away, are my ears clogged too? I'll never ever forget what he said, that's right Sherry, I need you to breathe for me, your doing fine, you're going to be ok. Ok, ok, I'm breathing. Can you hear me? Then I just closed my eyes or they were already closed, I don't know because still I could not see a thing. I really thought I was blind because the whole time all I saw was red.

    I knew that the Angel God sent saved me that night. Thank you Father. I was semiconscious and couldn't comprehend much of anything but I was able to breathe again. The oxygen mask gave me back my life. I don't know who called the fire department or how long before they arrived. But I do know that what seemed like an eternity, in actuality could only have been a few minutes. I can't even begin to try to explain how it felt to be able to breathe again. Yet, right before I passed out again in the ambulance I remember thinking we're gonna be ok, we was in a fire. Thank you God, thank you, you saved me…

CHAPTER 7

"BUT FOR THE GRACE OF GOD"

That was February 1, 1989 twenty-three years ago, when I was transported from Brooklyn to Manhattan's New York Wiell Cornell Hospital, the best hospital in NYC for burn injuries. I was rescued by the New York City Fire Department. According to the report, I arrived at the hospital at 4:00 am and immediately I was taken to the Burn Clinic. I knew that God saved me because according to the report, the firemen found me curled up in a ball on the floor right underneath a window, unconscious. My Angel knew that if I had found that window, I would not be here telling my testimony today because as sure as my name is Sherry, I would have jumped out that window to get out of that burning place. I would have fallen four stories below and died. There was nothing to land on other than the black gate with spikes on the top. I had just celebrated my twenty fourth birthday exactly one week before the fire on January 24th. I felt heartbroken because I had no business being in that house. I should have been at home. In a million years, I would never have been able to prepare myself for what happened after that. My whole life changed.

A few weeks after I came home from the hospital, this is what Cocoa and Shainne told me. Shainne at the time was a teenager; she was at home sitting down watching television when the telephone rang. She picked up the phone and someone said Sherry's dead, she died in a fire last night. That's what the person on the other end of the phone said and then hung up. Shainne jumped up holding the phone in her hand, she stood there frozen for a second then she started running around the living room screaming and crying hysterically. She was home alone and did not know what to do or who to call. Cocoa was on her way home from work at the time the call came in and Shainne couldn't get in contact with her because back then there were no cell phones. Although ma and daddy lived downstairs while we lived upstairs both of them were also at work. Shainne was all alone, a kid and she had to deal with what she had just heard all by herself. As soon as Cocoa put her key in the door, the next thing she knew, Shainne practically broke her neck running down sixteen steps to meet her at the door. She was crying, screaming and hollering. By the time Shainne hit the bottom step, she dropped to her knees. Immediately Cocoa knew something was terribly wrong for Shainne to be carrying on like that. Instantly Cocoa felt weak to her knees and her heart started beating real fast. The first thing she said to Shainne was, Where is Telly? My niece's name is Shantel, we call her Telly. Telly is Cocoa's daughter, who at the time was around seven years old and the way Shainne was so hysterical, Cocoa thought something bad had happened to her little daughter. Shaine was screaming uncontrollably saying no, it's not Telly It's Sherry! Oh my God, a man called here and said Sherry's dead! Cocoa they said she died in a fire. What, did you just say? Ring, ring, the house phone is ringing again. Cocoa was completely in shock after hearing the news. She was walking up the stairs by instinct, feeling like she was in a dream, knowing she had to answer that phone call, but dreading to. This time the caller said. Sherry was in a fire but she didn't die. She is in the hospital, and they told her what hospital I was in and again hung up the phone. Cocoa now feeling sick in her stomach, sat down, her legs feeling like rubber. Who is this? she was screaming into the phone. Feeling like she could pass out, she just held the phone in her hand. It had been at least 2-3 months since the last time she had spoken to her sis. And the worst part was the last time she had saw me, we had a terrible argument because I stole fifty dollars from her and Cocoa had cursed me out so bad and kicked me out. She was so angry at me. I had completely destroyed all of the trust from my family members. They were so worried about me and so mad at me, yet they never turned their backs on me. Whenever I would go home, all I heard from them was that I needed to get help but of course, you know by now, I was not trying to hear any of them. Remember I did what I wanted to do and that has been my biggest problem all my life. My family knew that my drug use had gotten out of control because the only time they saw me was when I really needed some money or when I really needed to come to the house to steal something.

 My God, ma was out of her mind with worry about me. The last thing Cocoa had heard about me was from Roxy who had told her, Cocoa please go get your sis, she is doing real bad. Roxy told Cocoa that she tried everything to get me out of that crack house, but I would not leave with her. Roxy was just as close to Cocoa as I was, so she told her everything. Roxy had told Cocoa that the last time she saw me, I was so skinny and looking real bad. She told her about the fights with Tee and everything. She told Cocoa and Ramel to go to Bushwick and check up on Sherry to see for yourrself. But the problem was Roxy left before she could tell Cocoa the address. Later on after the fire, Roxy said she thought they knew where I was living. Cocoa felt so bad because that same weekend she and Ramel had decided they were gonna find me and even though they did not know exactly where I was staying they were coming to Bushwick to look for me. But they never did make it in time. Ok Cocoa think, think, what should I do? Snapping back into reality, I know let me call somebody, I know I'll call Ramel. Ramel she said as she tried to tell him what had happened, and all the while the butterflies in her stomach were jumping around like crazy. Ramel oh God, sit down, I got to tell you something. Girl what is wrong with you? What happened? Ramel, Sherry was in an accident. What! What you mean she was in an accident. What kind of accident? Ramel, Sherry is in the hospital. She was in a fire; she was burned real bad. The hospital said they don't know if she is going to make it. What! No, no, no! He broke down so bad, he just could not believe what happened to his lil sis.

I had been unconscious for the past three weeks since I was admitted to the hospital. I had gone through several grafts on different parts of my body during this time. It couldn't have been anything other than The Holy Spirit that breathed on me and caused me to wake up. And all I remember thinking was, "Oh My God, I'm alive". The first thing I saw was white creamy stuff all over my arms and legs. I was laying down in a bed, when I looked up there was this heating system sort of like a canopy covering the top of my bed. I'm in a hospital. A Nurse came to me, she seemed so happy to see me awake. She was smiling saying, hi Sherry. She introduced herself to me and told me I was in Cornell Hospital, in the burn unit and that I was unconscious for the past few weeks, after being in a house fire. As I looked around, I started noticing other people who looked very sick to me. I saw a man whose entire head was covered in what looked like a white cloth or bandages and all I saw was blood. Everywhere I looked I saw people with the creamy stuff just like I had on, somewhere on their body. For a few minutes, I just laid there wondering, what is all of this? I couldn't really remember what happened. I just knew I was so happy to be alive. The Nurse told me that my family had been there with me the whole time. She explained that the past couple of weeks had been extremely emotional for everyone. But all I saw was her lips moving, did she say I was in a fire. It was funny to me because I could not move my fingers, my arms or my hands; they were in a full cast. The whole scene was very weird. I started remembering a little bit of what happened. By the time some of my family members came to visit me that day, I was fully conscious. I had found out that I was brought into the hospital by EMS at 4:00 am. After the Doctors performed all the skin grafts and surgeries, they told my family that there was nothing more they could do for me. It was now up to my will to live and God. They informed everyone that I really needed their prayers because I had a 50-50 chance of living or dying. Everyone was telling me about all the drama of the different reactions from my family members after getting the news about the fire. One after the other they all fell apart. After my little sis got the phone call, she broke down and then when Cocoa got home from work and Shainne was inconsolable while telling Cocoa what happened, Cocoa fell apart. Cocoa called Ramel and before the end of the evening, the whole family had heard. Here's the funny part, now that everybody knew I was ok, the majority of them was scared to see me for fear of the unknown. The Doctors had told them how I was doing and of course Cocoa had ten thousand questions about what I looked like and if this was burned and was that burned and it was so crazy. Everyone took turns coming to visit me at the hospital. Mina was in St. Thomas at the time, so she was a complete mess. She had to catch the next flight to N.Y. I was told that my father stayed at my bedside day and night. He never left me, the whole time he just sat there watching me crying and crying. My uncles, Aus, Maakal, my brother Ramel and all of my cousins Brina, Neecie, Eve, Audria, Rachelle, my aunt Glo, Rita, they all came. Even more family that I can't name, it's too many. They went home and begged ma please don't go, she don't look good. I was unconscious the whole time they were coming. I did not have a clue what was going on. By the time my aunts and girl cousins came to see me, they were passing out and fainting all in the hospital and everything. Everyone was hysterical. Ma told them, you crazy! All you get ready to come and take me to see Sherry right now. So daddy took her to the hospital. Ma said she didn't care how I looked, I was her grandchild and she had to be there with me. She did admit later on that even though she was so scared, she was prepared because she prayed that I did not die. In fact she had her whole Church praying for me, the same Church that we used to go to when we were small children. She said that when she walked into that room and saw me lying in that bed, she was so happy. She told me that she did not care how I looked, she just started crying. She said my head was as big as a watermelon and white as snow. My whole body was swollen and of course I was covered in the white cream. I must have been a sight. Last but not least were two of the biggest chickens of all, Cocoa and my aunt Leila. She was the same one who put the baby doo-doo on my thumbs. They came to visit me at the hospital together because they are the scariest of everyone in the family. Before they even got into my room the rest of my cousins who were already there, started coaxing them saying just go ahead, go on they said, she's in there. Literally pushing them to my room. They said that they were both terrified to see me because prior to them getting the call about the fire, Cocoa had recently watched a movie about the little boy who was in a fire and she said he was severely burned on his whole body. She had so many images in her head about what I was going to look like and it scared her to death. Finally they entered my room. I was just bugging out with my cousins and they came in, it was so emotional. My sis hugged me so hard and so did my aunt. We laughed and cried and cried and laughed. Then after a while, they felt better. She said I didn't look half as bad as she had pictured. Cocoa laid in bed with me as I told them what happened and they told me what they knew.

  That was all just the beginning. I was admitted into the hospital on February 1, 1989 I was not discharged from there until nearly two months later on March 27, 1989. Every day was a journey for me. I was in real bad shape. Weeks later, when my casts were taken off, I was so hurt. When I saw the scars on my arms and hands for the first time, I thought look at me. I had burn scars all over my arms. On the outside I laughed because I still could not believe that I was in a fire but on the inside, my heart broke into a million pieces.

I must have said it a thousand times that I cannot believe this. But it wasn't that I could not believe it, I think it was more like how will I ever get over this.

CHAPTER 8

"I WILL CREATE A NEW SPIRIT IN YOU"

It was bitter sweet for me because from the moment my eyes opened, I have always been so grateful to God for saving me. I know I am blessed. I know that if not for the Grace of God, I would not be here today sharing my testimony. To me, my life was saved but in order to save me, I had to sacrifice my outer beautiful self. Which is why there has been created in me "A New Spirit". And then the real test began. I had to learn how to walk again so everyday my Nurses would come get me. At first my grueling work outs included just getting out of bed. I remember the first time they helped me, it took two Nurses to hold me up. I could not stand up by myself because I had been bed bound for so long. When I finally did get up, it felt like a thousand needles were going up and down my legs, sticking me. As the days passed, it went from me getting out of bed, to walking around in my room. Then I started walking in the hallways. A few weeks later my Physical Therapist wanted me to start going up and down the stairs. After a long while with the help of those wonderful Nurses and a lot of hard work, I was able to walk on my own. Another huge challenge for me was that I was not able to use my fingers because of the severe burns on my hands. I found that out one night when I was in my room after my sisters left and I went to open a can of soda. I could not open and close my fingers. I had to call for the Nurse to help me. I couldn't hold my fork and spoon, forget about using a knife. So I had to relearn how to use my hands again it took some time, but one day I was able to use my hands again. I regained my full vision, which in the fire, I thought was gone forever. One day I was alone in my room, it was morning so I had just showered and was sitting in my bed. I was trying to comb my hair when my Nurse came to my room, she asked if I wanted a mirror so I said yes. When she handed me the mirror, my normal reaction was to hold it to my face. I did not think twice about it, I just looked into the mirror. It was the first time that I had seen my face since the fire. Now, this is probably the most emotional, I had become since the fire because for some reason I had not a clue that my face was burned too. And when I looked in that mirror and I saw my face, I cried and I cried and I cried. I could not believe that my face had got burned. And what was more shocking was that the whole time my family came to visit me, no one had ever said a word about my face. I grabbed the phone and called Cocoa, crying on the phone I can't believe that you never told me my face is burned. Huh! Sherry Oh my God, you didn't know? Oh boobie, I'm so sorry I thought you knew. I can't believe you haven't seen your face in all this time. We both cried about that but after a while I said ok then so this is what I'm dealing with. I think that is when it really hit me for the first time and I finally had to admit it yes, Sherry you really were in a fire.

Then one day something so shocking happened. I was in my room again when my Nurse came to me and she said Sherry do you want to go see Glen? I said Glen, who is Glen? She said Glen is the man that was brought in with you. He was in the fire with you. Oh my God somebody was in the fire with me. I don't know anybody named Glen. So I tried to think real hard, who in the world is Glen but for the life of me I couldn't remember. She said he is in the room next door. You can go see him whenever you are ready. Immediately my heart started pounding, what is she talking about? I wanted to go see who this person was so I put on my little housecoat and pretty pink slippers my sis bought for me. I looked in the mirror to make sure I was ok,. I grabbed my pole with my I.V and I went to see who this man was. My heart started beating faster and faster the closer I got to the room, then finally I peeked in. Oh my God, I almost dropped to my knees. In complete shock, I saw the man my Nurse was talking about. He was not somebody named Glen it was J!

CHAPTER 9

"BOND FOR LIFE"

My God I just started crying. It was surreal. He was sitting in a chair by the window. I could not believe my eyes. It was J. We were in the fire together. It was his voice that I heard calling my name over and over again in the fire. We looked at each other and when he saw me, he broke down crying. His face still looked the same to me, only his whole body was very swollen. I sat down near him and we could not take our eyes off of each other. It was a feeling like I had never known in my life. It was unreal. Here we were after everything we had been through. We made it out. Both of us made it out alive. I searched every inch on J's frame. His face showed signs of the scars in particularly around his nose, but it was not that bad. J are you ok? He was just looking at me tears in his eyes. He shook his head yes. J we were in the fire together. Do you remember? He shook his head no. Sitting there we held each other and we cried together. It was the first time I had ever seen J cry.

We began comparing our scars. It was so crazy. He showed me his arms which were badly scarred. Both of his arms were burned but he still had his brown skin. On his left hand his pinky and ring finger was bent down and permanently stuck inside the palm of his hand. Then he showed me his back which was the area that was most damaged on his whole body. I could see where the Doctors had performed skin grafts but the result was his back was covered in black thick scar tissue. His stomach and chest were severely burned. He had some scars on his legs, but overall he was very lucky. We figured he must have fell face down when he passed out which is why he sustained the majority of his burns to his back. Now it was my turn. First of all my beautiful hair was half way gone. I guess the heat scorched it because it was not burned in the roots, just shorter. It was evident that the majority of the damage I sustained was to the front of my body which means that when I fell unconscious I fell down on my back then I must of curled up into a ball, which is how the Fireman said they found me. My scars are very visible. Looking at my face you can see scars covering my forehead which is why I have worn bangs since the fire. Now I know why I could not see anything during the fire, it was because my eyes were burning. On my nose you can see the scars clearly. Right above my top lip I have keloids. My throat area is severely scarred going straight down to my breasts. When I look at my breasts I still don't understand how only the top portion got burned. I guess God wanted to leave me with a reminder, because they are still beautiful, just different. Both of my arms are covered in burns except at the crevice just above the surface of my elbows which were not too badly scarred. The reason this area was not burned is because I was so terrified that I kept putting my arms up towards my heart holding myself, praying for a way out. One of the hardest parts on my body to look at is my hands. My hands bear the marks of the horror of what I went through that night. I was so desperate to find a window or the door that I just kept feeling and touching any and everything, trying to find an escape. One that never came. My hands show evidence of my fight to survive. My shoulders and the top of my back have scars. It seems funny that I have no burn scars anywhere below my breasts on my body except for a patch on my left butt cheek. I can't imagine that I sat down on something and burned my behind, but apparently somehow my left thigh got burned. Looking at my beautiful legs thank God they were not burned, however, the doctors took the skin from my legs which they used to do the skin grafts on my arms and hands, so the color is slightly different than my normal caramel complexion. I can actually see where they cut out patches of skin off my legs in the shape of rectangles.

Overall the doctors said I sustained 3rd degree burns to twenty percent of my body. J just looked at me while I revealed to him my new self. It was the same way I looked at him while he showed me himself. A look of complete amazement, it was a time that can never be erased from my memory. J had felt my pain just like I felt his. In that moment, we shared a bond that could never be broken. We went through hell together but for the Grace of God, we both survived. I saw death that night. I felt it and I tasted it. It is a feeling like no other. It's a fear that is unexplainable. To this day, I have to sleep with a night light on because I have a fear of darkness. One day my cousin was in my hospital room visiting me, we were just chatting about the good old days when in walks Roxy. I could tell that she was crying. She held me so tight and all I could do was smile. I was smiling because I knew it was the only way she would stop crying and I did not want her to cry and plus I was sick of crying so I laughed. It's my fault sis, I am so sorry, she was squeezing the life out of me and crying her eyes out. Stop it, it is not your fault. I let her know that she does not have to feel bad it was not her fault. Every choice that I made, I made. I don't blame you. I was the one who decided to smoke crack. And I was the one who chose to move in. After that first time Roxy took me to the "building" she would come over at least twice a week to see me and hang out. Roxy witnessed me and Tee going at it plenty of times and each time she was right there throwing down with me. I can't tell you how many times Roxy and Tee went at it. He hated whenever she came to see me because he knew that I loved my sis and if he messed around, I would leave with Roxy and he feared I would leave him. She begged me a thousand times to leave him. She would say come on sis, look I got money.

And she would show me a handful of money because she knew that was the bottom line. But no matter how much money she had I was not leaving because I had all the drugs I needed right there with Tee and all the craziness.

She'd say let's go out sis, you want to go hang out? Roxy begged me plenty of days. She would try to think of any place she could think of, just to get me out of there. But of course I wasn't trying to hear her and nobody else. That has always been my biggest problem, I have the hardest head in the whole world and when my mind is made up about something, the only time it will change is when hell freezes over. What was amazing about this whole thing is that Roxy's mother is a Pastor (I Will Always Love You Pastor Schoels). I can't tell you how many days and nights her mother prayed for both of us.

I can remember so many times after hanging out and feeling so tired, we would go or rather sneak upstairs to spend the night at Roxy's house. We would come inside in the middle of the night. Ms. Schoels would be on her knees Praying and crying for all of our souls. Shantel, mommy is in the other room visiting J,. She was praying over him and she didn't even know J Roxy and I laid in the bed together and I showed her all of my scars. She cried again and again but I kept laughing. I had to laugh while I showed her my hands because it was surreal and she said Sherry stop it, stop laughing it's not funny. But it was all I could do not to cry, looking at my beautiful hands all scarred. Roxy kept feeling that I blamed her, so I told her that I forgive her and she knew that I meant it. A little while later Ms. Schoels came in and we had a Holy Ghost time praying and pleading the Blood of Jesus over all of us.

In the days that followed, everyday J and I spent time together in the hospital. I would go to his room, we would play checkers or cards and talk for hours. He would come to my room and get me, so that we could take a walk around the hospital. Every day we visited the burn clinic where I saw all of those small little babies and children who were in a fire. It broke my heart to imagine what they must have gone through. I'll never forget the pain I felt for each and every one of them. It was so hard for me to comprehend it all because I know what I went through as an adult. But just to have to think of all those little babies suffering through that nightmare was unimaginable. Seeing their little faces and bodies all scarred is an image that haunts me until this day. Honestly I was so scared because when I saw those children so badly burned, I was seeing me. I started to wonder what it was going to be like when I got released from the hospital. But nothing could have ever prepared me for what I was about to face. That day when I saw my face I think it was the first time I cried about my own scars. That's because when I woke up in the hospital three weeks after the fire fully conscious, the only thing I remember thinking was that I was so happy to be alive. I could not believe that I survived. At that moment, I did not care about the white cream I saw all over my body or the casts on my arms. I did not even care that I could hardly move my body or anything. I just knew that God had saved me and the only thing I felt was absolute gratitude to my Heavenly Father. But the hardest times for me came when my family and friends went home after visiting me all day and J was in his room for the night and the Nurses had already did their rounds and checked in on me. Now it was just me, myself and my scars. I felt such sadness, guilt and shame. I was sad because I felt ugly. Looking at every inch of my body alone with myself, it was so personal. For the first time in my entire life I felt ugly. Even with my family's complete support, there was nothing anyone could do to sooth my pain. It was then that I started becoming very self-conscious. When I examined my scars I admitted to myself that they were horrific. I did not need anyone else to confirm that for me. It was just how I felt from the deepest part of my being. Waking up for me that day was bitter sweet. Yes, I can't explain to you how grateful I was to be alive. But on the other hand seeing what I looked like now was without a doubt the most unbearable thing I would ever have to deal with. And I did not have a clue how I would do that. All I knew was one day I went to sleep and I was quote on quote normal and beautiful and the next day when I woke up and I was no longer beautiful, instead something horrible had happened to me. I felt ugly, but I was grateful (God's Grace eventually changed all that). In a moment my whole life changed. Life as I had known it would never be the same. I lived with extreme guilt. Guilt because I knew I had no business being in "the building" in the first place.

All of the people in the building that I had considered my friends, had been telling me, Sherry why don't you go home? A very good friend begged me to leave. Tee is gone Sherry, why won't you just go back home? In the weeks that led up to the fire, a lot of things were going on. For instance Gee had just left and I did not want to leave J. He was stressed about everything. Even though Cynthia and I were going at it something terrible, and she was serious that she wanted me out, J really did not want me to leave. Ok, ok, I'll stay until after the Holidays. I told myself, but Thanksgiving came and left, I was still here. Christmas came and left, still here. By the time January 24th came (my birthday), I should have been went back home, but in my heart, I was just confused and afraid. Looking back now I had plenty of warnings and numerous chances to leave, but I did not listen to that little voice within my spirit. I knew it was not the same hanging out in there anymore. Sure enough that feeling that something bad was going to happen, well it did.

I was so ashamed and embarrassed about my scars. I was embarrassed in the hospital, so I imagined what it would be like on the outside. I could not look anyone in the eye, because I felt ugly inside and out. And I knew that if I felt ugly and it was my body then what must I have looked like to everyone else. I had a lot of anxiety coming up to the day that I was going to leave the hospital. I would finally be going home a little less than two months. I was looking forward to going home but I was terrified. The week that I was going home was so sad for me because I had established a close relationship with my wonderful Nurses and Doctors. I thanked them by drawing pictures and writing letters to them for showing me a lot of love and for the care that they provided to me. I felt like they all helped to save our lives. J and I talked every day and it was funny that I was leaving first. It seems that although J's scars were less evident than mine, his were actually more life threatening. One of J's lungs had collapsed as a result of the fire. Initially when the Doctors broke the news to J's family, they were actually informed to begin making funeral arrangements because the Doctors did not expect him to make it. J was in a coma for almost 1 month. His Doctors said it was a miracle that he survived and had made a full recovery. J would be leaving the hospital the following week so it was all good. The arrangements were made and guess what? finally I was going back home. Cocoa and my grandfather would come to the hospital first thing in the morning to pick me up in the car. The night before I was leaving J and I was playing cards in my room talking, laughing and joking like we normally did but this time it was different. I was scared and he knew it. I was the first one to be leaving and it felt very funny. He tried to comfort me by telling me that he would be out next week and that everything was going to be ok. A few weeks prior to me leaving the hospital, I was measured for my burn uniform that I was instructed to wear 24-hours a day. Also I had a special mask that was molded to fit my face that would protect my scar tissue from the sun. Then the day really came. I had butterflies all inside my stomach. I was an emotional wreck! I felt happy, sad, nauseas, and anxious I was a mess that morning. J helped me prepare myself as best I could. Cocoa and daddy came to pick me up and then it was time to go home. I told J that I would see him in a couple of days, because even though I was discharged from the hospital, I would be coming back every week for Physical Therapy. My first appointment to come back for a checkup was in one week, the same day that J would be discharged, so I told him we would take him home. J was going back to live at his mother's house, while he recovered from his injuries.

CHAPTER 10

"BEHIND MY SCARS"

This is the day that I had waited for but it was also the day that I dreaded for so long. I was leaving the safety of the hospital and going to face the big bad world. J and I said our goodbyes. I promised him that I would come pick him up when he was discharge the following week. My heart was beating so fast, after all, the last time I was outside I was what we refer to as" normal' and now after being in the fire and surviving, I was no longer "normal". It was time for me to face myself. So my Nurse wheeled me downstairs and with my sis by my side I was off I was going back home. I had my balloons and all of my momentums that I had acquired from my family throughout my stay in the hospital. But most of all, I had my new scars. The day that I had been waiting for had finally come. From the time I regained consciousness, I was asking my Doctors, so when can I go home? They would say soon Sherry, very soon. We just need to make sure you are 100% ok. All that time I thought I was so anxious to go home. Until the day really came and when it did come, all of a sudden I was so afraid. I was paralyzed by my fear of leaving the hospital. For the past two months I was safe and secure in the hospital. I never felt different because the Nurses and Doctors never once made me feel different or ugly. From the moment I first opened my eyes, the Nurses and Doctors showed me nothing but love, care and concern. I guessed it's because they are trained professionals. As far as the patients, well they looked just like me in one way or another. Also I just figured that after seeing people with burn scars all the time, it's probably more traumatic for the survivor than it was for the medical staff. Nevertheless, going outside was something completely different for me. All I knew is that the Devil kept telling me that there was a whole world out there just waiting to see me all burned up. (Get thee behind me Satan). Although everyone had heard that I was in a fire, the only people who had actually seen me were my family and closest friends. But now as I was getting closer and closer to going out of that door, my heart started beating really fast. I wanted to cover myself up especially my face. I did not want anyone seeing me at all. The only thing I knew was that I was ugly and my only concern was getting into my grandfather's car ASAP and getting home. And never, I mean never coming back outside again. It was a long drive from Manhattan to Brooklyn. All the while that I was sitting in the back seat of the car, my sis and daddy was talking to me, but I was in a fog. My eyes were looking around watching everyone, funny how it takes a tragedy for people to take notice of life and all of God's creation. As I watched everyone going about their lives, for the first time in my life, I began to take notice of the little things. I saw all kinds of people some were beautiful while others were not so pretty. I saw fat, skinny, tall, short, whites, blacks, Chinese, Jews, I mean it was very interesting to see so much diversity. I watched the birds, trees, grass, sky, cars, airplanes, taking it all in. I smelled the air. I watched lovers and couples holding hands, laughing together, they looked so happy, just the intimacy that people share and then I got so frightened. For the first time in my life, I had to wonder would that ever be me again. Never before did I have to worry about getting a man. I had any man I ever wanted. I was the one who did the refusing. I was in control of who, what, where, when and how. I had always gotten what I wanted, when I wanted it. And as soon as I looked down and saw myself, I quickly began to realize from now on, it would be a very different ballgame for me.

So we pulled up in front of the house and I just looked out the window at our house. This is the house that I was raised in. It was the only true place I could ever call home. I was so sad when we arrived because after all that I went through, when I had the chance to go back home as the Sherry that I was, I did not want too. And now I am coming back home as the Sherry I did not want to be. I knew everyone on our block and everyone knew me. At least they knew the old Sherry. Boy was I ashamed to let them see the new me. All I could think was wow, it took all of this for me to be where I needed to be, at home where I know I was loved. I just laughed to myself as I always do when it is all I can do to keep myself from crying. My sis already knew what I was going through because I confide everything in her. She knew I felt funny and she understood that I was embarrassed. She felt so bad for me. She did her best to encourage me not to worry about any of that. She would say, sis it doesn't look as bad as you think it does and of course I looked at her like she had seven heads. As soon as we parked I grabbed what I could and jetted in the house. When I walked in the house that I lived in all of my life, I felt at home. It had been several months since the last time I was home. I felt like a little girl again, like I was safe and warm. But a funny thing happened upstairs, my little niece Telly had not seen me since before the fire she was too young to visit me at the hospital. So the first time she saw me, I had on the outfit I was told to wear, in addition to the mask which by the way I could not stand to wear. My sis tried to prepare her as best she could about what happened to (auntie) Sherry, but we found out that nothing could have prepared my niece for what she saw and felt. At the time she was only seven years old. I went to reach out to hug her and she ran straight into her mother's arms. We both realized that she was scared to death. I felt like I could have crawled into a hole. My own niece was afraid to look at me. Who could blame her, though after all I looked like a mummy, all wrapped up in my Burn Garments. I was told I had to wear it every day, all day to protect my skin from getting keloids. Unfortunately for me by the time summertime time rolled around, you couldn't even pay me a million dollars to wear that thing under my clothes. At least I did try to give it a shot, even though I felt like a dang fool, not to mention what I looked like. And the one time I called myself wearing it, was summertime and 90 degrees outside, of course I almost died again, from heat exhaustion. I'm sorry, I just could not do it. Eventually I ended up paying for it though, because instead of my scars healing nice and smoothly, they ended up healing nice and lumpy. The color was made especially for me, supposedly to match my skin tone and so as not to look so obvious, but of course it was very obvious. I was supposed to wear this plastic mask on my face and I'm sure I looked worse than Jason from Friday the 13th. At least they tried to make it a clear colored mask so you could still see my face. The eyes, nose and mouth were sculptured to fit my face but none of that helped me out in the least. I was just a mess and no one had to tell me, I already knew it. I was so very grateful for all of the time and effort that was put into getting me those necessities, after all it took my Nurse almost a whole day to measure every inch of my body, from the crown of my head to the tips of my toes, but baby it just wasn't working out for me at all.

My sis tried so hard, she said, look Tell see it's Sherry it's ok, don't be scared. After I realized how terrified she was, I said Cocoa it's ok, don't force her, in her own time, when she is ready, she will look at me. My niece held on so tight to Cocoa's leg and she squeezed her head into her mother's leg and refused to look at me. And over the next couple of days, every time she had to see me, Telly would run right past me. When that happened which was every day, my sis and I would just look at each other and start cracking up. It really was funny, even though deep down inside Cocoa knew I was devastated. I felt a little better over the next couple of days when instead of running, Telly would walk past me real fast, but at least, by now she started saying hi Sherry, as she was running to her mommy. I would just start cracking up. After a while she would come and sit down with us and I would see her peeping at me. By the end of the week she finally started feeling a little more comfortable with me and she began to come to me on her own and we would talk and laugh until we got as close as we were before the fire. I will never forget that experience. I will always remember what that felt like. Even though it was my niece and she was only a little girl and I know she did not intentionally want to hurt my feelings, it did. And subconsciously I guess all of those situations contributed to me knowing what it felt like to be completely rejected. But that was only the beginning, over the next couple of days, I had visits from all of our neighbors who had heard that I was home from the hospital. One by one, people came by to visit me. My sisters knew only the people who were genuinely concerned about me were allowed to come see me, our closest friends. The other people who just wanted to be nosey, well let's just say they will have to see me another day another time. By the end of the week I had definitely answered my own question, yes, Sherry you really were in a fire. I began to understand that what happened to me was tragic but that was to say the least because when I said before that my whole life had changed, I quickly realized that, that was an understatement. You can't imagine how hard it was for me getting adjusted to this new self. I mean my self-esteem and self-worth went from one hundred percent to zero. I had never been embarrassed about my looks before in my life. I mean of course I had a bad hair day here and there or needed the fashion police on a few occasions, but nothing major, nothing that couldn't be fixed. But now here I was feeling like the ugliest duckling in the whole pond. Nothing I put on felt right. I just wanted to cover myself up. I didn't want any scar on my body exposed. Thank God I had long hair because I was able to cover my forehead up with my bangs. For a minute I even contemplated becoming a Muslim or at the very least just dressing like one. But I decided against it, I knew I would look and feel like a dang fool. Instead I wore long sleeved shirts and pants everywhere I went. Unfortunately for me, I could not do anything to cover up my hands. I was released from the hospital in the Spring, it was March, so I just prayed hard for Winter to come ASAP, so then at least I could wear gloves all day, every day. But I was not prepared for what was to come next. You guessed it, what comes after Spring, yep Summer. The Summer of '89, my first Summer after the fire was the worst period of my entire life. Prior to the fire, Summertime was my best time of the year. I was always fly wearing Tee-shirts, tank tops, back outs, shorts and mini-skirts, not to mention the only bathing suits I wore were bikinis. Now I couldn't wear any of that and I was truly heartbroken and distraught. The last thing I wanted to do in the Summertime is cover myself up. That's when I really realized this having these scars is going to be worse than I ever imagined. Do you know what a problem it is to have to cover yourself up at a time when everyone else is trying to take off as many clothes as possible? No, well let me be the first one to tell you, it is horrible. Forgive me, but there is no honest way to say it than to admit that I was just plain miserable. By the middle of the summer I was experiencing major depression. Seriously, I just wanted to die. Everywhere I looked I saw the latest fashions but every time Cocoa and I went shopping, all I could look for was long sleeve this and long pants that to cover myself up. And as if that wasn't horrible enough, not only did I have to look for long sleeve clothes, I had to find material that I would still feel comfortable in, so I needed sheer material that would keep me cool. Imagine it's 90 degrees outside not including the humidity and I have to wear clothes to cover myself up, trying to hide my scars. After suffering the first year, I began to hate the Summertime and every year was the same thing. When I knew Summer was near, I would become so depressed, in fact I dreaded it. The hardest thing to do was to find Summer clothes that I could wear that allowed me to keep cool and plus be the prettiest burn victim anyone has ever seen.

I was ok at home because remember our good old balcony. I was so happy to see it again. In the daytime I would hang out on the balcony with my family where really no one could see me and at night we would sit on the porch. I could hang outside without really being around everyone. Sitting outside like that was fine, as long as I could hide myself from everyone. But the first time I had to really be outside away from sitting on the porch was the week following my discharge from the hospital. I had my physical therapy appointment at Cornell hospital and the only thing that made me feel good about going back to the hospital was because I knew I was going to pick up J. Finally it was his time to get discharged from the hospital. He was going back home to stay at his parent's house. My grandfather and I promised him we were going to drive him home that day. I was anxious because I knew I was going to visit the people that I had made friends with (the other patients in the hospital). I also felt happy because I would see my Doctors and Nurses again. It's funny but I did miss all of these people who had become a part of my life in the last two months. So daddy drove me to Manhattan every time I had an appointment and he even waited for me to get finished with my therapy sessions every week, no matter how many hours it took. And he never once complained. My whole family supported me and has never left my side even through years of lying, stealing from them and deceiving them.

They have been there for me even when I rejected their love, help and concern. I am blessed to have the family that I have. They all knew there was no way I was ever going to the hospital unless I was getting a ride. During this time even thinking about riding a train or bus was inconceivable to me. Even though I had been going outside, I was definitely nowhere near ready for public transportation. I was not going anywhere far from the house. Everyone tried to make me feel good but due to my own complex, my self-esteem was at an all-time low. I began watching people's reaction to me everywhere I went. It took me years to get over how people reacted to me. In the beginning it was just too painful. I was not accustomed to people staring at me in a bad way, and I didn't think I would ever get used to it. So I held my head down most of the time. I would not look any one in the eyes with the exception of my family. I noticed immediately people's expressions, some people looked at me in shock, disgust, confusion, amazement or unbelief. So many people looked at me with deep sympathy, while others showed a hint of enthusiasm. I guess looking at me, they understood that I have been through something and whatever it was that I went through, I survived it. But through it all, I had to and I still have to deal with being looked at differently. So we arrived at the hospital. As I was walking inside, I notice the stares and glances and immediately I become very self-conscious. It is a feeling like I can't explain. So I just block the people out and focused on doing what I came there to do, because as much as I wanted to, I realized that I can't run from people the rest of my life. So I get on the elevator, my first stop was to go to

J's room. As soon as I reached the floor we had shared, I began to feel safe again. I went to the Nurse's station to visit my Nurses and Doctors. When I got to the window, they were as happy to see me as I was to see them. Well, look who's here they said. It's so great to see you getting around by yourself. There is someone anxiously waiting for you. I started laughing because knowing J, he's been ready to go since early this morning. We got caught up on how things were going since I left the hospital. After a few minutes of chit-chat, I excused myself because it was time to go see J. I walked into his room and he was sitting in his favorite chair looking out the window. Wow, I say to myself, it's going to take some getting used to seeing each other this way. J smiled and I smiled back at him. So what's up baby? I see you ready to go. I looked at J, he was moving slow. His body was still swollen but not as much as it was a couple weeks ago. I looked in his face and I thought to myself, thank God, he was lucky because he only had a hint of scar tissue on his face. His hands looked so big. I checked J's two fingers which were still closed shut and I wondered how he is going to manage to do the things that he was accustomed to doing without full use of his hand. As I watched J from head to toe with his clothes on, I just didn't know how he would deal with this new self. For a minute we just looked at each other and all we could do was shake our heads. Yes, me ready long time, J says in his Jamaican accent. All the time I was wondering, is he really? Was J. really ready for what lies ahead? In the past week I had a taste of what our life is like now after the fire and all I was thinking is, baby you better buckle up and strap in because it's going to be a long, long ride. J I'll be right back I have to go to physical therapy, it shouldn't take too long ok, daddy is waiting for us downstairs. Yes mon go on, I ain't going nowhere anyway. As I left J's room, I stopped by the Nurse's station to find out if all of the paperwork for his discharge was completed and informed the Nurse to get his wheelchair ready. She told me she is going to take care of everything. After I finished my therapy session which basically consisted of me doing hand and arm exercises, I went to the burn clinic. I just had to see my little babies. I got the same feeling that I did when I was a patient and J and I would leave our rooms and take a walk to the burn clinic. My hands got all sweaty and my heart started to beat real fast. I was still so scared to see all of those people especially the little babies in cribs but I just had to go. As I watched them, some were playing with toys while other children were just laying around in bed, clueless of what their lives would be like growing up as a burn victim. My heart broke because their little lives had not even started, yet here they were scarred for life. Silently I said a Prayer for all of them and for J and I then I left feeling familiarly sad.

About an hour later, I arrived back at J's room. I see the Nurse helping him into a wheelchair. I said, well let's do this. Thanks mon for everything he says to his Nurse. She just laughs and I said really you all are the best. I'll see you soon. There is a man dressed in a hospital uniform, he is there to escort us downstairs to the ground floor where daddy is waiting for us in the car. Downstairs J gets out of the wheelchair and we thank the man and turn to go out the door. Outside I can see daddy's car, J walks slowly towards the car. Oh daddy, thank you so much for waiting all this time for us. Mr. Malone how you doing Sir? I'm fine young man, my grandfather says, getting out of the car to open the door for us. How are you doing? I guess you must be glad to be going home, huh? Yes, mon. My grandfather did not meet J until he saw him in the hospital one day when my family was visiting me. I told them about J. and introduced him to everyone. Over the next few months, I got to meet J's family too. Prior to the fire, no one in my family had ever known anything about J and I had only met his parents one time when he took me to their house. An hour or so later, we were back in Brooklyn. We pulled up in front of J's parents' house. I heard myself saying daddy you go on home, I will see you a little later. J will make sure I get home. Tell ma I'll see her later tonight. Mr. Malone, thanks mon, thanks for everything. Sherry are you sure? Because when I leave from here, I'm not coming back this way to get you. Yes, I'll be ok daddy, don't worry. I kissed my grandfather bye and I got out of the car with J. We watched him pull off, as I waved goodbye. It was high afternoon when we arrived at J's house. We rang the bell and his mother came to the door, she was smiling at both of us. We all went inside where J's father was in the living room watching T.V. When I took a good look at J's father, I was amazed at the similarity. J was the splitting image of his father. Mr. Hutchy was a tall slim man well-kept and very handsome. He had the same golden brown complexion that J had. I just kept looking at the both of them saying to myself, wow J looks just like his father. Mrs. Hutchy, J's mother is a small chocolate woman and instantly I could see that she is beautiful. She had it going on. She was wearing more gold jewelry than I was and her hair was the latest fashion. I could tell that she was something else in her younger days too, because she still had it going on and mama had to be at least in her late sixties, when I first met her. My spirit took to J's parents. From the first day I met mama, she welcomed me into her home. And after several weeks of going to visit J, I became a part of the family.

 I met all of his family, including his two sisters, Yvonne and Pee and his three brothers, Coury, Orvin, and Onelle. I found out real soon that J's sisters are crazy. I love them and I had so much fun whenever I was hanging out at J's house, which was mostly on the weekend. I was always fascinated with his sister Yvonne because she was like this movie star or someone very elegant. I don't think she knew it, but I used to just love to sit down and watch and listen to her talking. It was amazing how she would go between languages. You would never even know she is Jamaican because she uses the American accent so well. But honey at home when someone was getting on her nerves, ooh child, watch out because the Jamaican in her surely came out and it was a whole different ballgame. She is a ball of fire. Every time I saw his sister

Yvonne, she was giving me some fly shoes or fancy clothes of hers. Look here "CHERYL", she never calls me Sherry and I just laugh because I love her accent when she is saying my name. You can fit this dress, try on these shoes and see if you can fit them, they nice right? Ooh Yvonne I love these shoes girl are you giving these to me? Yes mon take em. Me have some nice things me gon bring for you, me forget home in Long Island but me will remember to leave them with mama for you here. Thanks Yvonne, and any time you want to give some stuff away just hold it for me. I was so happy to get stuff from Yvonne because she wore the most expensive clothes, shoes and pocketbooks, everything was top dollar. Lord, girl where you going? Where is J? Look at you Cheryl you looking good child. Now that's J's other sister Pee. God I love Pee, she kept me cracking up. Pee will be asking you a hundred questions, but the funny part is, by the time you try to answer each question, she already gone off into something else. Your hair look so pretty, a ya real hair dat? Wow, it's so long and pretty, it don't even look real. Little girl what's wrong with you? That's her little daughter Natrina, she is talking too now. Whappen to you? Jamaicans don't say "what happened" they say "whappen". Cheryl you get fat girl. You look good. Alright me gon upstairs, I'll talk to you a little later, mon. You must come upstairs before you leave, hear? And as she is walking upstairs, she is still screaming at her daughter. God I love them, they are so funny. Of course I never even got the chance to tell her, J was downstairs. Every time I saw Pee she was going to some party. She wore the hottest clothes and her hair weave was always tight. Yvonne has six children. Her daughter, Terisha could be on Americas Next Top Model. She is so beautiful. Hi "Cheryl" how you doing? where is J? I'm good Terisha, how are you doing girl, you alright? Yea I'm fine. Ok I'll see you later, she says running out the door. Those teenagers are something else. But the thing that I loved about J's family is they never looked at me different. I mean because of the scars. I don't even know if they saw the scars. They didn't know me before the fire and from the first time I ever met them, they have loved me, treated me like I was a part of the family and always made me feel so special. And Yvonne's sons, well let's just say she definitely has her hands full. But Yvonne knows how to handle all of her boys, she loves them so much. The cutest thing is that all of their first names starts with the letter D. Yvonne's husband, he's so handsome. He has always been there for J and I. From the bottom of my heart, I thank you for everything P. Many days you Saved us when you didn't even know it. J loves his brother-in-law, he talks about him all the time. Pee has four daughters, her oldest daughter is Carlisha, but instead of calling her by her name, I'll just call her sexy because that is the best way to describe her. She is about my height with a body that looks better than Halle Berry and Jennifer Lopez put together.

She wears her hair long and she wears the sexiest clothes, even her shoes are sexy. The funniest thing about Carlisha is that I have walked to the store with her plenty of times and I have witnessed men almost crash their cars into each other, just trying to catch a glimpse of her walking across the streets. I would look at her and she'd look at me and we just busted out laughing. The thing I love the most about Carlisha is not only is she beautiful, she has a beautiful spirit and she has a heart bigger than anyone I know.

Carlisha loves her uncle J and he adored her too. Whenever J saw Carlisha, he would say whappen sexy? And she would laugh. Pee had three younger daughters too, Tiff, Marsha and the baby Natrina. So she definitely had her hands full. On the weekends, I just loved staying over at J's house because it was like at a fashion show or something. All of his sisters and his niece would be getting ready to go partying Friday or Saturday night and it was pure drama going on. By the time they finished getting dressed they looked like super stars. The clothes they wore were like costumes glistening in the darkness. The parties they went to were usually video-recorded and they brought home the DVD. I couldn't wait to watch them on the DVD. The camera man takes close-up shots of the women. Some ladies wearing shiny short-shorts, and lace stockings, pointy boustieres or brassieres, belly-shirts and cut-out tee's. They were wearing boots that come up above the knees with high, high heels. And they wore all kinds of big flashy gold and diamond jewelry, covering their ears, nose, neck, fingers and hands. They wore the latest hair weaves, in various colors, including blue, gold and red. Some were real short while others were extremely long. We would all sit around in the living room watching the tapes of the Dance Hall Parties, especially mama. She would be the first one sitting down to watch. Me, J, his sisters and brothers, all of us, cracking up laughing. All of us there having a good time. J was the oldest child,. His brother Coury's fiancé is Contessa. Contessa is even crazier than both of his sisters. Contessa is a big, beautiful and crazy light skinned sister, and from the very first time I met Contessa, I loved her. She hung out with J and I and made sure we were good (love you sis). Contessa ended up saving my life in more ways than one. She has always been there for me. The thing that I love about her is her presence, she has a very demanding presence. When she walks into a room, everyone has to stare at her, that is just the way it is. She has been through some things herself but she always comes out on top. But even with all of the fun we had with his family, I noticed something every since the day I dropped J home from the hospital, I could see that he was going through something.. I knew just what he was going through. because I had experienced it already. He was going through a depression. We were both depressed. I did not expect it was going to be easy for him but I was not prepared for just how hard it was going to be. Life wasn't the same for either one of us. Many nights we were alone we talked to each other about our circumstances. I knew how J felt and he knew how I felt. The truth was we were both feeling pretty bad.

CHAPTER 11
"THE RELAPSE"

I knew it was going to be hard for J after getting out of the hospital but I didn't know just how hard it was going to be. Both of us were devastated after the fire. Depressed and feeling hopeless, we did what we knew we could do that would take away the pain we felt, we relapsed. After everything we had been through together in the past year, the drugs, our relationship, all the happy and sad times that we shared, meant nothing because after the fire, we realized that there was nothing either one of us could do to comfort the other. And so our way of not dealing with the pain we felt, led us right back to the thing that almost caused us to lose our lives, the drugs. One day while we were at J parents' house in Flatbush it happened, sitting in his basement room, J said, yo mon, me soon come. Ok J, you want me to come with you? No, stay here wait for me. J left me there, so I watched T.V. while I waited for him to come back home. A little while later when J got back, he did not say a word, but what I saw him do next, sent a chill through my body. "The little white rocks looked so innocent on the table" but this time I knew the destruction they were gonna cost. I watched in amazement as J put a rock in his pipe and puffed long and hard. When J sat the pipe on the table, before I knew it, I picked it up, put a rock in it and took and long hard pull, and just like that we were back on a mission.

After the fire I had promised myself that no matter what, I would never do drugs again. I hadn't had any drugs in my system for the two months that we were in the hospital and then just like that, I chose to give it all up. After waking up in the hospital, and seeing my new self, I knew that it was going to be hard. But the first time I saw J in his room after the fire, I said yes Sherry, this is going to be real hard to deal with, for both of us. Over the past several months, I saw the hurt every time I looked in J's eyes. Because it was the same hurt I saw in mine every time I looked in a mirror. The truth is that neither one of us were dealing with the aftermath of the fire well at all. The past couple of months were the hardest times of my entire life and I started to feel like I'm all burned up now, what difference does it make. The first couple of days after we relapsed were bad enough on J and I, but within a month's time, we were back out there and it was as if we had never stopped using drugs. Only this time it was a whole different ballgame. You see before we never had to worry about where we would get the money from to buy drugs because we were the drug dealers. When we lived at the "building", we never really had to go outside to buy drugs because we sold the drugs right in the comfort of our own home. Going from never having to think twice about your appearance, what you look like or what you are wearing, to dreading for anyone to see you, is a horrible, horrible feeling. Before we looked like "normal" drug addicts, we fit right in but now things were very different, we had the scars. Every time we had to go to a spot to cop our drugs, it was like we were two Aliens. I was still feeling very uncomfortable in my new skin, so going outside was extremely traumatic, not only for me but for both of us. Whenever J and I finished the drugs we had at home, we had to go out into the world, which meant facing everyone. J still had hustling skills, only now he wasn't selling drugs. I found out that he was an expert horse race player. One day in particular I remember having a panic attack because J and I had to get on the train together. We ran out of drugs and the only way to get more was to go to the Racetrack so J could bet on horses and win some money for us. Shortly after leaving the hospital, I had developed a fear of being outside especially in the daytime. At night wasn't as bad, I could hide myself in the dark. I would not go out in the daylight, not even for a million dollars. I did not want anyone to see me, I didn't even want to see me. So on this day I was a wreck and long before J and I even got outside, I began to feel anxious. And by the time we got outside I was a mess, walking down the block leaving his house, in the broad daylight. I noticed the stares, my heart is pounding. I knew from the rare times that I was out alone whether I was going to the grocery store or going home after leaving J's house, how people stared at me, but it was nothing compared to the stares we got when J and I were outside together. The burns to J's face was not as noticeable as mine, however if you looked real close, they were visible, as were the scars on his neck and his hands. As for me, one look and you could see scars all over me, on my face, hands, arms and neck. Just everywhere, so needless to say, every person that passed us on the street, couldn't help but to stare at us. It is a very uncomfortable feeling, people staring at you everywhere you go. To top that off feeling the paranoia from the drugs in our system only made it a hundred times worse. Whenever J and I were outside together I felt like crawling into my own skin or better yet under a rock. By the time we got off the A train in Queens, it wasn't until we got back outside that I started feeling a little bit better. At least when you are walking you are constantly moving, so even if people stare, it is only for a few minutes, however just sitting on that train with all eyes on us was unbearable to say the least. I didn't know what to do with myself. The walking only relieved some of my anxiety, but it never really disappears. Once we were inside the track, J went right to work. He would get one of those race track newspapers, and we would go sit down. After J studied all the horses and jockeys carefully, he would tell me which horse was gonna win. How much you want us to bet Shantel? I don't know J, you are the expert, you tell me. J would pull a couple of dollars out his pocket and he would tell me exactly what horse we would play to win. Then we would just chill. We were able to watch the race on the big TV screen. Ready, set and they're off!! Bells ringing and everyone in the Arena starts screaming, go, go, go, including J and now he is standing up yelling, go on mon, go on, yes mon. J would get so excited watching his horse running down the lane faster and faster all the way to the end of the line. Sure enough, by the end of the race our horse won. J and I would be so happy, we would crack up laughing. Sometimes we would stay for a while longer and bet on more horses, but really we always knew when it was time to go. Back outside, the funny feelings are back, just ignore them Sherry. Don't look anyone in the eyes and then you won't see them looking at you. After a while I learned very well how to block people out because that was the only way I was able to deal with the new me. Back on the block J would run in the spot to cop our drugs and cigarettes then we rushed back to our small room in his parents basement and we would stay down there until all the drugs were gone. This went on for months and before J and I both knew it, we were worse off than ever.

I had been staying back and forth between J's parents' home and at home with my family. I was able to keep the secret that I was back smoking crack for a while but another one of the worst days of my life came when my sis found out that I was getting high again. Cocoa was there for me through it all, from day one. Those years ago when she first found out I was using crack, she was devastated. She was so mad at me. Cocoa begged me to stop. She tried everything to get me to stop. The last resort was when she stopped speaking to me. I couldn't blame her, after all the sister that she had known and loved all her life, messed her life up so bad. I was her hangout partner, her home girl. Growing up Cocoa and I were inseparable, we did everything together. We were like twins. It hurt Cocoa so much to see me strung out on drugs. Then when I was in the fire, it broke her heart. She felt bad because she was coming to get me the same week J and I got burned, literally. And after God had saved our lives, the only thing I was sure of was that it would not be good for her or anyone in my family to know that I had relapsed. I knew that finding out that I was back smoking after everything I had been through would nearly kill her and probably destroy every drop of love she had for me. Cocoa started getting suspicious because when I was at home I would stay locked in my room all day or all night using drugs. Sherry, I know you are not in there doing crack? Let me find out you are smoking again. No, I'm not smoking, girl you crazy. I am just watching TV, relaxing. Sherry open up this door and why do you have your door locked anyway? What are you doing in there? Child, leave me alone, I'm not doing anything. My sis must have noticed that the past couple of months, I was not myself. At home I isolated myself from my family, which was a dead giveaway, because prior to my relapse, all I did was hang out in the living room with my nieces and Cocoa.

Oh by the way, my niece Telly is not afraid of me any longer and instead of her running away from me, now she just stares at me. Shainne always checks with me to make sure that I am ok. But she has become a young lady now, so she is doing her own hanging out with her friends. I hardly get to see her much lately. Ramel lives with his fiancé and their three children, in Coney Island. So I hardly get to talk to my bro much either. If they only knew what was going on inside me. Ma and daddy are downstairs and every time I came home for a couple of days, my ma would be so happy. She always made sure I had everything I needed. One day when I was at home, I was hanging out with ma downstairs. She just kept looking at me, then she started to tell me about when she first heard that I was in the fire. Young lady, if you had ever seen yourself those first couple of days in that hospital bed. I really thought we was gonna lose you. Everyone tried to tell me ma, please don't go in to see Sherry. Ma, she don't look the same. I know they were only trying to protect me but I told them take me to that hospital I am going to see my granddaughter I don't care what she look like. Ma what did I look like? Your head was as big as a watermelon and your skin was white just like those walls. When I walked into your room and saw you all I could say was, my God! Look at my Sherry. Tears rolling down her face and now rolling down my face too, we both cried. Ma I'm sorry, I'm so sorry for all the hurt I put our family through. If I thought she would understand, I would have told her ma, my heart is broken. Look at me, I have to live the rest of my life like this. I can't take it, the people staring, even looking at myself hurts so bad and some days I just don't know what to do. I couldn't break ma's heart again by telling her that I am smoking crack again. I couldn't tell ma that I am so strung out on crack, I can't think straight. How could I tell this woman who saw me almost lose my life that some days I get so depressed that I don't want to live like this. After the fire and even on my worst day, I have never contemplated suicide but I sure felt real, real bad. So I just put a smile on my face and kiss my ma all over her face, go back upstairs in my room, lock my door, put a rock in my pipe and pull long and hard and forget about all my pain. Over the next couple months I bounced back and forth from J's basement to our house, until the day finally came. Sherry open this door right now and I'm not playing. Running around my room I grabbed the can of Air Fresher spraying like a crazy woman. Next I tried to straighten myself out the best I can, trying not to look like the dang fool that I did look like. My heart was beating fast and I knew I was busted. You stole my money! What are you talking about? I did not steal your money. Stop lying Sherry, I know how much money I had and you are the only one smoking crack in this house. No one else in here has any reason to steal anything but you. Screaming at the top of her lungs, Cocoa did everything accept kick my behind and put me out, at least not yet. She told me what she'd do that day with a look in her eyes that I could never forget and that I don't ever want to see again. I stopped cursing years ago, however to make the point on Cocoa's anger this day, I will say my sis said, if I catch you in here smoking that "stuff", I am going to kick your "you know what so bad", you stupid "you know what", and she slammed my door so hard, that after she left, I stared stupidly at the door for a few minutes and when I snapped back to reality, I checked to make sure all the walls were still in place. I know she was crying. I could see it in her eyes. I felt like the dirt underneath our shoes. I felt like I wanted to cry but I couldn't. I had cried a thousand times already. I just sat there looking stupid. I was so bad off that I had started back stealing from my family. I stole money from my sis and when that ran out, I stole things from ma and daddy's basement to go sell. Month after month, I sunk lower and lower and lower. The days when I stayed at J's, he and I would go to 34th street so I could boost. J was an expert horse race player and I was an expert at shoplifting. I had learned how to boost when I was a teen, so it was nothing for me to walk into a store with not a dollar in my pocket and walk out with a couple hundred dollars in merchandise. I did not even think twice about it. Boosting and betting horses became our new nine to five hustle, seven days a week. I would go to at least four or five big time stores every day and shoplift. Each time I left a store, J would be waiting close by to take the bag full of merchandise. The next store that I went into I was empty handed, once inside the store, I would grab one of their shopping bags and fill it with their merchandise and walk out with a bag full of clothes, appliances or whatever. When we were on a mission, I didn't care about my burns, scars, and the people staring at us, or anything. I was too far gone to care about any of that. By the time J and I left the city, we had bags and bags of merchandise to go home with and this is where J took over. As soon as we got off the train at Franklin Avenue and we hit the street, J went to work. J could sell you a pair of old dirty shoes and make you think you were getting a sweet deal. He had the gift of gab and throughout the night little by little, every item that we boosted earlier would be sold that night.

    I practically lived at J's house because by now I was too far gone to continue to stay at my home. My sis was done with me.. She couldn't get over that after almost losing my life, that I would ever use drugs again. Cocoa loved me, but she hated who I had become. In her eyes I was a liar and a thief and she couldn't trust me in the house. She never turned her back on me. I always knew she was there for me, but we were not girlfriends or sista girls anymore. The only thing she would do for me is get me the help she and I knew I needed. But it wasn't time yet. Other than that she was disgusted with me to the point that she did not want to see my face. Over the next several years J and I were basically living like two burned bums on the street. We slept in our little room in the basement at his parents' house every night but we were in the streets most of the time. Either we were stealing, copping or bumming. J's parents knew what we were into but they never once put us out.

I think mama felt sorry for us (bless her soul) because she always made sure we had a big plate of dinner every evening. We would be coming in and out of their house, all hours of the day and night and we always had bags in our hands. I knew things were bad when we found ourselves out on the streets with the other crack addicts at 3:00, 4:00, 5:00 and even 6:00 am, broke, busted and disgusted looking for the next hit.

No matter what, we tried to make sure to get inside before the crack of dawn, when all the decent people were coming out going to work because it was too embarrassing. We lived like vampires. The few times when I went home to visit ma and daddy, I would go upstairs to see if my sis was going to talk to me that day. J do you ever get sick and tired of this "you know what?". Yea mon, me know what you mean, one day we gonna stop this. I'm telling you mon, one day. Yea I know one day we will J. We had that conversation a thousand times over the next five to six years, yet every day we got up and went to work hustling, came home and smoked crack. But something started happening. The game wasn't the same anymore.

Every day we had to deal with the stress of the drug lifestyle and it really started taking a toll on J and I. Whether it was dealing with the "other" crazy people we came into contact with at the spots or the fear of getting busted shoplifting, which also had me paranoid, in addition the paranoia you feel from the drugs too. So the boosting game was quickly getting played out as well. Month after month, it became more difficult to shoplift with the new alarms on everything in the stores and the high tech store cameras hidden all over. This made it a lot harder for J and I to continue to support our habit. We were definitely running out of options. The worst feeling in the world for an addict is running out of money and drugs. Just trying to figure out how to make money was getting real tiring and with each passing day, we were getting so sick and tired of being sick and tired. I know exactly what it's like when you are "feigning" for the next one. I know from experience that when you become so desperate for the drug, you will do anything and everything to get the next one. When I hear about people selling their children's milk and diapers money or someone spending their bill money for drugs, I know how it is. I had girlfriends that did it. It's no joke, it's real, it's raw, it's horrible, but when you get to the point that you are so addicted to the drug and nothing else matters more than the drug, it could easily be you too. You can't imagine what that must feel like having to decide, ok I will feed my child later on but right now I need this money for a hit, it's heartbreaking. I knew plenty of females and males that were forced to sell their bodies to get drugs. J and I never had to go there, because we were hustlers and we knew how to make money. But that didn't make us any better than the next crack head, because honestly, we were just one hit away from being them. People are out there selling their young children for a hit, a shot or a fix, whatever the preference. J and I did something one day that was bitter sweet for me because I think it helped me to see that this is not the life I wanted for myself anymore. But it also made me know just how bad off I really was to do something so stupid.

As I entered the "building" instantly I felt the creepiest feeling I had ever felt in my life, besides when we were in the fire. It was like walking in a cemetery. The building did not look the same. It did not feel the same and it definitely did not smell the same. It had been almost a year since the last time I set foot in there and all the while, I just kept looking up the staircase. From where I was standing I could see the handrails going all the way up to the 4th floor. It looked so scary. You can do this Sherry, you have too. I need to know, go on you will be ok. But the truth is I began to feel nauseas. I thought I would vomit. I couldn't take it any longer standing there on the first floor, I heard myself say, "P take me upstairs. No mon, for what? you don't wanna go back up there. Listen if you don't take me up there, J will, so stop playing, I want to see it. P called J and in a few minutes, all three of us were on our way back up stairs. As I started walking up the steps, starting from the 1st floor I was amazed at what I saw, of course my heart is beating so fast. I walked past the two apartments on the 2nd floor nothing, 3rd floor still nothing. As soon as I reached the end of the 3rd floor stairwell I stopped dead in my tracks. Looking up I saw it, the same two apartments that I had walked past a thousand times before, with the dingy white walls. I remembered it so well but now they were black and they looked to me like charcoal. Ba, boom, ba boom, my heart is racing faster and faster. My body started trembling. Hold on to the stairwell Sherry, you are ok just go on, you can do it. You have to do it. If I thought it was creepy downstairs on the first floor that was nothing compared to what I felt now. Slowly I walked inside the apartment my eyes wide open. Desperately I looked around searching for an answer. Why? I kept thinking over and over again. As I looked around, I noticed that some of the rooms were damaged, and other rooms were not. It still smells like smoke, can't be after all this time. I went from room to room, again I asked myself why is it that some of the walls were covered in the black charcoal while the other rooms were barely touched. Wasn't the whole apartment on fire? It was so hard to understand how only portions of the apartment were damaged. By the condition of the rooms, I could tell no one was occupying the place. Our bags of clothes were still there, the same old furniture was still in the apartment. I assumed that no one had been living in there since the fire. J and I just walked around from room to room, looking at each other in pure amazement. This was the place that we had once lived in, laughed in, got high in, now it was nothing more than a death trap. I remembered all the so called fun times I had living there and also I remembered the fights, arguments and the days that I was so stressed out too. I took myself back to the night of the fire and I remember thinking J and I was gonna die in there. And I felt trapped all over again. J help me, I can't breathe. I played the tape over and over in my head. My legs feel weak, like I'll fall down. My soul hurt. After just a few minutes of being in there, all I could remember hearing was the Fire Inspectors words when J and I were in the hospital. We are sorry to tell you this Ms. Graves, but this is being considered a suspicious fire. Somebody tried to kill us J, they wanted us dead. They set the place on fire and left us to die. I know I was drugged, but I don't know if J was drugged too? He definitely was sleeping real hard earlier when I tried to wake him and tell him about the argument with Cynthia. He was so out of it, he was still asleep when he told me not to worry about Cynthia, he wanted me to lay down and get some sleep and that is what I did. Whoever it was that set that fire waited until they knew that J and I both were knocked out and then they came and set the fire. I wonder how long they stood there watching us running around blindly in the pitch black and screaming at the top of our lungs. How long did they listen to us begging and pleading for help and fighting for our lives. And I wonder how long they waited before they walked off and just left us there to die. Whoever set that fire, caught us out there that night at our most vulnerable moments, while we were asleep. Because they knew that was the only way they could have hurt us. I felt sick to my stomach. Inside I cried. I cried because I couldn't understand why someone wanted us dead. I couldn't understand how any human being could do something like this. Why would someone do this? No answers came and when I couldn't stomach it any longer, I walked out of there and left the apartment that day. I walked back down the stairs in a daze. And that was the last time that I ever went into the "building" again. In my heart the 4th floor was dead to me and it still remains that way nearly twenty three years later. The Sherry that I had known and loved died in the fire that day, she was never to be seen or heard from again. I was only twenty four years old and my life would never be the same. It took years for me to get over the fact that someone planned to kill J and I. What had J or I done to someone that would make them want to kill us in such a horrible way? For years that question went unanswered. It no longer matters because God has a different plan.

CHAPTER 12
"IN TREATMENT"

Over the next few months things had gotten very critical for J and I. By this time several years had passed since the fire and by now the drugs had taken complete control over us. I never dreamed that it could happen to me but it did. I had lost every drop of self-respect, dignity, and pride, to the crack. There were many nights when we got so desperate and with no more money left from what we hustled during the day and no more drugs left, J and I found ourselves on the street, scheming with the other drug addicts. We were experiencing some of the lowest points of where the crack addiction would take us to. We no longer cared. As dangerous as it was, J and I would walk in the hood in the middle of the night, for miles to a train station in Park Slope Brooklyn, where we would panhandle or beg strangers for money. Imagine for just a minute what the both of us must have looked like to the people coming off the train in the late night hours. Here we are with burn scars covering our bodies, two grown people, begging these strangers for their money, hard earned money. I am sure some of them were coming home from working hard all day and just wanted to get home. I know those people had to know we were drug addicts. You might be thinking to yourself by now, they have to know that this is their "Rock Bottom" right? Yes, we did know that was "one" of our rock bottoms but sad to say, J and I had more rock bottoms to come, before it was over. Usually after getting the money we needed, we would leave the train station and go back on the block, cop more drugs and go home. It was always the same thing, as dawn set in and with the last little bit of drugs gone, there was nothing left to do now but go to sleep or think. I would lay in bed, I always liked to stare up at the ceiling, starving and feeling so tired. You don't even think about food or rest when you are constantly on the move trying to hustle up money. J, I am getting so tired of this we have to get some help. I don't want to do this no more. There has got to be something better out there for us than living in this insanity. For the thousandth time we had our talk about getting help. Our problem had always been that even though we both knew we needed to get into a program, neither one of us had the capacity to actually do anything about it. Before we ever could make any true attempts to look into a program, there was always another hit from somewhere. We would tell ourselves, ok we are gonna do drugs just one more time. That was always our excuse, but that one more time turned into a million more times. One day J shocked me, Shantel I'm ready whenever you are. You find a place for us and I will go. Stop playing J, you serious? Yea mon, I'm tired of this. It would happen but not just yet, one last rock bottom experience. J and I got involved with some loan sharks while hanging out in Brooklyn. Over a period of several months, we found ourselves in a hole so deep with these loan sharks, that the only way out was for us to start back hustling for them to repay our debt, which only took us deeper and deeper into debt. These loan sharks knew that we would never be able to climb out of the hole we had dug for ourselves, so they continued to supply us with their drugs to sell and of course J and I would smoke up more than we would ever sell. It seemed like we were on a suicide mission and after I ended up having a gun put to my head one night by the loan sharks, J and I knew it was that time. We had to go so we did.

Sometimes I am heart broken when I think about my journey, our journey together. J and my friendship developed because he saw how Tee treated me and he never liked it so he always protected me from Tee. And after Tee went to jail and Gee cheated on J, he didn't trust her any longer and their relationship ended. The more time we spent together, the closer we got. J made sure that I had everything I needed and by then we were in love. And after all of that, we ended up having to go through all of what we went through, it could have been so different for us if we weren't addicted to drugs. For me using drugs started out as fun and games back in the days. Smoking a little weed here and there, you know just bugging out, hanging out with friends. But it went from weed to cocaine and from cocaine to the crack and after about ten years in the game, I finally realized I lost, the game was over. It was over because there was nothing left. We were pretty much homeless, broke, busted and disgusted with nowhere to go. I felt like I had wasted ten years of my life. But did I really? Later on I found out that every experience comes to teach us something, and there are lessons to be learned.

My sis had put me out a long time ago. She told me when I wanted help to come back home. We had played ourselves out around the way by J's families house too, so we couldn't hang around there anymore. What it came down too was either we were gonna stop using crack or we were gonna die out there. And, finally that was our "rock bottom". I'll never forget the day, it was August 14, 1995. My sis and I walked into 25 Avenue D a Residential Substance Abuse Program in lower Manhattan. A couple of days before that, I was on a mission and I ended up at ma's house. In my old room stressed and desperate for a hit, all of a sudden out of nowhere Cocoa grabbed me by both of my arms and before I knew what happened, she stood me right in front of her, my back to her face. Face to face with the mirror. Look at yourself Sherry, she screamed at the top of her lungs, just look at yourself. Crying, she held me close to her and wouldn't let me move. There I was standing in our hallway looking at myself in our full length mirror hanging on the door. But for the life of me, as I stood there staring at myself, I couldn't see what she was seeing. Yes of course I saw my scars which by the way, it had been a long time since I even cared about the burns. But she was talking about something much, much deeper than the burns. She held me there for a few minutes and really made me look at myself.

After that she just let me go. She walked away and went into her bedroom. A few minutes later I went and laid down on her bed beside her. It felt so good because it had been years since we had done anything like this, many, many years. Girl do you wanna die out there? What is it going to take for you to stop Sherry? Because the way you are going, that's exactly what is going to happen if you don't get some help. And for the first time in a long, long time, I listened to what my sis was saying. All burned up, but of course I was still feigning for just one more hit, I finally surrendered. Laying there on my back, tears just rolling down my face, looking up, I frantically searched Cocoa's ceiling trying to find an excuse why I couldn't go into treatment yet. But, there were no more excuses and I had to accept that, it really was over.

I found out that no matter how "low you go" God will meet you in your lowest places and bring you up and out. And set you on a higher place. Are you ready Sherry? I will do everything I can to help you, if you will let me. I love you so much and only you can make the decision to stop hurting yourself and everybody else. There was nothing else to be said, so I just watched as my sis got the Yellow Pages and began looking for a Substance Abuse Program for me. A few minutes later, she picked up the telephone and within seconds I heard her dialing a number. Hello, can you tell me about the services you provide? Really, and did you say this program is long term, twelve to eighteen months? What are the requirements for someone to come there? Do you accept walk-ins or do I need to make an appointment? Well, can I schedule an appointment right now? It's for my sister? Yes, her name is Sherry Graves, she's thirty years old, no, she doesn't have any insurance. Sure, this Friday at 9:00 am is fine. That's all I heard, everything after that sounded like, bla, bla, bla, bla, bla. Since the ceiling wasn't talking back to me, I pretty much figured, oh well, I guess that's it. Sis made me stay there that night, because she knew beyond a shadow of a doubt that if I left there, you couldn't buy me a million cracks to come back Friday morning for that appointment. I might as well have been turning myself in to do a jail sanction, because honestly that's what it felt like. But I have to admit, it felt so good being home again, even if it was only for a few nights until I went into the program. I took a long hot shower. It felt so good just being able to take a shower and not have to rush or peep out expecting something to jump off. After that I put on some p.j.'s. I laughed so hard to myself because it had been years since I wore pajamas. So I stayed with my family that night, we had dinner and cracked up laughing, catching up on the "going on's". Later on that night when I laid in my bed, it was just me, myself and God. I felt at

Peace for the first time in years. I slept like a baby in my nice clean bed, in my old room. Thank you God. I knew in my spirit that he had saved me, again.

The next day when I woke up, I remember thinking that was the best rest I had in a long time. That morning Cocoa and I had breakfast and chilled for a while. She said, come on get dressed we're going somewhere. We got in her car and she took me shopping to pick up some cosmetics, a couple outfits and other things that I would need. Later on that evening I called J, because I really needed to talk to him. Ring, ring he picked up the phone. J had been back living at his parents' house. Hello J it's me. Shantel what's up baby? J listen to me, I have to tell you something for real. My heart was racing again. I felt nervous and anxious inside. I'm going into a program tomorrow. Word!! Yes, I am. I know it sounds crazy but I gotta do it J and now is the time. He didn't believe me at first, but after I told him Cocoa made some calls and got me an appointment, he started to believe me. I told him that I was serious this time and that I would be in contact with him. J, I love you, take care of yourself, I will call you as soon as I can. My sis and I talked for hours last night and I felt closer to her then than I had in a long time. We were bugging out together just like old times. I guess it was because deep down inside we both knew that she was saving my life.

Friday came and talk about butterflies in my stomach. Cocoa drove her car to the train station and we left it there. It was going to be a long ride to Manhattan but it was better and cheaper than paying for parking in the city that would cost at least a million dollars. As we sat together on the train with my big suitcase, I knew that Cocoa was trying to make me feel better by laughing and telling jokes, but the truth was my stomach was doing flip-flops. Sure enough, I was having a panic attack. I felt like I was gonna throw up. I'm thinking twelve to eighteen months, this is some "you know what". How can I get outta this? But I knew that there was no way out, the only way out was through. I had to go through what I had to go through. As we got off the train and walked down the streets, the closer we got to the building, I thought I was gonna pass out. I was having heart palpitations; my hands were all sweaty I was sure-nuff about to lose it. When we got right in front of the building I said, sis, wait! No, seriously hold up! I need a cigarette. I tried puffing for as long as possible, so after finishing the cigarette, she gave me one look and I knew, stop playing, no more excuses. But something happened when my sis finally pushed me through the door and I walked inside, it was like another world.

The building looked brand new. It was so bright, clean and pretty. People were everywhere. There was a lot of stuff going on, instantly I was like, "what the, you know what". My sis walked up to the desk and I saw her talking to the receptionist. My legs felt wobbly, so I just sat on a chair scoping out the whole scene. A few minutes later she came towards me and asked me if I was ok? Yea, you mean besides feeling like I'm about to jet? Yea I'm good. We both laughed, but she knew I was serious. This sista approached us. She introduced herself as one of the Counselors. I said, what's up and told her my name. She was a chunky big thing, light skinned and looked like she would put a foot in somebody's "you know what" if necessary, but on the cool side, know what I mean. She told Cocoa and I that we could talk for a few more minutes but that there was a lot to do and basically sis had to bounce. I held Cocoa so tight as we both fought back tears. As pretty as the place was, I didn't want her to leave me there. I wanted to go back home with her. I wanted J, but most of all I just wanted, "one more hit". You can do this sis, I will be right by your side the whole way. Call home as soon as you can. We will come visit every chance we get, ok. She kissed me, waved goodbye and walked right out that door, tears still in her eyes. By the time she left, all I could do was wipe away my tears, grab my bags and follow big mama into the room she asked me to go into. And just like that, the drug life that I had been living the past ten years was about to be over. Inside the small office, I pretty much signed my life away, at least that's what it felt like. We went over this paperwork and that paperwork, by the time we finished, I was never so happy. Next, big mama called for an expeditor and when she saw the expression on my face, all she said was, just chill you will get familiar with the process real quick. Five minutes later, this sista girl came into the office carrying a clip board in her arms. She looked almost as tore up as I did, so I figured she must be new too. She and another female gave me the rundown, as they both escorted me to the showers. They told me that I needed to take a shower so of course I almost went off, because number one, I knew I wasn't stinky. I had just taken a shower before we left home this morning. They both laughed and said it was the rules. Everyone new has to take a shower with quale and have a body search once they are admitted into the program. All I'm thinking is Lord, Sherry I don't know if you are really ready for all this. Now, mind you outside I was good with people seeing my scars, after all the people I surrounded myself with, they were getting high too and they could care less about my burns. But this was a whole different ball game for me it was way too up close and personal. So I noticed the sistas was still standing there right in the bathroom with me, so I'm like ok, I'll take the shower. I'm waiting for them to leave, when I notice they looked like they were ready to hang out. Are ya'll trying to tell me that you gonna stand right here while I get naked and take a bath? When they both shook their heads yes, I just shook my head, laughed to myself and you know what I'm thinking right, :what the you know what". The way I saw it, there wasn't any sense in prolonging it, so I just did something that I wasn't used to at all, which was "follow directions". They searched me and every piece of clothes and property I came in there with and when they were finished, we left the bathroom and they took me to my bedroom. This was another trip because when I walked into the pretty room, I quickly noticed there were five other beds. Again, when they saw the expression on my face they laughed and I didn't even have to say a word. Basically I would be sharing the room with at least five other chikita's and I knew I was not gonna like this at all. Things started getting real uncomfortable very quickly. Getting used to living in a room with all these women was one thing, but it was ten times worse for me. Up until now my scars were mine, very personal, the only people I really had to share them with were my family and J. I never had to hide from them. But now I was forced into exposing myself in a very, very personal way. I was not ready nor was I prepared to do that, but the bottom line was, I didn't really have a choice, if I was gonna be staying there. So I had to ask myself what was more important, getting the help I knew I needed or hiding myself. How would I ever be able to face my fear? I realized from day one in the program that I was feeling very self-conscious again, so in the beginning it was really hard for me. I had always felt different ever since being in the fire, but who cared before. When I was getting high, I was too tore up to give a second thought to it. When I had to cop some drugs, it was in and out. People still stared, but I was so far gone, I didn't give a care. But this, this was something totally new for me and it took a while to get with that program and if that wasn't enough to deal with, after all of that, those two sistas took me back downstairs to meet "the rest of the family", I'm thinking "the rest of the family", ya'll are bugging. Ya'll are really trippin. It didn't take long to realize I might as well just buckle in because this was definitely gonna be a long, long ride.

The reason the whole building was so beautiful and clean was because it was brand new. The Educational Alliance, Pride-Site 2 was a Residential Substance Abuse Program in Lower Manhattan, only a hour away from home and the place that would become my new home for the next year and a half. Pride-Site has another location about ten minutes away, also called Pride-Site, but its #1 and it's an all-male facility. One day we had to go to Pride-Site #1 for a meeting and after seeing their building, I was so glad to be in #2 because we were chillin and basically they weren't. Pride-Site 2 is a co-ed facility which was sometimes both a good and bad thing depending on the situation. I later that found out. When we walked into the huge family room, there were at least fifty people in there. Some of them were watching TV, others playing cards, some just kickin it, others listening to music, just basically chillin. As I checked the whole scene, I thought to myself, this might not be so bad after all. It was Friday night which they called Cool-Out Night, clients were allowed to hangout until at least two to three in the morning and although everyone was still being monitored by big-mama and whatever other counselor was on shift for that night, it was definitely a good time, considering. Everything took a little getting used too but by the morning I began to just go with the flow, which basically was just a part of my great adaptive skills, know what I mean. The whole weekend turned out to be good, even though everything was structured and I do mean everything, we still managed to have some fun. I learned that there were various phases or levels in the program. Basically the longer you are there, the more privileges you earned and the more freedom you got. Those people who were close to graduating, pretty much managed the house and I couldn't wait to get there. As a new jack, I was pretty much on lockdown. I had to be escorted or as I considered it followed around everywhere, even to the bathroom and this went on for a week. Oh! And to top it off, no outside contact, the only exceptions were medical or court appointments. So that meant besides my initial phone call that I was allowed to make on my first day, (of course I called home and spoke to my sis) no phone contact. I thanked Cocoa and let her know I will be ok, but there would be no contact with family or friends allowed after this call. I told them, listen I need to speak to my family. They told me trust me, your family knows that you are doing fine because your sister Cocoa has already called here two million times. I was pissed when they told me no contact with anyone for at least a month. The only reason I wasn't outta there right then was because the counselors assured me that I will have phone privileges in a few weeks, plus I would be able to go home on a pass soon, of course with an escort. They explained that the privilege procedures were put into place early on because there were people who were allowed to contact family and friends, but it became evident from the number of voluntary clients who left after contacting loved ones, that it is not in the best interest of the clients to let them have contact too early in their recovery. In some cases there were negative influences and the counselors found that people were being convinced to leave the program by family members after speaking to them on the telephone. For some of the clients who realized that they missed their families and hearing from them influenced them to leave. There were other people who after hearing news from home, sometimes good news other times bad news, would forced many people into leaving. Understandably so, there were many reasons why it was not conducive for clients to have any contact until after they have established a basic foundation and developed goals and objectives to work a recovery program. All I kept thinking about was that I needed to speak to J.

Over the next couple of days I started to get a little more comfortable with the process. Quite a few people that were in the beginning phases of treatment were unemployed and/or they were not in school. These people were given a job function to perform within the facility. A few weeks later I laughed my behind off when I was given the job as Expeditor, which basically means anyone in this function is considered "the eyes and ears of the facility". The job of expeditor had approximately five or six different stations in which a person was assigned a location to monitor the comings and goings of everyone. The Expeditor must know everyone's whereabouts at all times, especially each staff member. Here's a quick rundown of the jobs from the top position to lower level. First there is a Senior Coordinator, a Chief, and the Department Heads who oversee each department crew including the kitchen workers, maintenance workers, medical workers, and expeditors, all of these positions were held down by clients. Of course, even the top positions which were the Senior Coordinators, the people in these roles still reported to the Staff, if and when there were serious discrepancies. The Counselors made the final decision. There were Cardinal Rules which included; no drugs, no sex, no violence or threats of violence. These rules were enforced to the maximum. Failure to comply in any way was grounds for termination. It was cool this way because the clients basically managed the house which gave us a feeling of some control and it made us feel important. However if you were in a role and messed up, the staff really came down extra hard on us. As the days passed by, I was shocked to learn that I actually started liking the program. I began meeting new people and slowly but surely I even stopped caring about the chikitas in my room seeing my scars.

I began to say to myself, It Is, What It Is, I got tired of trying to hide my body every time someone came in the room, which was constantly especially since a part of the expeditor's job is to do hourly checks in the whole facility. That meant checking every room.

The first week there I was given a Social Worker. The only thing I knew about a Social Worker then was that they were the ones at BCW who came and took your kids when the child was neglected or abused. When I met my social worker, my whole life changed. I'll never forget him, the coolest white man I had ever met in my whole life. Mr. Carl Feinman, he was so cute, that is, in a bald headed, sexy, goofy walking, kinda way. What I liked most about Carl was that he always let me be myself and after several months of weekly individual sessions with him, we got to know each other. He knew when I was pissed off about something so he never held any punches with me he was just straight up. He'd take one look at my face after I would storm into his office, huffing and puffing, about to blow the house down, (without knocking, mind you) and all I heard was, "WHAT THE HELL IS WRONG WITH YOU NOW? Excuse me but that's what he said, not me. I'd dump on him and he'd let me whine, then if there was nothing else going on, he'd kick me out of his office just like that, and I'd feel so much better. This pretty much went on the whole time I was there. I began to love Carl. He was like the white father I never had. And although nobody could ever replace my real father, Carl was there for me when I needed him. He was real, he was caring, he was supportive and loving but most of all, he didn't put up with my mess. Carl was the one who motivated me to want to become a Counselor. Some days after talking with him for about an hour, I would just look at him and say Dang, don't you have anything else better to do other than just listening to me? He'd just give me that look like, you know I'm about to kick you out right, I'd laugh and say I wanna have your job. I just want to chill like you are and I know I can do your job Carl, probably better than you too. And he'd just smile and shake his head at me. Carl had five other clients on his caseload and every chance he got, he told me that none of them got on his nerves the way I did, and I'd just say yea, and I love you too. Every other counselor knew I was a spoiled brat, so pretty much if anything went down concerning me, nine times outta ten, they just sent me straight to Carl's office. I'm guessing they musta said let him deal with her behind. The weirdest thing happened about two weeks into the program. I'm standing on my point in my new job function as an "Expeditor"(don't laugh), when all of a sudden who comes walking in the front door but J and Contessa with these big bags. You could have blown me over with a feather. I'm like J and Sis, what the "you know what" is what I'm thinking. Now mind you, I haven't spoken to J since I got here because we weren't allowed any phone calls the first month. So to see them here, I was really trippin. After bugging out with them for about five minutes, yelling and screaming like some fools all up in the lobby, I caught myself and remembered where I was, especially with everybody looking at us like we were all crazy. Ya'll wait a minute, I'll be right back! The first thing I had to do was go tell staff what was up. Now, Ms. Young was the Counselor on duty, she was that one, you know the one that did not play. And I sure wasn't up for any drama with them finding out later that not only did I know J, but that he was my husband. Oh, did I forget to tell you that the year after the fire, J and I got married on my Birthday? Yes we did, January 24, 1990. One day we went down to the Court House and we got married. So I knew that I needed to let the staff know our situation. Immediately after I notified Ms. Young that my husband was in the lobby, all I heard was her voice screaming I need someone to come relieve Sherry off 1st point, ASAP. As I was being pushed off the point by this girl, I yelled to J, I will talk to ya'll before you leave. And I was replaced by someone who did not know J or Contessa. Just in case you forgot who Contessa is she's my sis-in-law you know, the crazy one who used to live with us at J's parents' house. She would smoke crack with us and then put on this long behind wig and dark glasses (in the middle of the night) go outside and be on a mission with me and J. Anyway after about a half hour or so, I was called to come back to the front office. When I walked into the small room, J was sitting there and one look at his face and I knew it wasn't happening. Apparently J had tried desperately to get admitted into Pride-Site but because we were married, they shut him down. Ms. Young gave us the run down. She basically said couples were not permitted in Pride-Site, especially married ones, at least not at the same time. Understandably so, because that could cause problems for both people, as far as sharing issues, feelings and/or personal experiences in the groups and everything. But I was so glad that Ms. Young gave J some referrals for other programs right in the area. Just before J left, she gave us a few minutes of privacy. I begged him, J please, you gotta go and try to get into one of those programs that she gave you, as long as you are in a program, we can be in contact. I looked him in his eyes. J, if you're not in a treatment program, we can't have any contact at all. I can't even talk to you on the telephone. Promise me you will call them and we hugged. It had been almost a month since the last time I had seen J or even talked to him on the phone. So much has happened in my life since that time. Every day that passed, I was a different person. I wanted to tell him so bad, how good I felt being in the program. How good it felt that I did not have any crack in almost one month. I wanted to find out how J was doing, but there wasn't enough time. J call me when you get in the program. But he just looked at me and said, Go on Star, me talk to you later and walked away. On his way out, he hugged Contessa, grabbed his big bag and left. I thought about our life together and how J had saved me in so many ways, he saved me the million times Tee put his foot in my behind. He saved me even after Tee went to jail, by supporting me not only with drugs, but in every way that counted. He bought my food when I wasn't even thinking about eating, my clothes and whatever else I wanted. We were already close, so by the time we were in the fire, our bond was unbreakable. I had to get outta that room with the quickness because I knew if I stayed in there any longer, I would run right outta that door behind J. So as the tears were rolling down my face, I walked off. But I couldn't help feeling that J needed me. It was almost like he couldn't do it without me. Yes, we had talked about going into treatment and getting help a thousand times before but the plan was that we would do it together. Never once did I think we would not be in it together. It had been seven years, seven long years that J and I were out there together and after everything we had been through, I still couldn't do it, I could not leave. Not when I had just started to feel better, not after seeing that there was a way out and not after beginning to want something, anything better than the life we was living. For the first time I was scared to throw it all away. At the same time I was torn because I knew J needed me, but deep down I knew I couldn't help him until I helped myself. For a second, for some strange reason I began feeling alone and afraid. Looking back now, I believe when J walked out that door that day, a piece of me left with him and in my soul I knew it was the beginning of the end for him and I.

But when I saw Contessa's face in that moment, she was the only reason that I did not run out that door after J and I told myself, at least I had her. J was not able to stay at Pride-Site because of the conflict of interest, however Contessa was accepted. Somehow with her being there with me, I knew we would get through it together, "If Not for the Grace of God". So just like that, more changes in my world and I was so sad about J not being accepted in Pride-Site. That woulda been cool, I thought to myself, all of us in treatment together. In all the excitement with Contessa somehow I managed not to let my hurt get the best of me. But deep down inside, I knew it would never be the same. I grabbed my sis and held her tight, that's when it hit me.

What! my sis is here with me now. I'm thinkin all ya'll better watch out. Contessa is a thick-with-it, light skinned, beautiful, fearless sista with way, way too much attitude and just like me, she had got caught up in the drug game. Many days while we were in the streets hustling, it seemed like it was just no way out. She was addicted to crack and heroin too. Now many of you may know that is a deadly combination. Plenty of days I felt so bad for sis when she was sick, but Contessa always found a way to get what we needed. So over the next couple of days, I started feeling better and better. Pride-Site was a very structured T.C. Every day consisted of a series of meetings, groups, sessions, and various functions, which were designed to make the place run smooth as honey. One of my favorite times of the day was our Morning Meeting. Every morning the clients all gathered together in the huge Family Room to discuss our needs, issues, concerns and good feelings. During the meeting everyone would stand up as a family and recite our Philosophy. So here's a "Shout-Out" to all the people, the family who came to Pride-Site before and after me, this one's for all of us.

> **"We Who Have Come From Hell Seek To Deliver Ourselves From a Life Of Misery and Contempt Into an Existence of Happiness Within Our Selves and Others. To Know That Within Us We Who Once Understood No Salvation Has Come To Learn the Ways Of the Self-Fulfilled. A Goal In Which We Must Accept Ourselves For What We Are, Leaving Room For Change, Towards What We Shall Be. A goal In Which We Must Achieve Responsibility, Endure Pain, Overcome Obstacles, Achieve Self-Respect, Appreciate Love, Face Reality and Denounce All Evil. To Accomplish This Task Of Becoming Men and Women We Search the Help Of Our Brothers and Sisters, For United We Stand, Divided, We Stand Alone" (Pride-Site).**

I can't tell you how many lives this philosophy touched. I know as for myself, even after 16 years, the message in this philosophy still brings tears to my eyes. It was in morning meeting, every day we got the chance to say how many days we have been clean and sober. Everyone would stand up and take turns. I remember clearly my first time I had to say it because it was only my second day at Pride-Site. I'm sitting in the morning meeting just checking everybody else out. I quickly saw how everyone was going around saying their clean time, so I said to myself "they trippin" and I already knew I wasn't about to get up and make a fool outta myself. When it got down to my row, everyone else said their days clean, then came my turn. This sista-girl sittin next to me gave me the look like, what's up? So of course I was like, "what the, you know what" ya'll trippin. I just looked at the person that was going after me and one look at my face, I guess she realized it wasn't happening, so she went. But a funny thing happened over the next couple of days, I started feeling like I wanted to say my clean time too.

CHAPTER 13

"HE MET ME IN MY LOWEST PLACE AND PULLED ME OUT"

A couple of weeks after that first incident in the morning meeting when I had refused to say how much time I had been clean, some of the girls tried to encourage me by saying it was hard for them also in the beginning. Over the next several days after really listening to the other people share their experiences, one day I decided I wanted to stand up and I said my clean days. At first everybody thought I was trippin but you know what the more I did it, I began to feel so good about myself. First it was one day clean, then fourteen days, then thirty days but to hear myself saying sixty days and so on, and so on, it was like a "birthing". I'm telling you as sure as I'm breathing, back then I didn't even realize it but it was Pride-Site, and all of those morning meetings, talking in the groups, developing friendships, establishing trust, and getting real with myself, that first got me back to "Birthing Visions" again. After all, every little girl has visions but sometimes they can get snatched away by life. Everything we got in Pride-Site, we had to earn it. I'm talking about our privileges, that includes phone privileges, going home on passes privileges, job functions, all of these were earned privileges. It was all of these responsibilities that helped to give us back structure in our lives and it even helped to build up our self-esteem. One of the first privileges I earned was escorting other clients on passes, which I was ecstatic about because I was able to go outside. I had not been outside in weeks and it felt so good to be out in the world again. It started with me taking the new comers to their medical appointments, legal/court appointments, or home to pick up clothes or their important documents etc.,. And that's when I began to get my sense of "PRIDE" back. So by the time I was able to go out solo, "what", you couldn't tell me anything. I felt like an Eagle. I just wanted to soar, not fly away just soar, just like the Counselors said that first day. After about three to four weeks. I was able to make phone calls. I was calling my sis and everybody else at home, letting them know that I was ok. Everything was good except one thing that really concerned me, every time I tried to get in touch with J, he was never there at his parents' home. So I didn't know if he had gotten into a program or what. I just kept on Praying that he did. I told myself, maybe that's why he hasn't called me yet, because he is in the program and he had to earn his phone privileges too. In order for me to focus on my treatment, I had to just put J in a safe place within my heart. I never thought it would happen, but the longer I stayed in Pride-Site, the more my family started becoming so proud of me, especially Cocoa. Things were so good once Contessa moved in because by that time I was beginning to feel like Pride-Site was my second home. The weekends was as close to our party-at-the-nightclub-nights, as we would ever get, the only difference was we did it sober and surprisingly we had a ball, go figure.

From Friday morning to Sunday night it was so much fun in treatment especially since we were all given allowances. The Government provided the Public Assistance Funding which we all got. It paid for our treatment stay and every client received a weekly stipend, This money was supposed to hold us over till the next week, depending on your spending habits. So everyone including me pretty much lost their minds on Friday's because to us, it was our "payday", you know like at work. We were given between ten to forty dollars depending on your status in the program. Basically the longer you were there, the more you got. We could use this money for anything except sex or drugs. I had my plans on how I would spend my money before I even got it. Here's the rundown I had to figure out how much I needed for my hair weave (yes, I said hair weave), a pack of cigarettes (yes, I smoked cigarettes back then), a cheap and I do mean real cheap but fly outfit, and some munchies was all I could squeeze outta my allowance. But later on we found ways to make things happen, because everyone including me, was getting money on-the-down-low from our family on many of those passes home.

On the weekend, we would do store runs for food, soda, munchies or whatever. We could go shopping at the Malls. Some people put in requests to go to the movies. The very fortunate people were able to go home on passes for the weekend (if approved by staff), and we could go on a park trip when the weather permitted. Or if you didn't want to leave the house, we could just stay in and chill, watch TV or listen to music, all kinds of fun stuff. So basically every weekend we all just went ballistic, you know what I mean. Usually the weekend staff was somebody we could really chill with, like Sophia, Kendell, or Regina I loved them all. The first time I met Sophia it was about two weeks after I was admitted into the program. She came busting into our evening meeting one night. Sophia is a light skinned, African American straight-up, bring it if you want, to rough neck kinda female. Sophia was beautiful, I assumed she had to be in her thirties and she gave it to us raw. Wasn't no sugar-coating, playing around just blam! right in your face, it is what it is. Sophia shared her own experiences with drug addiction she talked about smoking crack, her experiences with the paranoia, the peeping out the windows, the doors and everything. So right there she had my attention because we knew she was real. I loved Sophia, all three hundred plus pounds of her but even though she was overweight, she took pride in her look, and plus she was straight up gangsta. We all knew she was on the down-low, but we never cared about that. We loved her. The first time I heard her going off about life on the streets, she screamed out, Who knows about saying yes to stuff when you know you really want to scream heck "NO! She was a little more graphic, if you know what I mean. She was addressing the people who had to sell their bodies for the drugs. How many times did you have to agree to do things that you would normally go off on someone for even asking you to do? Yea, but every addict knows about that, right ya'll? If she touched nobody else Sophia sure blew my mind and from that day I loved talking with her because I knew I could talk to Sophia about anything. I never heard someone come with it the way she did. I really couldn't believe my ears. Wow was all I could say, all the while bugging out because of her in-your-face style of putting-it out there. Overtime I learned each counselor's style and how they interacted with the clients. Kendell usually worked the weekend shift, which meant we could chill. Kendell was this African American handsome, kinda short, but not short enough to have a complex about his height, man. You could tell he was probably a player back in the day. I guess he was in his forties at the time. He was cool but trust me you couldn't play him either. Kendell knew what time it was, he would give us just enough rope to hang ourselves. Everyone loved when Kendell was working because he was rough but fair. Now Regina was the counselor that either you loved her or you hated her, and thank God for me I loved her. She's Puerto Rican, kinda tall; slim, pretty face, beautiful black wavy hair, and usually you can find Regina chilling in a two piece fly suit. Here's the funny thing about Regina you couldn't catch her without her favorite, Espresso. Later on, I found out why it was her favorite, basically espresso coffee will have you flying real high. Just in case you did not know, let me pull your coat, there are quite a few substance abuse counselors that were recovering addicts and at one time or another, they were strung out on drugs themselves. Our counselors were upfront with us, they did not hide their addictions and we appreciated their honesty. It helped so much because we always felt like they could identify with us and relate to our struggles and pain, because they were there before, themselves. Regina could be one of the coolest people in the world, but catch her on a bad day and let's just say, she wasn't the one to be playing with, especially if she didn't have her espresso. She also had a drug history. She was an ex-heroin addict who wasn't taking any shorts. Regina usually worked the weekday night shift and when that Sheriff was in town, we all knew what time it was. Especially for everyone that liked creeping around at night, doing what they knew they were not supposed to be doing. But those of us with any sense, knew that when Regina was working, don't even try to play that game. It was the responsibility of the chief and senior to select a night expeditor, which consisted of one male and one female, to make runs of the entire facility. What this meant was all night long, on an hourly basis every room in the building from the six floor to the basement had to be checked. A female would take care of the females' rooms and the male would check all the rooms on the guys' floor. As I mentioned earlier, Pride-Site has a few Cardinal Rule's and one in particular is that a male better not be caught dead on the females' floor and vice-versa, day or night, unless there was a very good reason. And even then, only if there was someone else present as a witness. Many people found out the seriousness of this rule the hard way, let's just say they played themselves right out, of the program that is. I assumed these rules were put in place to ensure the safety of everyone but the way we figured, it was mainly to see the "going's on" if you know what I mean.

The females occupied floors three, four and five and the males they had the sixth floor. One night Regina wanted to play one of her games because she loves playing games with us you know, anything to just piss us off. Back then, we called it pushing buttons. So one night she knew I needed to get some rest because everyone has to wake up at 6:00 am each morning except for the people in Re-Entry. So it was bad enough that she kept me up all night long talking one ton of nonsense, not to mention she had me running back and forth getting her espresso. Here's how her game went since she already knew that I was tired as you know what because it had to be at least 3:00 am. After hanging out downstairs talking with her, she would say, ok Sherry go on to bed, see you later, have a good night. But as soon as I got upstairs and took off my clothes and laid in my bed, an expeditor would come and say, Regina wants you in her office ASAP. I'd have to get back out of bed, get dressed and go down three flights of stairs. When I got to her office Regina's in their laughing her "you know what off" talking about, "what you want"? By the third or fourth trip up and down the stairs, I finally had it with her and by now all I was thinking was, damn the jokes. I screamed at her, in the morning I'm telling Carl what you did! I bet I'm gonna get all my hours of sleep back that you took from me, just playing games all night long! I stormed back to my room pissed off. On my way going up the stairs, I could hear Regina and the other expeditors that she was torturing that night, laughing their behinds off. I dived in my bed clothes still on. I was so tired, all I could say to myself was, crazy heffa!

Then there was Ms. Deb, oh my God!! Deb was like a female terminator. She is a dark skinned African American woman, at the time I guessed her to be in her forties. Ms. Deb is kinda thick, medium tall, she always wore her clothes tight, her nails were always meticulously done, and her hair was always hooked up. You couldn't tell miss lady anything. First of all her husband was the Program Director, Franklin AKA Mr. Terminator, and if you think she was tough, when Mr. Terminator was on the premises, well let's just say all one hundred and something clients was on point for real, for real. Ms. Deb was so tough, she even had the male clients at her facility scared. But in the mix of all that drama she brought to everyone one day, she surprised me and

I got the opportunity to see she actually has a soft side. One Friday evening she came to our campus, thank God she worked at Pride-Site 1, was all I kept thinking whenever she came to our campus. I imagined what all the clients over there had to deal with, having Ms. Deb in charge. But just because she did not work at our facility, of course that did not stop her from popping in whenever she wanted. Anyway this day in particular, she came through, I guess she just wanted to terrorize someone other than the regulars at her program. I was sitting in our lobby, you know, just chillin, minding my own business. Here she comes, Ms. Graves come here. You know what I'm thinking right, here she goes. Hi Ms. Deb what's up? Come here she said, where do you think you going miss? Ms. Deb you know I ain't going nowhere because you're not letting me go anywhere, now are you? Come here I wanted to talk to you. So she took me in the office. When we got in there, she told me to have a seat. She confided in me that she had gotten burned a long time ago on her leg. She showed me her legs and told me her story of how hard it is for her to wear shorts or skirts that expose her scar. I want you to know Sherry, that you are not alone. She gave me a hug and I was so touched by her, from that day on, I saw a different side of Ms. Deb. And even though she continued to be Ms. Terminator, I also realized that deep down she had a soft side.

I love all of the counselors at Pride-Site. We had so much respect for them. It didn't matter that some of the staff were former drug addicts, that only caused me and the other clients at Pride-Site to respect them that much more. We felt like if they made it out and got their lives together, so could we. When I think about the Vice President, Mr. Ray Kearson, man he is the coolest, African American man alive. He is classy, confident and as smooth as a chocolate candy bar. Mr. Kearson came through on a regular and whenever he did, you had better be on your p's and q's. He was the kind of man that had your back as long as you were doing what you were supposed to do. On the other hand, if you weren't doing what you were supposed to be doing, believe me you didn't want him to know it and you definitely didn't want him to see you in the building. Mr. Kearson, The Terminator and Carl Feinman were running the show. All three of them were like the dudes in the movie "Three the Hard Way", the only difference was Carl was the only white man in the crew. But he could have passed for a black man anytime and the funny thing was he loved playing basketball. You couldn't tell him that he didn't have game "way back when" lol. I loved all of them they are dear in my heart.

CHAPTER 14

"MY JOURNEY BACK"

By the time three months passed at Pride-Site, it had become my second home. I didn't understand it at the time, but the Sherry that walked in their front door months before, was being transformed by the experiences of my journey. First, I started feeling better about myself. I gained back my sense of self, my pride and dignity. I actually started liking Sherry again.

I talked to everyone at home every chance I got they were so proud of me. But no one was more proud than my sis, she kept her word from the first day, when she told me that we would go through the program together even though she was on the outside looking in. She helped me to get through by just being there for me, talking to me on the telephone and letting me know how much everyone was rooting for me. My family kept me motivated to want to stay at Pride-Site and get the help I so desperately needed. Some of the best times of my life were when we had Family Day at Pride-Site. This was where everyone's family members were invited to the facility for a holiday, a party or barbecue. We got to spend quality time with our loved ones. The days leading up to family day were always nerve wrecking for us and everyone's anxiety levels definitely increased. Cocoa and my cousins would come visit me whenever we had family day, it was so very special having my family there. I remember the first time they all came for a visit, we had so much fun catching each other up on the "going's on". Cocoa and the rest of my cousins all laughed at me, girl you are getting so fat, child what are they feeding ya'll? Look at you girl you look so good, there is something different going on with your scars Sherry, your face is clearing up. I just kept laughing and smiling because I was seeing what they were seeing, of course everything except the part about me being fat. They were so happy and so was I, for the first time in years. Early on in my treatment, I had asked ma and daddy not to come to Pride-Site because well, they were older and I didn't want them worrying about me anymore. So as long as they knew I was in treatment and getting better, they were ok. After my head started clearing up and my mind could focus on something other than the crack, I began to get a better understanding of what the program was offering. Pride-Site offers Comprehensive Services and Interventions such as Vocational counseling, recreation, group and individual therapy, educational, medical, family, legal, and social services. But it wasn't until I really started looking at myself and where I was in my life, that I realized I was at Pride-Site for something so much more significant than just the drugs. I was on a Healing Journey. At first I didn't like what I saw when I started checking out my life. And for the first time in a long time, I wanted something better for myself. I was 30 years old and I didn't have anything. It hurt me so bad when I realized how much time I wasted all the years I spent doing drugs. I had dropped out of high school in the 11th grade remember way back when, when I thought life was just one big party? And I had never had a meaningful job, except when I worked at McDonalds as a teen. At the time, working at Mc D's was definitely meaningful to me because of how much I love Big Macs. And since I got to eat all the free Big Macs I wanted, well let's just say I was in heaven. But how many Big Macs can one eat before getting so sick and tired of them. So of course I quit. Growing up I always had everything I needed, either I got it from my family or my male friends. I did not see a point in working, my oh my, how I deceived myself.

As I mentioned before, at Pride-Site everyone had to participate in the program so in the beginning phases of treatment new clients were acclimated to the treatment process. A part of it consisted of us having a job function at the facility. This was done because for the first couple of weeks we were not allowed to leave Pride-Site unless we had a medical or court appointment or unless we had to go home to get clothes or personal stuff. Even then, we had to be escorted by a resident, someone who had been in treatment for several months. Once we were there for an extended amount of time and earned our privileges, we were allowed to seek employment opportunities, however many of the residents that were in treatment longer were already employed. Or you could choose to enroll in a vocational training program. Each job function lasted at least 3-4 months and then the staff determines the next job assignment. The residents were not allowed to choose a job. Early on in treatment, working as an Expeditor was a cool job. I always had to be on point because I never knew when one of the staff would try to test me because as you already know, they loved playing games with us. There were plenty of times when one of the counselors or even the Program Director would go in an office and then run out into a different area, just trying to throw us off. They would call one of the Expeditors and ask where is such and such. And of course by then no one knew, so I would have to run all around the building trying to locate the staff, which meant I had to get someone to cover for me, because you can't leave your area unattended. So once I got a relief, I had to run around until I found out where the staff member was. Expeditors had one of the most important jobs in the facility. We were responsible for ensuring the safety of everyone. But I sure was glad when that job was over. So when that job ended, I worked in the Medical Department in this role, I took care of scheduling the medical appointments for all of the clients as well as filing and preparing all the necessary paperwork. I had my own little office and everything. I enjoyed having a place where I could go to just to get away from all the drama. My office was where I went to get a peace of mind in the mix of chaos. Several months after that job was over, of all things, my next job, they made me the Department Head for B.O.P.S I still don't know what it stands for but I knew for sure the staff were just trying to be funny putting me in that role. Basically I was responsible for overseeing the Maintenance and Building Operations Workers and of course I hated every moment of it. I had to check the boilers, electrical and plumbing. I don't know how I lasted the four months in that job but what I did know was that I was so glad when it was over. The role that I loved the most was when I was chosen to be the Senior Expeditor. Everyone wanted to be the Senior or Chief Expeditor because being in either of those two jobs meant being in charge. The only person in a higher position was staff. As the Senior Expeditor, I was second in charge of running a house with over a hundred clients, it was a huge responsibility. But I did it very well and I loved every minute of it. By the time the job ended four months later, I was worn out and glad it was over.

It went from three months to six months and by then I had learned a lot about myself. I was finally growing up. I wasn't that lost little girl anymore. I was maturing into womanhood. I knew I was growing up because it was in Pride-Site when I finally, finally stopped sucking my thumbs. No one was more surprised about it than I was but I couldn't necessarily be in charge of running a whole facility and still be sucking my thumb, just not a good look, you know what I mean.

It seemed everything in my life was good except for one thing. I was worried about J, ever since that day he was turned down at Pride-Site. A couple of weeks after that, I got a call from J. he told me the same day he left Pride-Site, he was admitted into one of the Men's Program's. Turns out the list Yvonne gave him helped him get into treatment. But a month or so later, J called and he told me he was leaving the program. Shantel mon, me can't take it in here mon, me going back home. Me talk to you later, and he hung up the phone. After that conversation, it was a couple of months before I was able to speak to J again. I never dreamed that J and I wouldn't be together, not after everything we had been through. I knew it was going to be hard for him because we did everything together for the past six years and it was very hard for me too. I had been living at Pride-Site for several months now and every day that passed J and I got farther and farther away from each other. Everything was so different. I was so different. I was still trying to understand what I was supposed to be doing with my life. So much had changed in my life. I wanted to share some things with him, like J could you believe I haven't had any crack in 6 months? I wanted him to see me because I was looking good again. I was even feeling better. I was working and it felt so good to be responsible for something for someone. But deep inside I knew that day when J left Pride-Site, the day he tried to come into the program, I knew when he walked out that door that it was the beginning of the end for us, and it was. The bond between J and I could never been broken. But within the past year, we had started going in separate directions on different journeys. And even though it broke my heart, in order for me to continue doing what I knew I needed to do at Pride-Site, I had to put J inside a special place in my heart and he remains there today. The only reason I was able to handle J not being in my life was because I had Contessa, the rest of my Pride-Site family and especially my family at home. They all helped by encouraging me and giving me the strength I needed to get through my feelings. And I was so glad to have Contessa there with me at Pride-Site. Just seeing her face every day helped me get through another day.

Going through all the different phases of treatment was very challenging for me but every day I got stronger and stronger. Everyone in the program couldn't wait to get into re-entry, myself included. Re-Entry is the last phase of the treatment process and when I got there, it was some of the best times of my life. Residents in re-entry have it so good, this is definitely the place you want to be. If you made it to this phase it meant that you had proved yourself to the staff that you were responsible and trustworthy. It also meant that you were making better choices and had earned your due rewards. Things like phone privileges, weekend passes, full-time employment, and pursuing vocational goals, were just some of the privileges you earned early on in the middle phases. I remember the first time I was approved for a weekend pass, it felt so good to go home and hang out with my family especially without having an escort. It was a wonderful feeling. I can't even begin to explain the feeling I had just walking to the train station by myself and getting on the train, it was so different for me now. I looked around checking out everything and everybody. I realized I wasn't afraid any longer. I had been dealing with my fear of people staring at me because at Pride-Site there were at least 100 people coming and going on a daily basis. And after the first couple of weeks, it became impossible for me to keep on trying to hide my scars any longer, especially since I shared a room with five other women. I found out when I got into re-entry that another one of the benefits was you got a two-woman room, thank God, at last some peace. It was way too much trouble always having to cover up myself whenever one of the girls came into our room, so after a while I stopped. And it was like yes this is me, and this is what it is. The funny thing I realized was that no one treated me any different. I felt at home with everyone. I got along with all of my sista girls and the guys were like my brothers. We all looked out for each other and it was all good. But what I didn't know at the time was that it was all a part of the Divine Plan for my life. God was preparing me. So after getting off the train at Shepherd Avenue I was feeling so good inside. As a girl growing up I had been to this train station a thousand times before. Walking down the block I started reminiscing about all the times Cocoa and I drove with daddy to come pick ma up from work right here at this train station and remember how when she opened the car door we would jump out from the back seat and scare the crap outta her. I just laughed to myself thinking about back in the days. By the time I got to the house both of my sisters Cocoa and Shainne were so happy to see me and I was so happy to see them too. What's up girl? Look at you all grown up now, traveling by yourself, and you're not on lockdown anymore? What, I hear that. Looking at my sisters I told them ok, so ya'll got jokes and we would all start cracking up laughing. Hugging and kissing each other. It felt so good to have my family back but more important it felt even better because they were not angry and hurt any longer and they trusted me again. They didn't have to hide their stuff and it felt so good. And of course ma and daddy were both so glad to see me. I would go downstairs and sit with them for hours, watching TV and talking. It was just like old times. But the more I started going home on passes I noticed something different about daddy, he looked so frail sitting in his chair. Daddy had Diabetes and although ma took excellent care of him, he seemed to have aged ten years in the time since I was at Pride-Site and he seemed so sad to me. Ma is daddy ok? He looks a little sad. You know your grandfather, he is always quiet and ever since he lost his leg he has not been the same. Daddy had to have his left leg amputated because of the Diabetes not long after the fire and I think his spirit was amputated too, when he lost his leg. Daddy was never the same and I understood why he changed. My grandfather had always been a very independent man. He was a humble, yet confident, quiet, proud man who loved his family. He took care of the house, I mean he did everything, gardening, home repairs, he fixed this and that and he helped ma clean up the house. He was an active, hardworking man and when he couldn't do the things he loved to do anymore, he went into a shell and never came out. I would rub daddy's bald head and get him some cold water to drink, love you daddy. I always told him how much I love him.

Ramel lived with his family by now but he always made sure to come home and hang out with us too. I realized how much I had missed my family. Over the weekends when I went home, we all chilled, we laughed and cried and of course my sis and I went shopping. Those were very special times for me. It felt so good to feel welcomed at home again. It was a feeling that is indescribable and even though I had to be back to Pride-Site by Sunday night, it was all good. Over the past several months I went back home for weekend visits on a regular. Being in re-entry, I felt like I was on an extended vacation. I loved it because of the independence and freedom that came with it. At this point, the staff had pretty much taken off the majority of the pressure that they have to put on newer residents and they allowed us the freedom to make our own choices. In Re-Entry you are being prepared for re-entry back into the world and for some people it can be very frightening and intimidating. I was a little afraid to get back out into the world as my "new self". The self with no drugs in my system and the self with a new outlook about my scars, with me being clean and sober, now all the feelings I had about my burns resurfaced again but the difference was that I was so ready to face them head on and that is exactly what I did. When I think about it, I am so proud of myself because I wasn't mandated to treatment. I came to Pride-Site voluntarily, so I could have left anytime I wanted too but I didn't. And even though there were a million times when I definitely wanted to leave back then, I knew I couldn't. And when it was all over, I was so happy I stayed because staying saved my life, again. It was at Pride-Site that I got myself back. I got Sherry back and the best part of it all was that I was getting better than ever.

I walked inside of Pride-Site a crack addict, broken, busted and disgusted. Thirteen months later on September 26, 1996, seven years after the fire, my time at Pride-Site was over. And now it was time for me to live my life, it was time to step into my future. And I was so ready. I walked out of the place that had been my home for the past year and with no more crack in my system and my head on straight, I felt like I was on top of the world. And I knew right then there was no going back. "But for the Grace of God". But it was another bittersweet time for me. As I walked out the doors, I thought about every experience I had ever had at Pride-Site, from the very first day when I walked through the doors into that beautiful building. I remember feeling so unsure. I didn't know what to expect. I was scared of what could happen. I never dreamed that my whole life would change by coming there. Pride-Site gave me myself back, no it gave me my life back. I was so grateful for the program, to all of the staff, and to all of my peers. Going to Pride-Site helped me to stop smoking crack. I had wanted to stop for so long but I couldn't do it on my own. And if I didn't get anything else out of being in treatment, that alone would have been enough. Because it was such a tremendous accomplishment in and of itself however, it was all the other blessings I got too as a result of the time I spent at Pride-Site, that keeps me grounded seventeen years later. I learned the necessary tools that have helped me to stay off drugs and for me my Higher-Power, God has kept me. God has given me so many wonderful gifts but one of the best gifts He gave me is the man who also helps to keep me clean today, my Babe. Something so wonderful happened while I was in treatment, I met the man who would become my future husband. But one of the hardest things for me to do was saying goodbye to everyone, especially my Social Worker Carl Feinman. The night I was leaving Pride-Site, I had to tell Carl thanks so much for everything, for always being there for me and especially for putting up with me. I gave him such a big hug and I walked out of Pride-Site and into my future.

CHAPTER 15

"BABY STEPS"

Fall of '96 I was back out in the world again. It was just a little over a year and one month ago that I was so broken. I was at my rock bottom. I was ashamed of myself for all of the things I had done while I was on the streets. My self-esteem was at an all-time low. I hated myself and all of the scars that came from the fire. I felt so ugly inside and out. Not to mention I had no confidence in myself. I felt inadequate and unworthy of anything good. I had lost all of my values and morals, my pride and dignity. I was a mess. But now I felt like I was sitting on the top of a mountain looking all around and although I didn't know where to start, I felt so good. Because all of the things that the crack stole from me I was getting them all back. And even though I knew I was starting over from where I had left off, which was ground zero or better yet rock bottom, it didn't matter because I had been through the worst of my life and there was nowhere else for me to go but up.

When God pulled me out of the pit of self-destruction, He said, here, I want to give you some gifts and one of the first gifts He gave me was a Vision. For the first time in a very, very long time, I started seeing things that I had never seen before.

With not much prior work experience, I started praying to God for a job, after all I had bills to pay. My Babe and I had found an apartment about a ½ hour from ma and daddy's house which was great because I was able to go home and hangout with my family on the regular. My Babe is Dorian he and I met in treatment. It was around the time I was still dealing with not having J in my life anymore. So needless to say, I was going through all kinds of feelings. I was feeling better about myself when Dee and I met, however I was still at a place where I never thought I would have another relationship after J and I separated. It had been such a long time since J and I were together and although we were still married, our relationship had been over. J was in that special place in my heart where he will remain forever. I told Dee all about J, our life together, including the drugs, the fire, the separation and where I was in my personal journey. I don't think either Dee or I were prepared for the rollercoaster ride that we were about to take together but we buckled up and together we rode it out. Through the many, many ups and downs, in's and out's, the backwards and forwards, we are still standing, loving each other and growing stronger and better. But it has definitely been some ride. Some days we get off the ride and we are swaying back and forth trying to land on solid ground. Other days we grab hold of each other and we hold on tight, so tight. I never dreamed that I would have a man who would love me with my scars. When Dee came into my life, I was shocked that he wanted anything to do with me. One of the things I love the most about that man is that my scars never stopped his attraction to me. The chemistry between us was too powerful. Dee accepted me into his world and he has loved me ever since.

The apartment itself was not bad, it was in the Flatbush section of Brooklyn and it was all we could afford at the time. We rented a one room bedroom, using the only money we had, which was what we got from the money saved at Pride-Site. Even though we had to share the kitchen and bathroom we were so happy for our little room. But it was cool because our next door neighbors were really nice people. We had an older lady, she lived in the room right next to ours and a tall slim guy had the room next to hers. Our apartment building was right smack in the heart of the Caribbean! everyone in the neighborhood was Jamaican, Trinidadian, Haitian, or from one of the Islands, so we fit right in. The thing about using drugs is that many people use drugs to avoid dealing with their feelings and I had so many feelings that I did not want to deal with. But all of that was changing day by day. Dee and I were both working now but we had to save enough money so we could afford to move into a real apartment. The first job I got after leaving treatment was around October '96. I got hired at Radio City Music Hall. I absolutely loved this job, everyone in New York knows about the Rockettes and the Christmas Spectacular. First of all, I have always loved Christmas. As a little girl growing up, it was one of my favorite holidays. Cocoa, Ramel and I would stay up all night. I couldn't wait until 12 midnight to open up my gifts. I worked in the Guest Relations Department. I was responsible for seating our guests. I made so much money in tips, so my paycheck was like gravy on top of a steak. But the best part about the job was that I got to see the show for free every night. After I seated all the guests, we had to hang around to be available for our guests in case they got lost or forgot where they were seated, so I would stand or sit and watch the whole show. When I found out that we could even go back stage one day, I went back there and I was amazed at what I saw. I went behind the curtains and it was a whole different world back there to see all the actors running around like crazy people, I was laughing so hard. Some of the people were practically naked, some of them were wearing stockings and makeup, but everyone was changing outfits faster than I had ever seen anyone change clothes, getting ready for their next scene. I even got to see the Rockettes up close and in person, it was so much fun. By the time the next act was on stage, I was back in our area watching all the crazy people that I saw in the back doing their thing on stage. It was amazing. But it was a seasonal job so it ended after the

Holiday Season. In 1996 I got my next job. I was hired at Sprint doing Telemarketing. It wasn't a bad job and after working there for a couple days, I found out the skills I had mastered when I hustled in the streets, I was now using in a positive way. I had always been good at encouraging others, so motivating customers to try our "product" was especially familiar for me and within a few weeks, I became one of their top Reps. I was making lots of money. I stayed at Sprint about four years and I was grateful for the friendships I had established while I was there and the learning experiences too, but I knew it was time for me to go. Not to put telemarketing down or anything but I knew that wasn't what I wanted to do for the rest of my life, I wanted something more. But I began to notice something, whenever I was in the process of job seeking, all of the old feelings and insecurities resurfaced. Even though I had started feeling better about myself, about my scars, I was still working on improving my self-esteem. It got to the point where I dreaded going on job interviews because no matter how hard I tried to be positive, I felt inadequate in comparison to the other candidates. I remember leaving job interviews and going home telling Dee, Babe I don't think I'm gonna get that job, not because I am not qualified for the job but because of my outer appearance. I felt like someone else would be chosen over me based on the fact that they didn't have scars and I did. And that went on for years. Sherry listen to me, you have to stop doing that to yourself, you don't know what the employer was thinking, maybe you will get the job. They can't not hire you because you have scars, that would be discrimination. Yes, Dee I know that and of course no employer could ever say I didn't get the job because of my scars but deep down I always felt that if I didn't get the job, that my scars was probably the reason why. But God had a plan. It was at this point in my life when the pieces of the puzzle started coming together. By now Dee and I had moved into our first apartment together and what was so funny, it was right across the street from the room we rented, so we didn't have far to go. It was ok, it wasn't anything to write home about, but it was ours and I hooked it up the best I could. Just when things were going good, something happened that rocked my world.

CHAPTER 16

"GONE BUT NEVER FORGOTTEN"

Growing up, as you know, our grandparents raised us Ramel, Cocoa and I. And as I mentioned, we called our grandfather, daddy or pops. My daddy was a handsome man, skin as brown as honey. I guess that's where I got my honey brown skin from. Daddy brought the bald head into style because as far back as I can remember, he had a baldhead. He was like 6'2, medium build. He was not too fat or skinny, he was just suave. He was a family man. He did everything for his children and grandchildren. Ma and daddy had six children together, three sons and three daughters. My Mina is the oldest, then there is our aunt Lee, our uncle Aus, our aunt Glo, Roy was the next to the youngest (RIP, love you) and the youngest of the bunch, Maakal. While I was in treatment my sweet uncle Roy passed away, he was so young at the time. And now that I think about it, Roy was like daddy in so many ways, especially in regards to his suaveness. Both of them were quiet but when we had family functions, daddy talked nonstop. Roy has a son, lil Roy who looks exactly like him and his daughter Roz, she is so beautiful. When I was in treatment, I always told myself, the only reason I would have ever left Pride-Site was if someone in my family died. So when unc died and I stayed, I knew then that I had made the commitment I needed in my treatment process. The legacy that my unc left behind was his two children and if he were alive today he would be a very proud man. They are both doing so well, very respectful and loving. We all miss Roy so much and we try to go visit his grave, especially on Father's day. I loved watching daddy, he was pretty, you know what I mean, for a man. His nails were always manicured, his clothes looked like they were tailor made and his shoes always looked brand spanking new. In my whole life, I have seen daddy get upset maybe three or four times. And if we saw him and Ma argue a handful of times, that was too much. I have never witnessed my grandparents fighting ever. Daddy was a peaceful, gentle soul. He went to work every day at the hospital, he was a Janitor for more than thirty years. When my grandparents relocated from St. Thomas V.I. to New York, I don't even think I was born back then. They didn't have much but they worked hard and were able to get themselves a house. The same home that all of us were raised in. Daddy had been diagnosed with Diabetes for years and then shortly after the fire, he suffered a stroke. I remember my grandfather would drive for an hour and take me every time I had to go for

Physical Therapy. He drove all the way to Upper Manhattan every single time and he never complained. And he would wait for me sometimes for hours until I was finished and we would go all the way back home. I would say thank you daddy for bringing me to the hospital and waiting for me, I love you so much. And of course he wouldn't say a word. But I knew in his quietness he was saying I love you too. He dealt with the Diabetes and he even handled the stroke, but the final blow to his self-esteem was not long after the stroke, he had to have his left leg amputated. So he couldn't get around as much on his own anymore. Ma took care of him with so much love, she prepared each meal specific to his dietary needs. She did everything for him. But no matter how much she did, it seemed like when daddy realized that his life would never be the same again, he kinda gave up. It seemed like one day he was full of life and the next day it seemed my daddy had aged ten years. At home he would be sitting in his chair asleep. He had always been a quiet man, I mean like I said; the only time we could get a word out of him was during family occasions such as Thanksgiving or a Barbecue. Daddy was not accustomed to being dependent on any one for anything. He was a very proud man; he had been all of his life. His disability had a devastating impact on him emotionally. He worked all his life and when he was not at work, he was at home taking care of his house. He took pride in his family and instilled morals and values in all of his children and grandchildren. The house was always peaceful except for us kids running around like we done lost our minds. After his stroke, whenever I came by to visit ma and daddy, he would be sitting up in his favorite chair asleep. He would wake up and would just look at me while ma and I chatted. You want some ice water daddy? I would rub his bald head, kiss him on his forehead and get him some water. He loved ice cold water. Every weekend his lifelong friend Mr. Watkinson came all the way from the Bronx and he would stay for hours talking and laughing with daddy. You could tell daddy enjoyed having his friend come visit and hang out with him. Mr. Watkinson would bathe daddy, shave his face and rub lotion on and massage his leg and a half. Daddy was well loved by his brothers too, especially uncle Lar-Lar and ma's brother, uncle Darwinson. They both came by most weekends to keep him and ma company. Ma would cook fish, dumplings and fungie and they would spend the whole day together reminiscing. Those were the times when my daddy seemed like his old self.

December 19, 1997 I was at the house, I hung out with ma and daddy for a while then I went upstairs to check on my sister's and nieces, Shantel and Yany-Boo-boo those are Cocoa's daughters. Shantel is my beautiful niece, the one who was scared of me when I first came home from the hospital. Like I said earlier, she would run every time she saw me. And Yany is Cocoa's youngest child, she is our Naomi Campbell, she is going to model one day. I remember it like it was yesterday, we were sitting on Cocoa's bed bugging out like we always did, when all of a sudden the door burst open. It was my uncle Maakal, yo ya'll sitting up here making all this noise and daddy just passed out downstairs. Ya'll call 911, hurry up. What!! Oh my God we yelled. Running down the stairs, my sis had the telephone in her hand dialing 911. When I got to the top of the stairwell banister, I looked over and nothing could have prepared me for what I was seeing. There he was my daddy spread out laying flat on his back on the hallway floor. It was surreal. My ma was holding his head on her lap as she kneeled on the ground. She was saying something but there was too much commotion going on. His eyes were closed and he was not breathing. At first, we all thought maybe he fell down, but when we realized that he was not breathing, we knew something real bad was happening. 911 operator, what's the emergency? It's my grandfather he's a Diabetic and he passed out, his eyes are closed, he is not breathing. Yelling into the phone, my sis pleading please send an ambulance right away! Maakal is trying to do CPR, not sure he even knows what he is doing. Ok, try to calm down Miss, an ambulance is on the way. Step by step we followed their instructions. Put a spoon in his mouth and make sure he is not choking on anything. Can you tell us what happened to him? He was fine we yelled, he went to walk towards the front door and he fell down, we think he hit his head. Please somebody help us! Sirens screaming, red lights flashing, I heard the fire trucks and ambulances stop outside our house. The door was already wide open so they all came right inside. They started putting all kinds of equipment on his body. They are doing CPR. My heart had stopped. Please Lord please don't take him, not now. I begged. Fight daddy, fight. Don't give up I prayed. All of us stood around, some of us were on the ground watching, but I was still stuck on the banister. I just couldn't go any further. I stood there. I was stuck as I watched while they did what they do. When I was finally able to take my eyes off of my daddy, I looked around and I noticed for the first time that the house was full with his children and grandchildren. We were all right there watching in horror as the Medical EMT's tried desperately to revive our daddy. Monitors were going off. Needles were stuck in his arms. Someone had taken ma in the living room. She just sat in their chair numb, while all of this was going on. Her son, my uncle Maakal was right there with her holding her hands trying to comfort her. When I looked back at daddy, I saw the face of the two huge men they were taking turns working so hard on daddy, trying to resuscitate him at least the past 10-15 minutes. Then it happened, I watched as one of the EMT's pressed on daddy's chest one last time and then he just fell back on the ground, perspiration and sweat running down his face. The expression on his face said it all. Before he looked around at anyone in particular I already knew it. The man that had raised us ever since we were infants, the man that was there for us always, the man that was there for me when I needed him the most, was gone. Daddy was dead. The next sound I heard sent such a chill in my soul that to this day, I still remember hearing her voice echo all through our house. It was ma she screamed out so loud. I have heard that sound other times in my life. It's a sound like no other when someone loses a loved one. The pain one feels when they lose someone they love cannot be explained. Mina had just told ma that the man she had loved for the past fifty or so years was gone. It felt like time had stood still. It was unbelievable. Not fifteen minutes earlier he was fine. I had just left him, sitting downstairs in his favorite chair, alive. And now he was dead. After a few minutes, his son and the EMT's picked daddy's lifeless body up off the ground and placed him on our living room couch. They had to take my ma out of the room because she was too overwhelmed by her grief. It was just too unbearable for her and all of us too. After the shock of everything, I found myself sitting on the rug on the floor, right beside my daddy. I don't even know how long it was but I just sat there, looking in his face. He looked so peaceful. I was face-to-face with my grandfather and all I kept thinking as I sat there staring at him, was that I have seen him in this position a thousand times before. He looked just like he did when he came home from work and was sleeping on the very same sofa. His precious hands were crossed over his chest. I looked at him from the crown of his head to the tips of his toes. I even looked at his half leg, in complete despair and amazement. Everyone tried to get me up from there, but I just couldn't leave him. I just wanted him to wake up. I really wanted him to get up. But he didn't. The next thing I know, I could not hold it back anymore. I burst out crying and held him. Mina came and she had to drag me inside ma and daddy's bedroom. I kept screaming no, mommy please, no, no, no! She was crying too and rubbing my face, everyone was crying and distraught. Just like that, his life was all over. It wasn't until hours later that the coroners finally came and his body was taken away. Me and my sis just kept saying, did daddy just die? Can't be. How and why was all we wanted to know? It was really weird, ma said he was sitting in his chair just like I had left him when all of a sudden, he just got up from the chair and he walked down the long hallway towards the front door. He looked outside and on his way back inside, ma said that's when she heard a loud boom. When she ran to see what happened, she could not believe her eyes, daddy had fell down, half of his body was in the hallway. Daddy did hit his head really hard, we found out later on. But what we also began to understand was that he took his last walk around the house as a final journey. He went into a Diabetic coma and was not able to be resuscitated. In the days following, there was a lot of running around to do with making funeral arrangements. Everyone pitched in, we had to pick a suit for daddy, a casket, we had to find the right Cemetery, make the flower arrangements, it was so much. I mean every detail was meticulously planned right down to the color of his socks.

On the day of the funeral the Church was packed. Daddy was well loved not only by his by family but his lifelong friends, many of them flew in all the way from St. Thomas V.I. There to send him off with nothing but love. Ma was holding up really good until it was time for her to go to his casket. My heart broke for her. We all did everything we could to try and console her. We never left her side. I was so thankful that my sis lived right upstairs and Mina had been living with ma and daddy for a couple of years, so she had the family around her every day. They say time heals all wounds and I know that daddy's death left a huge void in my ma's heart and soul. However with all of us smothering her with love, as hard as it was, Ma is moving forward. I guess like all of us, she had her memories which could never be taken away. Daddy remains strong in all of our hearts. We visit his grave on Holidays especially Father's Day and his Birthday. (Daddy, may your precious soul rest in peace, miss you, love you, will never forget). Until we reunite again.

CHAPTER 17
"THE BIG WEDDING"

My family loves Quan. He and Cocoa have been together since forever. Our family loves him for Cocoa, they are so good for each other. Quan is what I like to call an "Old G", he is handsome, like dark chocolate and if I'm not mistaken, I think he thinks he is still a playa, lol, Quan. Seriously though we love him, he is perfect for Cocoa, especially since she has always been that girl, you know that girl you want as your partner, if you have something you need to get done. They had their daughter Yany together. She is their pride and joy and Quan has his oldest son, Shamal. He adores his son. And of course his daughter ,Tamia she is the youngest. Tamia is Quan's heart. The year was 1998, sis and Quan had planned a huge wedding. I think they had over 200 people attending and that was because ma kept adding on "one more person". Her one more person basically included at least a hundred people, plus the people Cocoa and Quan already had on their list. The closer it got to the big day, we were all running around like crazy people. The color Cocoa chose was a dark, beautiful purple and of course she was looking for the prettiest white gown. We all went with Cocoa to find the perfect dress. Mina, Shantel, Yany, Cocoa and myself, stepped into the Bridal Shop and there were so many beautiful dresses. Sis chose a couple of dresses and went to try them on. One by one, she came out to let us check her out and we were saying ooh that is so nice, ooh that is beautiful. This went on for hours. Sis, of course who is as picky as can be, was saying um maybe, no I'm not feeling this one, no let me try on a couple more. By now we were ready to strangle her. I'm saying look girl you look beautiful in each of those dresses, pick one and let's go. We were all laughing at each other. We had the salesgirls cracking up all afternoon. Then finally sis came out in "the dress" and had all of us in tears. She looked like a model, she was so beautiful. The dress was lace all around the top part and then long and flowing to the bottom, with a long, long train following behind her. One look at her and I busted out crying. Look at you sis, oh you are so beautiful. Yes, that definitely is the one, now go take it off because I don't care what you say, we are getting this one. OK, ok she's laughing I love it too, we are gonna get this one. We all shouted thank God. Cocoa's oldest daughter Shantel, our cousin Brina, and Ramel's fiancé at the time, Kim and Quan's sister were her Bridesmaids and of course I was her Maid of Honor. They all found their beautiful dresses with no problem, now it was my turn. We all knew finding my dress was going to be a challenge. My family knows how I feel about my scars, they have been dealing with it and with me since the fire. Finding my dress turned out to be even more difficult than finding Cocoa's dress. First of all, I was still not wearing short sleeves and we're talking the middle of summer, so it was pretty much next to impossible to find a beautiful long sleeve, lacey or sheer purple dress. So after leaving the Bridal Shop empty handed, we decided we are going to have to go to a regular clothes store. So we went on a hunt for my dress. Five stores later, we were like ok, this is not working, we were hungry, tired and hot. Sis maybe you could get one of the short sleeve dresses and wear the beautiful long gloves, they will cover your arms. At that point I was cool with that, so we began looking for a short sleeve dress. Then I spotted it, I saw this absolutely beautiful purple, sheer, flowing dress. It looked like it was sitting there just waiting for me to see it, it was perfecto. I LOVED it. The only thing was, we were going to have it retailored just a touch. I wanted to have the top of the dress cut so that we could use this sheer material I found, making it see through all around the top. Everyone was ecstatic when I tried the dress on and we knew that was "the one". I was happy, they were happy, we all had our dresses and we were good to go. The next day I took the dress to a tailor shop in Flatbush, told the lady my Vision and she said, I will take care of it. I picked me dress up a week later, tried it on and fell in love. The day finally came, oh did I forget the best part? Everyone has something a thing that they need to work on to improve and get better and for my sis hers is that she is late for everything. All week we were saying Cocoa you cannot, absolutely cannot be late for your wedding. She laughed about it, we joked about it and I bet on it. That night we had a ball, it's a wonder anyone got a drop of sleep. The morning of the big day, since everyone stayed at sis' house, we were all there. The guys of course were doing their own thing. We videotaped sis every step of the way, her nails were meticulous, her "hair weave" was flowing, her makeup was flawless and then she put "the dress" on and that just sealed it. She was absolutely glowing. We tried our best not to make her cry, so she wouldn't ruin her makeup. By the time we all got dressed, the beautiful white limo's were waiting outside. Milford Street was on fire and we were the Stars. I felt so beautiful in my dress and my long purple gloves did their job and to top it off I found this huge see through purple hat. I felt like Diana Ross or some big movie star. The photographer took shots of every single thing. It was the most exciting, wonderful, crazy day of not only sis' life, but the whole entire family. By the time we got to the Church, sure enough true to her game, she was late. We all cracked up laughing on the way because we were all late. We tried our best rushing all around like crazy people but the best part was that we had so much fun. Finally at the Church, I had never seen so many people! The whole family was there. All the guys looked so handsome in their suits and Tuxes, especially my Dee. And Quan, well he was looking like the Don. He was so handsome. They said their vows, Cocoa cried, we all cried, and laughed, they kissed and the Celebration was on. We drove to the beautiful place where the Reception was being held and we partied all night long. Cocoa must have a thousand wedding pictures, it was one of the happiest days of her life and our lives. Ma and Mina were so happy, even they had on their beautiful purple dresses.

There were only two sad things that day, daddy/pops was not there to celebrate with us. He had passed away a couple of months before. But he was there in spirit. And our father, Lis was not able to walk Cocoa down the aisle. My father the great "Lis", had been diagnosed with cancer several months before. The man that was so full of life, the family man, the music and food lover, was deteriorating right before our eyes. My father suffered so much, the cancer had taken everything from him. My father was a huge man, tall and thick. He had lost so much weight, he was as frail as an elderly man. The past couple of months Cocoa had begged daddy, please daddy, I will understand if you can't do it. Daddy it's ok, I can get uncle Aus or Maakal to walk me down the aisle. As long as you are ok and you are there, that's all I want. By now daddy could hardly walk two steps, let alone down an aisle but he wanted to walk his baby down that aisle so bad, he pleaded mommy, that's what he called Cocoa, I can do it, please let me do it. But when the moment came, my father couldn't even take a step, he was so weak. Yes, he did make it to the wedding but because he was so sick, we had to ask his wife, Cherelle to please take him home and let him lay down. Although he refused to leave, we made him go. Sis begged him daddy please let Cherelle take you home, I need you to go rest. It was only when she begged him that he agreed to go home and rest. Daddy would have done anything for us, that is how he was his whole life. So Cherelle got the car ready, she was taking him home. We were able to hold him up, Ramel, Cocoa and I, long enough to get a couple of quick pictures with him. He couldn't even stand on his own anymore. Even when I look at those shots today, I see how much pain he was in by the look on his face. Still breaks my heart even today. Cocoa and Quan got married a day after her birthday, June 6, 1998. It was a family celebration that will never be forgotten. Then something else happened that rocked our world.

CHAPTER 18

"ROCKED OUR WORLD"

A month after Quan and Cocoa's wedding July 18, 1998, the great "Lis", our beloved father passed of cancer and it truly rocked our world. He was so young, fifty four years old. Daddy had always been a heavy smoker, all of my life I remember him with a cigarette in his mouth. He was diagnosed just a couple of months earlier and by then it was too late for daddy. Growing up I never really remembered a time when we all lived together. I was the youngest of daddy and Mina's three children, too young to remember anything. But what I will never forget is how much daddy loved us.

After Mina and daddy separated he stayed in BK which stands for Brooklyn, for a while he lived in a house on Park Place and Nostrand Avenue. We were very young during this time. I couldn't be more than about six or seven years old. Daddy brought me my little red tricycle. I loved that bike I can remember riding that thing up and down the street all day long. Of course I could only go about two houses away and then come right back. If Ramel and Cocoa was outside, Ramel would take my bike and ride around all crazy and then give it back to me. We loved going to the corner store every minute to get our chips and then we would run back home. When we became teenagers, daddy had moved to the Bronx. We didn't know anything about the Bronx other than we didn't like it. There were too many big buildings and it was a long drive to get there. Even though it was only about an hour drive from Brooklyn to the Bronx, but it felt like forever to get to his house. I didn't really care though as long as he stopped to get me my two Big Macs, fries and a soda from McDonald's, I could ride all day. Daddy came to pick us up every couple of months. We loved spending time together. My father was a loving, caring, nurturing man. He would pick me up and put me on his shoulders and carry me around. He would make sure we had everything we needed. He had the funniest laugh. Daddy worked at a Gas Station in the Bronx and his mother our "Darling", that's what we called her, she lived right across the street from where he worked. Darling was a feisty little lady, she had some mouth on her. She told you exactly what she felt. Darling didn't hold no punches. I was very young and I don't really remember her but I know we used to go upstairs in this building with a lot of floors. When she passed away daddy was so sad. RIP/Darling "little feisty lady". We would run back and forth upstairs to her house and back downstairs to the gas station.

A FIRE WITHIN

Daddy hung out there after work drinking beers with his friends. He moved to a Co-op in the Bronx, it was called River Park Towers. Now that was a different story. Basically the building was a really nice project and we definitely loved his new place. The apartment was so nice and spacious and pretty. Daddy picked us up on Friday nights, usually by the time we got there it was dark outside, exactly what we loved. We would just drop off our bags and jet downstairs. It was a whole new world for us. Even though we didn't know anyone Ramel, Cocoa and I were chillin. Eventually we met friends out there and found out the Bronx wasn't so bad after all. It definitely wasn't the BK, but it was all good. By that time I was eighteen and smoking cigarettes and thought I was grown. One day daddy came to pick us up and I was outside smoking a cigarette. He got so upset and all he said to me was, "mommy you think that is cute, you think smoking a cigarette makes you a grown up. I don't like you smoking". And I looked at his face and he had a look that I had never seen on him before. All I could do was throw the cigarette away and I never let him see me smoking again. Years later when I was in the fire, it was my father who stayed by my bedside, day and night with me. Some days I didn't even know he was there, I would be asleep and when I woke up the Nurses would say your father was here with you all day. He sat right there just watching you for hours and then he would leave. Lis was the best father in the world. He showered us with love. Always instilling in us the importance of family I can hear him saying, mommy if I don't call you, you can't pick up the phone to call me? When is the last time you called your cousins? He is talking about our cousins on his side of the family, crazy Herb and his sister Bev. Ok, ok daddy I promise I will call you more and I will call crazy Herb too. My cousin Herb, I love him dearly, but I don't think his elevator goes all the way up to the top floor. He missed his calling too, just like Ramel because he definitely could have been a comedian and made lots of money.

Daddy had been right by my side, just like he always was. Now he was gone. His funeral was so sad all of us were there, his brothers and friends. Just like always, before we even got to the funeral parlor, my heart started pounding and my hands were sweaty. I don't think I will ever be ok with funerals. So I stood at the back of the parlor and peeked up front and saw his casket. I started praying Lord give me the strength. Ramel and Cocoa went up front and I ran up there because I didn't want to be by myself. When I looked at the man that I loved with all my heart I just cried. I thought about the last day in the hospital when Dee and I went to see him. Cherelle was there as she has always been. We love her so much, it had been so hard for her. She and daddy were married since we were little and she was the one who took care of him when he couldn't take care of himself anymore. So she was at the hospital too every step of the way, along with Cocoa, Quan, Ramel, Dee and I. We all had been to the hospital the past couple of months and every time we went daddy was worse off. But this day Cocoa called me, Sherry we got to go see daddy and say bye. The Doctors called and said they don't think he is going to make it past today. Unless you have experienced someone dying from cancer, you can only imagine how hard it is going through it with a loved one. Again I prayed. By the time Dee and I got to the hospital, no one else had gotten there yet and as soon as I walked in the room I thought I would throw up. The smell of death was in there, his body had completely deteriorated. If it weren't my father in that room, I could have never stayed, not even for five minutes. Daddy didn't even recognize me or Dee. He couldn't talk, I'm not even sure he could see. But I held him and told him, it's me daddy your Minna-Soda-Fats. I'm right here with you. Ramel and Cocoa are on their way here too. We will be right here with you daddy. Close your eyes and get some rest. Quietly I said the Lord's Prayer for my father. You are going to be ok. Go on daddy be with the Lord. You will not have to suffer anymore. We love you so much, don't worry, we will take care of each other. I held his hand one last time and when I couldn't take it any longer, I ran out of the room into the hall and cried my eyes out for my father. It hurt so bad losing him like that. The only relief was having Dee there with me and knowing that he was not going to suffer and be in pain anymore. But most important, just knowing that he was going to be with the Lord gave me Peace. The very next day my beloved father was gone. The funeral was over and we left the Bronx and headed back to the BK. And every year on daddy' birthday and Father's Day, just like I do for daddy/pops and Roy, I light a candle for Lis, RIP my love.

CHAPTER 19

"BETTER AND BETTER"

By 1998 Dee and I were good, we were still on that rollercoaster ride but at least we weren't on bumper cars. Although there were many times it felt like we were. Every once in a while I talked to J, he was living at his parents' house. J knew that I was in a relationship and he even wished me the best. It had been two years now since our separation and it was getting a little easier for me, so I checked in on J every couple of months. Every day I got up and went to work, I had to ride the trains to the city. By this time I wasn't having the panic attacks any longer. I think it was because I really didn't have any choice, I had to go to work. People stared at me all the time, whether I was on the train, in a store, walking down the street, it didn't matter, wherever I am people stare.

When I wasn't working my sis Cocoa would come and pick me up in her car and we would go shopping and hang out pretty much every weekend. Year after year I began feeling better and stronger, but the fire never leaves me. And the crazy thing is, I still haven't gotten over that I was in a fire. I don't know that I ever will. I would look at my scars and think, God you really saved me. The summer was always the worst time for me, even after all this time I continued to struggle with summer clothes. I had never been outside with short sleeves since the fire. I refused to let anyone other than Dee and my family see me so exposed. It seemed like every year the people staring at me bothered me less and less because there was nothing I could do about that. So to make me feel better, I would find clothes that I could keep cool in and feel comfortable wearing. The majority of my shirts would be lace or something sheer without exposing too much skin. Pants and skirts weren't a problem; my legs were not burned although I do have a huge patch on the back of my left thigh. Remember, that's where they removed my skin to use for grafts in other places on my body. The first couple of years were the worst for me and I felt so bad for Dee because I drove him crazy with my mood swings. He would come home from work and see my clothes thrown all over our bedroom, it looked like a hurricane in our bedroom. That was because in the morning when I was getting ready for work, there were days I would go through three or four outfits until I felt comfortable enough to walk out the door. Of course by the time I felt comfortable, I was running late, so I would have to leave everything until I came home that evening. And as if that weren't enough, I also drove him crazy every time we went outside together. When Dee and I went out he wanted to hold my hand or kiss me and I felt so uncomfortable. I would let his hand go and it would make him uncomfortable. It took us a while for us to get comfortable with each other. I never wanted him to feel embarrassed, so before we left home, if we were going out together, I would ask Dee, how do you feel with me wearing this? Or I would ask him how does this look to you Babe? Basically I drove him absolutely nuts. But he never stopped showing me love, whether we were inside or outside, Dee was always Dee. He wasn't the problem; I was because I wasn't comfortable in my own skin. But God had a plan. Over the past several years, little by little, God has put me in situations where I had no choice but to interact with others. The more I had to ride the train whether it was to work or to an appointment in order for me to deal with my feelings, I started reading books. I started enjoying reading Spiritual books. Some of my favorite books are by Pastors, Ministers and Gospel Artists. Joyce Meyer has been teaching the Word of God since 1976 and she has been in fulltime ministry since 1980. Joyce is the bestselling Author of more than seventy inspirational books, including "Approval Addiction" and one of my favorites "The Confident Woman". The book "A Confident Woman" has been such an inspiration in my healing journey. Joyce encourages women by sharing her personal journey from insecurity and self-hatred, to developing self-confidence and realizing her full potential. The book reminds us that "women are a precious gift from God to the world. We are creative, sensitive, compassionate and talented" (Meyers-A confident Woman, 2006). It was reading her book "A Confident Woman" that gave me the courage to step out in Faith. Joyce gave me keys to identifying my own barriers to confidence, and she outlined the steps I needed to take to become more independent. Joyce explored the seven characteristics of a woman with confidence, which include a woman who knows she is loved, who refuses to live in fear, and who does not live by comparisons, "if onlys" or "what ifs". She spoke into my spirit, sharing these very tools that were life changing for me. By the time 1999 came around, I was going from feeling better to feeling renewed. And then it happened again, I got news that rocked my world.

CHAPTER 20

"HEART BROKEN"

I will never forget the day my heart broke, August 1999. I went to visit P, she was the Jamaican lady, the last one that moved in with us at the "building". Throughout the years we had kept in touch from time to time. P had moved from Schaeffer Street and she had stopped using drugs. It had been a long time since I last saw P, so one day I decided I was going to check her out. Knock, knock!! Who is it? I heard the familiar voice yelling through the door. It's Sherry, girl open the door. And what happened next I was not prepared for. As soon as the door opened, all I saw was P drop to her knees, screaming Sherry, oh God, oh God. P what's wrong with you? What happened? you ok? Girl what is going on? Sherry you didn't hear? Hear what P? You are starting to scare me now tell me what happened? What are you talking about? Sherry J is dead, he died. After P said those words everything else sounded like bla, bla,bla. I saw her lips moving, but I wasn't hearing what she was saying and I definitely wasn't understanding. I felt weak in my knees. I had to sit down on her sofa. P what did you say? Me telling you mon, J is dead, he died today. Me heard it from me friend, she said in her Jamaican accent. No that can't possibly be true, J can't be dead, I had just seen him.

I went to visit J at his parents' house two weeks before. We sat at the kitchen table and talked for a while. J are you ok? as I am sitting down looking at J I noticed something different in his eyes. J your eyes look funny, are you ok? Yes mon, me good. How are you doing? he asked. I'm good, I'm hanging in there. Sherry mon me just want you to be happy. You think I don't know you have your man, it's all good mon. Don't worry about me you just live your life and be happy. J I'm good and I am happy. It was getting late so after we finished the delicious dinner mama cooked, we talked some more and I said come on, I gotta get home. Come walk with me outside and wait until my cab comes. On the way out, I looked in the living room and said good night mama, good night Mr. Hutchy, see ya'll later. You gone, ok we talk to you next time, they said as I walked out of the door. We were outside by the time my cab came, as I was about to get in the cab J said, so that's how it is now? I can't even have a kiss bye? I kissed J on his cheek and I turned around and got in the cab. I headed home, never did I think it would be the last time I ever saw J again.

I snatched my cell phone out of my pocket dialing mama's house. Ring, ring, ring the voice on the other end of the phone was mama, J's mother. Mama please tell me it's not true, where is J? Sherry, my dear I was gonna call you, yes darling J is dead. Oh my God mama I can't believe it! I'm so sorry. Mama are you gonna be ok? Is everybody there with you? Yes, mon everyone is here. Mama I gotta go, I will be over there as soon as I can. Mama what happened to him? We will talk when you get here. Ok I love you, I told her and I hung up the phone. I cried sitting on P's sofa. We hugged each other and I cried and cried. My spirit was hurting inside for J and when I thought about our last conversation, I cried some more. J's autopsy said he died of Natural Causes, J was only forty seven years old. He was thirteen years older than I was. When I got to the house, I just hugged mama. She started telling me what happened. Mama said J was downstairs in the same little room he and I used to stay in and he wasn't feeling good all night. Mama made him some food which he could hardly eat. Every time mama went down to check on him, he looked worse and the last time she went to check on J, he asked her to take him to the hospital. The ambulance came and J was taken to the hospital and he died that morning. I was devastated even though we were not together, and even though I had moved on with my life, I thought J would always be around. He died so unexpectedly. It was a huge loss for his family, mama and Mr. Hutchy, all of his sisters, his brother's, and especially his son Kris. But for me, I lost my buddy and my partner, there was a bond between J and I that never did get broken, even in our separation. J had been and he always will be, right inside that special place inside my heart, where he will remain forever. A part of me died when he died, the part that he held in my heart. We almost died together, but God saved both of us. And then ten years later, God called for J to come be with Him. I still don't know why, but he will forever be a part of me. Everyone was there, we all hugged, we talked about J and we ate dinner, just like we had done so many times before. I told Mama and Mr. Hutchy how sorry I was for J and they knew I meant it from the bottom of my heart. Later on I left and went home. I told Dee J had died and he just held me, and I cried some more. The day of J's funeral, I asked Dee not to come. Mommy and Cocoa came with me and when we got to the funeral home, there were so many people there. I saw Mama and Mr. Hutchy, the rest of J's family and some of his friends. Mama had saved a seat for me right up front with the family. I was shaking all over, I was so scared to see him. So I refused to look over at his casket. We all cried and talked about J and his life. The Minister went up and gave an awesome Eulogy for J. It brought everyone to tears. Then it was time, it was time for everyone to go view his body and say their goodbyes. I was already crying, I am never any good at funerals. I get really nervous and scared. My palms of course were all sweaty and the tissue I had in my hand was soaking wet from all my tears. I knew it was not gonna be good for me, but by the time I got to the casket and I saw J just laying in there, it was like time stood still and it was all I could do, not to drop to my knees and tell him how sorry I was. I was sorry for him dying. I was sorry for all the pain I know I caused him after we separated. I was so sorry that he would never get to see his grandchildren. I was sorry for hurting J. Maybe if I never went into treatment J would still be alive I thought. Maybe he died of a broken heart. I cried my heart out for the man who took care of me when I couldn't even take care of myself. J was one of the sweetest, kindest, and the gentlest man I had ever had the pleasure of knowing and being with in my life. He was a peacemaker, a singer and a lover. I will never forget all the times we shared and although it was not the best of times because of the drugs, he made them the best. He made me laugh so hard and when I wasn't laughing I was smiling. Goodbye J... I will always love you. By the time my sis held me to get up and tried standing me up, she had to escort me out of the parlor. It was way too much for me to deal with. After the service was over, we went back to J's house for a while and that was it, just like that J was gone. Even until this day, I still call his family. Not a Holiday passes and I don't call mama and Mr. Hutchy. I tell them all the time how thankful and grateful I am to them both for all the years they put up with our mess. They never once turned their backs on J and I, even when we were at our worst. They let me live in their home, knowing I was a drug addict. They fed me when they ate. They loved me even after J and I separated. For that I will always and forever love them.

CHAPTER 21

"9/11"

In the year 2000, there were a few changes in my life. I had left Sprint and started working at the New York City Department for the Aging. I worked in the Elderly Crime Victims Resource Center, doing the agencies Intakes. And this is where the shift in my career first started. Ever since I left Pride-Site, I knew I wanted to be a Social Worker. The seed was planted and the Vision was there. I just had to figure out how to implement it. I learned so much valuable information working in the Crime Victims Unit. I learned about Elder Abuse and all the many ways people take advantage of seniors. As the intake worker, I was the first line of communication for victims seeking help. I couldn't believe some of the conversations I had with the victims. These were elderly people who were very vulnerable and many of them fell prey not only to violence perpetrated by strangers, the majority of the calls I received, the victims were abused or neglected by family members. The different forms of abuse to the elderly included but are not limited too; financial, verbal, psychological, and physical and unfortunately many of the callers were victims of sexual abuse. After about a year of working there, I became so interested in wanting to understand people and why we do the things we do. The New York City Department for the Aging was located at 2 Lafayette Street, New York, N.Y.

September 11, 2001, I got dressed for work just like I did every day. The train ride to the city was a normal ride. The train was crowded as it usually is in N.Y., nothing out of the ordinary. But what happened next changed history not only in N.Y,. but worldwide. As I got off the train on Chambers Street and I headed up the steps, I didn't notice anything too different, maybe it was because I was rushing to get into work. But by the time I walked inside our building, I noticed there were a crowd of people standing by the elevators and since our Dept. was only on the 3rd floor, I decided to walk up the stairs. As soon as I opened the Exit door to the stairwell, I realized something serious was going on. There were people all around. So hurriedly, I went into our office. And there they were, all of my colleagues standing by the window and I'm like, what is going on? What are ya'll looking at? Haven't you heard? There's been an attack at the World Trade Center, look Sherry, you can see the Airplane sticking out of World Trade 1! When I went to look out of the window, I couldn't believe my eyes, there it was just like a scene from a movie. This huge Airplane sticking out of the building. My heart started racing as I ran to my desk and grabbed the telephone to call my family. I needed to tell someone what was going on, not realizing by now the whole world already knew we were under attack. It was being broadcasted all over the news. My question to my friend standing by her desk was, Anne ok, why are we still here? They are saying the other buildings in the area are being evacuated. A few seconds later all I heard was this loud thunderous sound. In shock and amazement everyone was looking out of the window screaming, oh my God, oh my God! The building is collapsing. The building is collapsing. Two seconds later I heard it, that heart wrenching scream that I had heard years ago when ma realized that daddy had died, it was coming from the office. And the loud scream that I heard was the familiar sound of someone losing a loved one. It was one of the Supervisors, she had just learned that her son who was a New York City Fire Fighter was in the building, he was one of the first rescuers to arrive on the scene. She didn't know if her son was dead or alive. All she knew at this point, was that it was confirmed by someone, he was in the building. By now I have my pocketbook in my hand because I was about to be out of the door. I was terrified. Quickly glancing out of the window, I saw what looked like dominos but it was the huge building, World Trade 1, crumbling to the ground. No one knew if we were still under attack. Our building was just a couple of blocks from the World Trade Center and basically, it was time to go. By the time they got the Supervisor who was screaming together, everyone was running around the office and no one knew what to do, whether to leave or stay. The Program Director didn't even know what to do. Go, everyone just go! They didn't have to tell me twice, by the time we opened the office door to leave, someone burst in screaming, EVACUATE, EVERYONE MUST EVACUATE THE BUILDING! Before he finished screaming, I was already downstairs. And again I was not prepared for what I was about to see. Anne and I were running down the stairs holding each other and of course I had on heels. Sherry take off those shoes. Do you hear me, take off those shoes. I'm looking at her like she is crazy. Girl just come on, I ain't got no time to take off no shoes. I definitely wasn't stopping to take off my shoes. I didn't know if our building was gonna collapse next or what. I just needed to get out of that building and get outside. But when I walked, excuse me when I ran out of the building and stepped outside, I was in complete shock. Outside looked like a War Zone. There was smoke all around; you could hardly see two feet in front of you. And everyone that passed me by had dirt and chalk looking stuff all on their clothes. People were running and some people were walking really fast. It was unbelievable. I'm running, in my heels behind Anne. I told her I could run in heels, I have done it plenty of times before.

 My cell phone in my hand, I'm calling Dee, no answer. Cocoa, no answer. Ma, no answer. No wonder, I had no service. Now I'm running with no service on my cell phone. My heart pounding even faster. Oh my God!! We were right in the heart of Ground Zero, just one or two blocks away. There were hundreds if not thousands of people all around. No one knew where to go. Of course, I started having flashbacks of the fire, only this time it was daytime and I could see what was going on. Which I said later on, didn't make it that much easier, it was still very, very frightening. Oh did I forget to say that I am directionally challenged. After I found out the trains were not working, the severity of the situation really began to sink in. Wait a minute!! No trains are working, NO TRAINS ARE WORKING! How in the world am I going to get home? All the way to Brooklyn? Oh My God. What is going on? I was headed to Brooklyn and Anne lived somewhere in Manhattan, so that meant we had to go in separate directions. Which also meant Sherry, you are on your own, again. Even though I didn't want to walk all the way from Manhattan to Brooklyn "in heels". Even if I could, I didn't even know where I was going. Sherry how do you walk to Brooklyn? It was so scary. So I did the best thing I knew to do. Excuse me sir, do you know the easiest way to get to Brooklyn? What part of Brooklyn? Anywhere, I just need to get across the Bridge. Oh! You just have to go that way, the Brooklyn Bridge is that way. Thank you, thank you very much. Sherry you are gonna have to wear these heels until you can't take it anymore. So I'm headed in the direction the man told me to go. Every couple of blocks the people headed in the same direction would be screaming run, run and everyone would take off running. Finally I found the Brooklyn Bridge and when I stood on the Bridge and tried looking to see how far a walk it was to get to the other side, I almost cried. I said Sherry girl make sure you always keep a pair of flats in your pocket book from now on.

I started the long, long, long walk across the bridge with the thousand other people going to Brooklyn. The funny thing was I met people while we were walking. This sista girl was headed towards Flatbush and so was I. We ended up walking together. After a while I kicked off those heels and walked in just my stockings, me and the other hundreds of women who all wore heels to work that day. I was so worried about everyone because I still didn't have any reception. No one seemed to have reception. I didn't know if my family was ok. Or if they even knew we were under attack. It was a horrible feeling. I had ran out of work that morning around 9:30 am and I didn't get home that night until 10:00 pm, because even after I finally crossed to the other side in Brooklyn, I still had to walk to Flatbush. At least I had reception back on my phone. I called and everyone was ok. Later on I found out that Mina had to walk across that Bridge that day too.

I will never forget that day. All of the people who lost their lives, it was just heartbreaking. The next day I went to work, the area looked like what I imagined hell to look like. It was dark and gloomy looking; there was dirt and all kinds of debris all around. During lunchtime I walked around the corner.

Of course the streets were closed off to pedestrians. But I did get to stand on the corner and look down as far as I could to where the buildings collapsed. I couldn't see from where I was, but what I did see was enough.

Over the next couple of weeks things started getting cleaned up. The stores reopened. Businesses were back in business, as we were trying to move on from that horrible tragedy. Everywhere you looked, you saw the ribbons and pictures of lost loved ones. People still missing. Others who died. Even after eleven years, it still is very clear in my mind. My heart goes out to all of the people who lost their life and the people who lost a loved one on that day.

Recently I saw on the news that they have finally finished the new World Trade Center and hopefully the families can find peace. My cousin Brina lost a very good friend of hers that day, he died in one of the buildings. It was so hard for her, but over time, she is healing from her loss with the help of her family and friends.

CHAPTER 22
"LIFE CHANGING"

In 2001 at age of thirty six, I made a decision that would change my life forever. I decided I was going to college. One day I came home and said to my Babe, sit down, I want to tell you something. Dee, guess what? What baby? I'm going to college. You are? Yes, I told you one day I'm going to be a social worker. That's great, Sherry go for it. At the time Dee probably thought I was crazy or something but I was very serious. I was still working at the Department for the Aging and I knew that I was going to be a Social Worker. I had that Vision since 1996, when I left Pride-Site. And now I was about to make it happen. I never dreamed that I would go back to school, let alone college. But God had a plan. The funny thing about it is that when God has a plan for our lives, whether or not you want it, it does not matter. He just guides you in the direction He wants you to go and you follow. I know that because I had no intention of going to college, however the journey that has been placed in front of me caused me to pursue a college education. And at the time, I didn't even know what the plan was. I was just walking in my Destiny. As an adult I realized that it was a huge mistake dropping out of high school in the 11th grade. I was working forty hours a week and knew that it was going to be a challenge working fulltime and going to school fulltime, but I never let that stop me. So I researched some local colleges and found Audrey Cohen College. It was located in Manhattan. I went to the school one day to start the registration process and I was told I would have to take a placement test. I aced the exam and I was in. At the time, I didn't even have a high school diploma or a GED. I Majored in Human Service and when I started classes, a new world opened up for me. I found that school was so interesting, because my classes focused on the thing that I was interested in the most, people and addictions. Right up my alley. The first day of class, I arrived, sat down in my seat and checked everyone out. Of course they checked me out too, but that was cool. A strange thing started happening over the past couple years, I was hiding myself less and less. I wasn't afraid any longer to look people in the eye. I wasn't holding my head down any longer. I was beginning to break out of the cocoon I had put myself in since the fire and I was about to bust life wide open. And after the first couple of semesters, it wasn't whether or not Dee thought I was crazy, because I knew I must have been nuts. Me and my schedule was crazy. I worked all day and went to class at night. But you know what, I loved it.

Some of the course offerings included Self-Assessment & Preparation for Practice, Values & Ethics, Promoting Empowering Change, Developing Empowerment through Supervision, Professional Skills for Counseling, Models of Counseling, Legal & Ethical Issues in Counseling, and I had to do Field Placement. I still don't know how I found the time to do all the things I was doing, but honestly, I didn't even have the time to stop and think about it. I just did it. I squeezed my field practicum in volunteering at Catholic Charities, where I provided treatment services for the Mentally Ill Chemical Abusers (MICA) patients. I managed a small caseload of about five patients and I provided treatment planning. I met some wonderful people at Catholic Charities but there is one lady in particular who taught me so much, her name was Ms. Susie Steinhart and of course she was a Social Worker. Susie showed me what real compassion is, she was excellent with the client population we served. Her patience and dedication was exceptional and I learned so much watching her interact with the patients. It was a valuable experience. My professors at Audrey Cohen were great, I was amazed sitting in class just listening to them teach us about life. Year after year, I continued to do my thing. I had a couple of friends, it was cool, all of us overcoming challenge after challenge. And then the day finally came, Graduation Day. I had prayed for this day for years and it was here. My family was ecstatic, it was one of the happiest days of my life. Dee, Cocoa, Mina, Ma and some of my cousins came and they were taking pictures and videotaping, smiling and crying, all at the same time. Me a graduate and not a high school graduate, I was a College Graduate. I put on my cap and gown and I walked down that aisle and I have never been more proud of myself. All of the old feelings, the low self-esteem and no confidence was replaced more and more and I was getting back all of those things that I had lost when I did drugs. The confidence that I was gaining was not just the result of the degree that I had earned. But it was a gift that God gave to me because the confidence that I was gaining was not in myself, it was the confidence I had in **God**. Because I knew beyond a shadow of a doubt that I could never have done any of it without Him.

CHAPTER 23

"JUST GETTING STARTED"

And God wasn't finished with me, not at all. As a matter of fact, He was just getting started. A couple of months after I graduated with my Bachelor's degree, one day I came home and I said Dee guess what? Yes Babe? I'm going back to school. Oh yea, wow? Yes, I'm going to get my Master's degree. I told you I am going to be a Social Worker he just looked at me and shook his head. Go for it babe, you are something else. So I enrolled in the Master's program at Long Island University-the Brooklyn Campus and it was on. By now I know I am walking in my Destiny for sure, because there is no way in the world I wanted to go back to college again. But there I was a couple weeks later, sitting in class. Still working fulltime and back in school fulltime. This time it was the meat and potatoes. I was pursuing a Master's degree in Social Work with a concentration in Alcohol and Substance Abuse and I was in heaven. I had this opportunity to learn about my own former addiction. I couldn't wait. The Alcohol and Substance Abuse concentration at LIU incorporated various methods and systems of practice and by the time I graduated, I was prepared to work with individuals, families, groups and the community at large. This concentration also prepared me to work in settings ranging from community-based organizations and from mental health clinics to the criminal justice system. I gained valuable knowledge, skills and the values to deliver alcohol and substance abuse counseling and to perform assessments; clinical evaluations; treatment planning; case management; and client, family and community education. In addition, I became completely familiar with the social works professional and ethical responsibilities as well as the documentation process.

I left the NYC Department for the Aging by the end of 2004, after four years. I was so grateful for my time there. I learned so much from working in the Crime Victims Unit, it helped me to understand the vulnerabilities of our seniors and how to ensure they are being treated with dignity and respect.

That same year my life would change in a way that I never dreamed. One night as I was laying in our bed, when in my Spirit I heard, I want you to tell your story, your testimony. So, I said ok Sherry, it could just be a flashback or something, so I didn't pay any attention to it. I told Dee about it and that was it.

We had moved in a really nice basement apartment in the beautiful Canarsie section of Brooklyn. I had found this place for us a couple of years earlier so we moved from Flatbush. But the strangest thing started happening to me. Every day at work, I began "telling my story". And at first it was not on purpose. It was to help someone through a situation they were dealing with. God is so awesome because before I knew it, I had already started telling my story (that was my "light-bulb" moment).

I will never forget the day, it was September 27, 2004 I sat down to my computer and put the date on the top of the page and I wrote a prayer to God. Thanking him for giving me my testimony. And from that day on, I promised God I'd share my story to inspire others until the day I take my last breath. And I gave God the Glory, Honor and Praise for this gift of life that he gave to me. I started writing "A Fire Within" that same day and when I think about my dreams they are coming true. I'm walking in my destiny and with a purpose. And there is no stopping me now. I can't help but to think it was all worth it.

I got hired at Samaritan Village, a Residential "Substance Abuse Program" in Jamaica Queens in 2005 and I have been in my element ever since. God the Author and Finisher knows exactly the plan he has for our life, and the plan that he has for mine is dynamic. Everything that I was learning at school, I was applying at work. I was so fascinated learning about the Disease of Addiction. It felt like I was now living my life on the other side of the drugs. I loved being a substance abuse counselor at Samaritan and over time, I let my Program Director, colleagues and the residents know about my former life. And I found out that just like at Pride-Site, the majority of the staff at Samaritan was also former drug addicts, including the Program Director. Some of them were in recovery and others were not.

The apartment I found in Canarsie even though it was in a basement, was perfect for Dee and I at that time in our lives. It was in a pretty two family house. The block was so nice, clean and peaceful we even had our own little backyard, it was so cool. It was good for us to have some peace for a change, to me Flatbush was cool too but it always reminded me of the jungle. There was always so much noise and drama. So by the time we moved to Canarsie, the slower pace and the calm that came with it was so good for us. I lived in BK my whole life and in almost every borough, East New York, Bushwick, Bed-Stuy, Brownsville and Flatbush, but I loved Canarsie the most. I felt safe, there was no drugs and crime going on at least not on our block, that I knew of. The apartment was closer to my family, it was maybe a twenty minute drive to ma's house.

Dee had his little room where he had his music system setup which was really the boiler room but it had enough space for his system and he enjoyed it so much. That's where he went to get his peace of mind after a hard day at work. Dee is a real D.J., he goes by the name of "Deentertainer". Playing music has been his passion since he was a teen. He used to drive his grandmother Ms. Shirl and his mother, whom we refer to as mama, over the edge, making all that noise, blasting his music in the house every day, which is so funny because he got his love for music listening to them playing music at home at that time. But over the years, he has taken his love for music and he uses his gifts to be a blessing to others by playing music at weddings, birthday parties, catering events, family gatherings, outings, picnics, whatever. Dee loves what he does in music, however it is what he does professionally that especially exemplifies his talents. Professionally Dee is an awesome Chef, he manages one of Georgia's #1 Barbeque restaurants, there are locations all throughout GA. His cooking style and techniques are phenomenal and his dishes are so pretty; sometimes I hate to even eat them and mess it up. Dee can cook most anything however; he specializes in Entrees and Cuisines. As he continues to work professionally, his dream is to one day have his own entertainment and catering businesses, which he is expanding more and more, playing music and cooking at various events, both in New York and Georgia. Dee has taken his skills to even higher levels now and is working hard both professionally and personally.

Some of our most precious times in Canarsie that we shared together was when Dee would have the music blasting and back then he had speakers that were bigger than me. Playing music is his passion. He can play music in a club or in a boiler room and still love it. Our little joke was Dee would have the music blasting and on the weekends, he would take me to the club and we never even left home. He has hundreds and hundreds of my Old School jams. We would be at home having a party, we had so much fun. He played all my favorite songs and I would dance my booty off. He had his little clubroom and I had everything else, lol Dee.

Seriously though shortly moving in we got a dog his name was Blue (RIP/My baby). Blue was a Chow. He was charcoal gray with a curly tail and absolutely beautiful. Shortly after getting Blue, we got Na-Na, she was our cat. One day I saw a tiny mouse in the house and I told Dee, Babe please go to the A.S.P.C.A and get us a cat. The next day when I came home, all I saw was this pretty little cat roaming around our bedroom and Blue messing with the little baby. She was the same color as Blue and from the very first day, I fell in love with Blue and Na-Na, and Dee.

My personal journey has had many heart breaking experiences along the way but the one that crushed me the most was finding out that I couldn't have any children. I found out when I was in my thirties and it just about broke my heart because I love babies. Most every woman wants to experience motherhood, I played with my baby dolls until I was fifteen years old and giving them up even then was traumatic. So when I got the news, I was so devastated. At eighteen I contracted Pelvic Inflammatory Disease, it was an infection that I got from the then, love of my life, his name is Pudgy. I still don't know where he got that name from. But one day I was so sick, I was throwing up and I couldn't stand up, let alone walk. Cocoa took me to Kings County hospital right away. We waited for hours to be seen by a Doctor and when I finally got in the little room and told the Doctor my symptoms, he just gave me a shot and sent me home. Over the years it never really bothered me because I didn't have time for a baby back when I was doing drugs anyway, so it wasn't until almost fifteen years later when I knew something was wrong. I went to another Doctor's office and I told the Doctor my medical history and my concerns so he wanted to do a procedure. The procedure was done and in a couple of days, the results were in. When I came back for my follow up, as soon as I saw the Doctors face, I knew it wasn't going to be good. Have a seat Ms. Graves, ok what Is it? I can see by your expression it's not good news. Ms. Graves have you ever heard of P.I.D? it's a STD infection. Actually yes, I had P.I.D when I was around eighteen years old. I went to Kings County, the Doctor gave me a shot and sent me home. I'm so sorry to tell you that the Doctor was not supposed to give you a shot and send you home. You should have been admitted into the hospital and treated. The Doctor showed me the LABS and he pointed to my fallopian tubes. He showed me what looked like two balloons the size of an orange, covering both ends of my tubes and said they were badly scarred. That's the reason I never conceived. He did inform me that In Vitro Fertilization was definitely an option but by then I was already in my thirties and felt like I'll be ok. I'm so sorry Sherry, I really am. I'll give you some time for yourself. I thanked him and he left me in small cold little white room. I took a moment to get myself together and I left the Doctor's office that day feeling so hurt inside. The older I get it hurts a little less. One day years later I ran into Pudgy and I told him. I saw tears in his eyes, he apologized to me and I knew he was being sincere. Pudgy already had two children at the time, so he was hurt that I would never have any children because of him. His apology helped me to feel a little better and what really helps me is because I have eight wonderful nieces and nephews and they are such a blessing to me. I can't believe how fast they are all growing up.

Shainne has her two children now, she loves them more than anything in the world. I remember when she first got pregnant, we were a little scared but happy. We have always been very over protective of her and even though she was in her twenties, we still were like hold up, wait a minute. Her fiancé Mikale, man did we give him the third degree. Do ya'll know what ya'll are getting yourselves into? Are ya'll going to be able to afford a baby? By the time all of us finished with them, we realized that we just had to let our baby sis grow up and fly. Just like everyone else, she has to live her life too, but no matter where she goes, Shainne knows we have her back. Each month as her little belly started getting bigger and bigger, we fell more and more in love with the idea of her getting ready to be a mother. And her fiancé Mikale we absolutely love him. Thank God he is in her life. Shainne and Mikale are perfect for each other. He may have been young when they first got together but he is so responsible. Mikale will do whatever it takes to make sure his family has everything they need. He is also a comedian, he keeps us cracking up. Mikale's personality is kinda like Ramel's, he is that fun, loving guy. But he also takes care of his business. God couldn't have given our lil sis a better guy and guess what after all of the worrying, they are taking care of their children and doing a darn good job at it too. So by the time the baby came, everyone made sure they had everything they would need, especially Mikale and Shainne, soon after, lil Mikale was born. Mikale looks so much like his mother. He is kinda quiet and shy but I ain't letting all that shyness fool me, I know he can be a handful when he wants to be. Growing up he enjoyed dancing all the time. One weekend the kids were hanging out with Dee and I at our place. Of course Dee had his music blasting, we were partying hard. Mikale jumped up and was like ya'll wanna have a dance contest? Dee laughed so hard, he has never forgotten that day, we had so much fun. And we definitely did have a dance contest. I hate to beat a little kid but you know I rocked all of them. But I had to give it up to my lil man, he did his thing too. A year or so later and baby makes two and there came Myasia. When we found out Shainne was pregnant for the second time, we almost fell out. Girl what are you trying to do build your own football team or something. But sure-nuff, we were having another lil baby. Nine months later out came the most beautiful baby girl I have even seen in my life. She took our breath away. She had the most beautiful eyes, nose, mouth everything was so pretty. She had a head full of curly jet black hair. You couldn't help but to run your hands through her hair all the time, it was just too pretty. She is definitely another one of our Modeling Queens. And of course Myasia looks just like her daddy. She loves Art so we are all inspiring her to go for it. She can draw just about anything. Her artwork is so creative and beautiful. I already know that one day she is going to make so much money doing what she loves. Wow they are all growing up so fast. The last time I saw them, they were almost as big as me

And then there's my step children, Dee has a daughter her name is Nataila and his son is Tony. They have been in my life since they were little. I love them so much. And now we are grandparents, Nataila had a baby boy a couple of years ago. Dee's grandson is the cutest little thing, he makes me smile all the time. We absolutely adore him and then there's my God daughter, she is my cousin Adrie's daughter. Her name is Melody and she is growing up so fast and so pretty. I'm good, I have many blessings in my life. It's just every once in a while, it hits me and I think I would just love to have had a little Sherry or Dee. So after I came home and told Dee what the Doctor said, he hugged me and said you already have two kids and anyway I don't need no more, I'm good. So I surrendered it and gave it to God, as I always do when it is something I can't handle. And I continued to focus on finishing school.

Long Island University Brooklyn Campus' is a 60-Credit Masters of Social Work (M.S.W.) degree program. My concentration was in alcohol and substance abuse, the program is accredited by the Council of Social Work Education (CSWE), and it meets the highest standards of academic excellence. The program provided a step-wise progression of generalist and specialized practice. In my first year the curriculum included eight foundation areas of policy, practice, human behavior, field practicum, diversity, populations at risk, and promotion of social justice and values. It introduced the components of generalist practice with systems of all sizes and provided me with an understanding of generalist practice that distinguishes between generalist and advanced content while supporting the integration of specialized knowledge and technologies into a generalist perspective. It also introduced me to principles of interdisciplinary collaboration, preparing me for work in interdisciplinary fields of practice.

In my second year the curriculum builds upon the first year and gave me an understanding and demonstrated mastery of psychosocial assessments, administrative theory and practice, and diversity sensitive practice. The research curriculum in my second year supported the substance abuse concentration by demonstrating application of research methodology to substance abuse. I received a generalist background that included a conception of generalist practice, an eclectic knowledge base and an understanding of the relationship of values, diversity, populations at risk and promotions of social justice to the social work professional role with systems of all sizes. I established wonderful friendships with some great women and men at LIU. Together we faced challenges and overcame obstacles and worked our way past each semester.

I had to make some sacrifices which involved giving up my weekends to attend classes, that part wasn't so cool because the weekend was when Cocoa and I hung out. We loved going shopping together. She would come and pick me up in her SUV and we would just chill. Dee would go Uptown to hang out with his boys, we would usually get home around the same time. But when school started all that changed. I did what I had to do and we hung out when we could, which was still cool. By this time Cocoa and I were as close as we were when we were little girls playing hop scotch and jacks. Cocoa would say to me, go ahead girl, I am so proud of you Sherry, you are doing your thing.. Everyone in my family was right there with me the whole way through. I would go to the house after school most weekends to hang out with ma and everyone or Cocoa would come over to our place, it was just like old times. And when I wasn't in school or hanging out with Dee or my sis, I was working at Samaritan. Even though I loved my job, it was a huge responsibility. I had a caseload of 20-25 clients and there was a lot of documentation involved. I prepared weekly progress notes and treatment plans for each client. I facilitated the Addiction Education and Relapse Prevention Groups, Conflict Resolution Groups, and Individual Sessions with the clients on my caseload. It was a lot of work but it was so good for me. I was at a place in my life where I was doing a lot but it was manageable.

The clients on my caseload continuously encouraged me to finish my book Ms. Sherry I can't wait to read it, I heard from each of them every day. Every chance I got after work or on my days off, I would go to the computer sit down to write in "A Fire Within". The name 'A Fire Within" came from my cousin, Neecie and her husband, Kev. One day Mina and I was at their house for a visit and we were talking about the book and Neecie said, Sherry I have a name for your book and I want you to think about it and tell me if you like it. She said the name and I fell in love with it. The Fire Within me is my passion to let everyone know how God saved me in so many ways, to let everyone know where He brought me from and where He is taking me too. And most importantly, the Fire Within is my passion and I can't stop telling everyone how awesome He is.

I had dreamed about this day ever since I left Pride-Site ten years earlier. I can remember telling my Social Worker Carl one day I am going to have it like you. I am going to be a Social Worker. And when I graduated with my Bachelor's degree, that was a life changing experience that I will never forget. But Graduation Day with my Masters, that was a whole other level for me. I'm that girl, you know the one that was out there addicted to crack cocaine for years. I hustled drugs and shoplifted to support my habit. And I put my life in danger to get drugs. Someone actually tried to kill me. And at my worst time when I was at some of the lowest places of my life, I panhandled at train stations, begging strangers for money, just to get the next hit of crack. Those were the times when I had lost every ounce of dignity, morals and values that my family instilled in me growing up, to the drugs. I had no more self-respect and I didn't have any pride left, but I'm here standing stronger than ever. And I knew right then and there as sure as I was standing that this was all a part of the Master Plan that the Author and Finisher had for my life. I was walking in my destiny, it was part of my Journey, one of the best parts and times of my life. I felt like a Shining Star and I was. So I put my cap on my curls, made sure my gown was straight and my heels were looking good. I did my Naomi Campbell walk, as I strutted across that stage and I accepted my degree that I worked so hard for, from the faculty at Long Island University. It was one of the happiest days of my life and I was so proud of myself. It felt so awesome knowing my man and my family was sitting in the audience watching, taking pictures and shouting for me. As I took my degree, I hugged my favorite Professors, Dr. Jones and Professor Myricks and I stood beside my fellow classmates as the audience applauded and shouted at the top of their lungs. And as if that wasn't enough, what really blew me away was, I graduated with

Honors. Standing on that stage that day, I thought about my life, the good and bad and I surrendered everything. I gave it to the Lord. Have your way with me Father. I know this is bigger than me, it has to be. I knew that in and of itself, I could never have accomplished what I did that day. I trust you to use me to fulfill all the plans you have for my life and I am eternally grateful to you. By the time I walked off that stage, I was more humble than I had ever been in my entire life. My life has been a rollercoaster ride as far back as I can remember. I've had up's and down's and I have had so many twists and turns, I have gone backwards and forward and through it all, I am still standing. Then in October 2005 something happened and once again, my world got rocked so hard

CHAPTER 24
"MY SHINING STAR"

"My Shining Star" is my Ma, as a matter of fact she's everyone's shining star. Her name was Indiana she was born on February 27, 1923 in the beautiful Island of Tortola, the British Virgin Islands. After several years ma moved to St. Thomas V.I. where she married the man she knew and loved from childhood, Austin and from this fifty year union would emerge a family that "Indiana" or "Indie" affectionately called "Ma", adored and cherished. A family for whom she would do anything. In the '50's ma and daddy moved their family to New York City where they lived the rest of their lives. Her children consisting of three sons and three daughters are a testimony of how a family raised with unconditional love and proper parenting can grow to be one that is cohesive, resilient and compassionate. Qualities indicative of both Indie and Austin. Ma was a proud, committed and lifelong member of Beulah Wesleyan Methodist Church for over fifty years. She truly exemplified the woman that is described in Proverbs chapter 31 who is a "virtuous woman whose price is far above rubies". Ma was a precious gift to all who knew her. A person whose love, character, sincerity, honesty and humility are rare and exceptional. She was a caring wife, mother, grandmother, great-grandmother, sister, aunt and friend who always sought to help others in any way she could. With the simple touch of her hand, a kind word, or a roaring thunderous laugh, ma knew just what to do to brighten one's spirit. Ma's one lasting wish was for all of her family and loved ones to remain kind and loving toward one another. That's her legacy to us.

I am so honored to have had the grandparents that I had. October 20, 2005 eight years after losing daddy (my beloved grandfather), ma went to be with the Lord. And even now after all of these years losing her still hurts. For some of the family it has gotten a little easier as time passes but for others in the family they still can't even look at pictures of her without bursting into tears. So for that reason I will only say we never had a funeral for ma, no we had a home going Celebration of her life and it was beautiful. Of course we cried at times, however we laughed more, remembering her. It wasn't sad for me that day because ma was not unhappy. She was happy and so full of life. Her laugh could fill an entire stadium. She was never angry she always said I lived my life and it was wonderful. And she always kept her faith, "Whatever the Lord wants" or "God willing", I can hear her voice echoing in my head. Those were ma's favorite saying's even until it was her time. But I will never forget it, everyone went up to express their thoughts and love for her and that was so special. But something else we did that was so uplifting and afterwards the whole Church was roaring, we clapped, laughed, cried and hugged, it was a wonderful way to Honor ma. One thing about her was that she had about a hundred hats that she wore to Church every Sunday, beautiful hats. All of her daughters, granddaughters, and great granddaughters, all decided to give Ma something on that day. So my cousin Charles at one point during the ceremony requested a moment of silence then one by one we each stood up wearing one of ma's hats by the time everyone looked, there were beautiful colorful hats everywhere because we were seated all around the Church. Seeing the different colors brought life to the service and I knew she was smiling and laughing that beautiful laugh like only she can do, for us. It was awesome. Ma was just too precious to us. She fought that cancer demon and if I may say so myself, I am so proud of my ma because for an eighty two year old, she kicked its ugly butt real good. Seriously though, what helps us feel better is to know that she did not suffer, to God be the Glory. Thank you Father for covering her with your Angels.

And to know that she is with the Lord who watches over each and every one us is the best part. Ma was all of the things that I already mentioned, but she was so much more. And so anytime I am feeling down or I really, really need her I just look up until I see the "Shiniest Star" out of them all. While we all miss ma tremendously, we have each done our part to ensure that her lasting wish and legacy continues for generations to come.

My Tribute To "My Shining Star"

Dearest Grandmother,

You will always be my "Shining Star"
Sparkling so bright every day and every night, even from afar,
Your smile, laugh, warmth and grace
Is buried so deeply within me it can never, ever be erased.
So caring, loving and giving of yourself,
No wonder God blessed you even when you were feeling your worst.
Although my heart is broken, it's a sadness I've never known,
My soul is rejoicing thanking God for all the years that I had you.
One day you were fighting, I said my God, my ma is so strong,

Then suddenly, as quick as lightning, you were gone.
If I could take your place, me instead of you, you know I would,
But, even if it were possible, you'd never let me, would you?
Dearest grandmother, the Lord saved you, by taking you away from me,
My breath, my heart, my soul, my joy, but, he told me stars are always and forever in the sky,
So whenever I need you, just look up and there you will be,
Just like always you and the Lord, both watching over me

I love you ma…and I miss you so much!! Rest in Peace my love, with all the other Angels.

CHAPTER 25

"A POWER MOVE"

The year 2007 brought about even more bitter-sweet changes. We had been living in our basement apartment for several years and then it happened. One day our landlord came to talk to Dee and I, he told us I'm sorry but I am going to have to sell the house. The tenants upstairs are so far behind on their rent and they are refusing to pay anything. I am in the process of taking them to court so I just want to let you guys know I am selling the house. You only have a couple of weeks but you really need to start looking for another place to live.

Dee and I were devastated; we loved our place and all I was thinking was why do we have to suffer because the people upstairs can't pay their rent. So we had no other choice but to start looking for another apartment. I looked all over Canarsie because I didn't want to leave the area. But everywhere we looked was so expensive. We always knew that we had a very good deal living in the basement and after being exhausted I had to accept it. We were not going to find anything in Canarsie. Dee we are going to have to go back to the jungle. Laughing he said to Flatbush, yes Babe back to Flatbush. Our time was running out and what made it even worse the landlord had started bringing potential buyers by who were interested in buying his property. It was so awkward, strangers coming into our home while we still lived there checking out our place. But we ran into an even bigger problem as we were looking for our place. We had checked out maybe 10 apartments and everyone of them said the same thing, no pets. Ok so by now we are desperate we have maybe another week or so to get out and nobody would accept us with Blue and Nana. I was willing to do anything even pay more if we had to but it wasn't about the money in N.Y there are not many landlords willing to rent to people with pets. We had to make a decision that once again broke my heart. Eventually I found this apartment in Flatbush not far from where we lived before and begged the landlord to let us keep our pets. I even offered to pay extra each month and still the owner flat out refused. He said ya'll can keep the cat but the dog definitely cannot stay. With no more time left we had to take it. Everything was packed up and all I knew was that we had to find a home for Blue.

No one in my family could take Blue. Cocoa already had a dog and no one else wanted a pet, they all have kids. We started asking our neighbors if we could give them Blue. The day before we were to leave we realized no one was gonna take Blue and our only choice was to take him back to the A.S.P.C.A. And we already knew what that meant if no one adopted him ASAP they would put him to sleep. Devastated again I cried and cried for my baby. I tried the best I could to tell Blue how sorry I was that we had to give him up. I took him to his favorite park and that is where I said my good-byes. He was looking at me like he knew something was wrong. He looked so sad. By the time I took him back home I was a mess. Dee you know I can't do it. Please you are gonna have to take him when I go to work I don't even want to be here when you leave. As hard as it was for Dee he had to do it. Dee loved Blue just as much as I did he was our baby. And just like we had planned by the time I came home from work the next day my baby was gone. I vowed to Dee that day we are going to get another dog I promised him that. So we moved into our next apartment and I quickly realized it was a mistake. Ii was in a two bedroom apartment back in the jungle in a four story building on Snyder Avenue. My poor Na-Na one late night I woke up and went into the kitchen to get some juice when I turned on the lights I saw a million roaches and my Na-Na standing there just looking down at all of them. She must have been saying what in the world are those things. I grabbed her up and ran back in the room and told Dee. The next day I tried to bomb out the place we took all the food out and sprayed the whole place but those roaches just kept coming back. I guess they were saying we are not going anywhere we were here long before ya'll got here. All I knew was this ain't going to work at all. After that my Vision was Babe we are getting out of here as soon as we can.

 The plan was to stay at the roach house and keep on looking for somewhere decent to live.

Then one day I said Dee I have been looking everywhere and I don't like any of the apartments I'm seeing. I'm going to start looking in New Jersey or Upstate New York I was tired of Brooklyn and I wanted to move far away. I was angry and still hurt that I had to give my baby away I was just ready to leave. So a colleague of mine at Samaritan Village lived in New Jersey so I was talking to her about her area. Oh yea, it's real nice where I live you should come check it out. We made arrangements and one day after work we hopped on the train and headed for New Jersey. A while later we got off the train and took a cab to her house. And right away when we pulled up to her house I knew it was definitely not going to work. I didn't like her area or any of the area's leading up to her house. It was not what I had in my Vision. I thanked her, we chilled out for a minute but I had to go I had that long ride back to BK. Ok Dee so N.J is out of the question. Babe you didn't see all of N.J. you only went to one part. I know Dee but I wasn't felling it out there we might as well stay out here from what I did see. Next stop Upstate New York. Another colleague at Samaritan lived in Upstate N.Y so we drove to check out his place. An hour and a half later I didn't even want to get out of the car that's how bad it was. But I didn't want to make him feel bad. So I went to check out his house and all I kept thinking was this definitely ain't going to work, so we left and he drove me back to Brooklyn. I didn't realize it at the time I was busy making plans and nothing I did seemed to be working out that's because God had another plan. After sharing my Vision with yet another colleague at Samaritan she said, Sherry you should move to Atlanta. I'm thinking Atlanta, GA. Yes I used to live in the ATL and it is so beautiful out there. Really so why did you leave? I couldn't find a job so I had to come back to N.Y. Thanks a lot I will think about it. She knew about my Blue and Na-Na and she told me they allow you to have pets in most all apartments and everything. I was renting an apartment it was only $700.00 a month it even had a swimming pool and tennis court and everything. You should call Anthony he lives out there maybe he can help you as far as job possibilities. Anthony lives in Atlanta? Yea he left here at least a year or so now, here is his call number, call him, and just like that she definitely had me thinking, seriously thinking. I ran home got on the computer and looked up apartments in Atlanta I was shocked and amazed everything I saw was more beautiful than the next. And everything I saw said WE ACCEPT PETS. Next I called my uncle Aus he and his wife moved to Atlanta a year or two ago I heard that he bought a beautiful mansion out there. And when I saw picture of his house I almost passed out they weren't kidding he really did have a mansion. I couldn't believe my eyes. Hey Unc its Sherry how are you? Hey Sherry I'm doing fine.

    Congratulations I hear you Graduated from college and finally stopped using that crack, good very good. I'm proud of you. Laughing I said, thanks unc but I really wanted to talk to you about something. I want to come to GA for a visit I heard you can find beautiful apartments out there for a lot cheaper than N.Y. Yea, you can definitely find cheaper apartments in GA, when were you thinking about coming down? I will call you back and let you know I have some things I have to work out first. Love you, tell Auntie hi for me. Ring, ring, ring hello can I speak to Anthony. This is Anthony who's calling? This is Sherry, Sherry Graves from Samaritan Village in N.Y. I'm one of the Counselors here, how are you doing? Anthony and I talked for a long time and just like Jacqueline said, Anthony really liked Georgia. He told me he worked in a hospital out there and he lived not too far from where he was working in place called Cobb County. He told me to go on line and check out his apartment complex and call him back.

    Hey Sherry I could talk to my Manager and see if she would be interested in interviewing you, I know for sure she is hiring for a counseling position. Really, that would be so great and I would certainly appreciate it. Hey

Anthony please check that out for me, if I don't hear from you I will call you back cool. Yea that's cool. Ok later! By the time I got off the telephone with Anthony I had a new Vision and I had already seen ourselves packing.

As much as I fantasized about Atlanta I knew that one of the biggest challenges I would have to face then was trying to encourage Dee to leave his family. His mama is his whole world. He was raised by his great grandmother "Big mama" and his grandmother Miss Shirl. I wasn't fortunate to meet his great grandmother, unfortunately she passed away when Dee and I first met and all I know is that he loved her so much, he always tells me about her. And his grandmother was his girl; Dee always talks about her too. The first time I met her Dee took me to her house in the Bronx, when we finally got to her floor I was so happy because the elevator took forever. Hi Ma'am I'm Sherry it's so nice to meet you. Oh so you're the young lady he keeps on talking about ha, nice to meet you. That's funny because all Dee talks about is you and his big mommy all the time and we both laughed. I'm sure he does she said what is he saying about me. Laughing all I could say was it's all good ma'am, it's all good. Over the years we had so many good times with Ms. Shirl and every time we went to the Bronx to see his family Ms. Shirl would say here young lady I want you to have this or here this is for you, she was always giving me her things.

One of the many things Ms. Shirl gave me was her two pretty scarves. Thank you Ms. Shirl but you have got to stop giving me things whenever I come over here. Child don't tell me what to give you now go'on over there and pick you some of those things outta that box, I want you to have them. Of course I was cracking up and all I could do was say yes Ms. Shirl thank you. I used those scarves to wrap my hair at night I had them for over ten years. And by then some of the strings were hanging off and the material was starting to stretch out and everything. But for some reason I could not throw them away. I love those scarves they were silky and when I wrapped my hair at night they were perfect. It was so sad when we lost Ms. Shirl to Cancer years later. Dee was so devastated and so was I my heart went out for him for everyone in the family. But he talks about his Big Mama and Ms. Shirl all the time as a matter of fact I must have heard it a thousand times from him you are just like my grandmother, sometimes I don't know if it's a good or a bad thing. And just like with the rest of the family that we lost over the years on their Birthdays and Mother's Day we light candles at home it's our way of keeping their memories alive. Each and every one of our families that we lost they are always in our Spirit. Dee has a joke that he tells me about Ms. Shirl, apparently that very first time when I met her when we hung out at her house, later on when she and Dee were talking about me, Ms. Shirl said, she sure is mighty friendly ha, Dee said he and Ms. Shirl cracked up laughing that night! Dee got such a kick outta that he is still joking about that even after all these years. I have a collection of our families pictures covering our walls we

A FIRE WITHIN

love looking at it and showing the pictures to everyone. Dee has his daughter Nataila when I first met her she was about 8 years old. She looks like Dee's mama and her mother Tawania. Nataila has Dee's attitude she is a ball of fire. Tawania and Dee were together for years they have two children together I think it's great that she and I get along, we hang out as much as we can, it's so cool.

And Dee's son Tony he's the youngest child. As a little boy I always thought he was shy but I found out the first time he came to spend the weekend with us that he is not shy at all. What I love about Tony is his love for pets he always played with Blue and Na-Na even more than we did. Holiday's we knew exactly what to get him a turtle, fish, a rabbit, he was happy with any animal. Mama had two children, Dee and his older sister Mona. I like to call her Mona Lisa. The first time I met her, it was amazing to me because she looks like a female version of Dee. Mona loves her brother so much, she has always had his back, no one and I mean no one could mess with Dee except Mona. Dee told me all the stories of how many girls and guys got their behinds kicked messing with Mona. And when I got to meet her I can tell he wasn't playing. She is tough and it don't take much to piss her off. Mona's daughter's name is Shanice and if you think Mona is tough, her daughter is ten times worse. He has his uncles and I just knew it was going to be hard to get Dee to leave N.Y. and move to Atlanta. I was sure he was going to think I was CRAZY for real this time. But Sherry once he sees how beautiful Atlanta is and how much money we can save with the rent being so cheap I'm sure he will want to go, you have to at least get him to think about it. I'll talk to Dee tonight when he gets home.

Ring, ring, hello. Hey Anthony this is Sherry. Hey Sherry I got good news. You do I almost jumped through the phone what's up? I spoke with my Manager and she is definitely interested in interviewing you for the counseling position. OMG I'm jumping all around in our living room, Anthony this is so great. I will speak to Samaritan tomorrow I need to get approval to take a couple of days off but it shouldn't be a problem Anthony thanks so much, I really appreciate everything. I will call you back by tomorrow. The next couple of days I couldn't get Georgia off my mind. I just kept seeing those nice apartment complexes and the signs that said Pets Allowed. I didn't know what to say to Dee I mean even I thought I was crazy thinking about moving to Atlanta. My family is in New York, St. Thomas, Florida and Georgia. I waited a little while after he came home from work and relaxed a little sitting on our sofa I said, Dee I need to talk to you come sit down with me. What's up Sherry? Babe you know I have looked everywhere for our apartment and I can't find anything decent. I've been checking out places all around Brooklyn, Queens I even went Upstate N.Y. and N.J. just to see if we could find something out there. We are paying all of this money and we are living in this roach infested apartment I can't stand it any longer. So what are you saying Sherry?

I talked to a couple of people today and I want to show you something on the computer. I took Dee to the computer and opened the pictures of the beautiful apartments in Atlanta. ATLANTA he screamed. Georgia Sherry, girl I'm not trying to move to Georgia. Dee I know it sounds crazy but we could have everything we ever dreamed of in Georgia. We are paying $1200 a month not including utilities for this piece of crap. Do you think we will ever be able to afford a house in N.Y. and even if a miracle happened look at what you get for the money you have to put out. In N.Y you pay all this money for mortgage and you don't even have a place to park your car you're lucky if you have a one car garage. No porch or backyard and not one tree. Look at these pictures, there is grass all over the place. All of these apartments have swimming pools and tennis courts and the best part Babe is they all allow pets. Look at all that we can have for only $700.00 to $800.00 or whatever we could afford. I know it is a lot to ask you to leave your family Babe but I am willing to leave my family too in order for us to have a better life. They can come visit us anytime.

At least think about please. Every day the Vision became more real for me unfortunately Dee was not going for it. And over the next couple of weeks the more I mentioned Atlanta the more we began to argue. My mind was already made up I was leaving but I wasn't leaving without Dee. So I did what I should have done in the beginning. God thank you for putting into Dee's spirit everything you want him to know. Thank you for showing him things to come and telling him what he is supposed to do. God is so awesome. Not even a week later I couldn't believe my ears when I heard my Babe saying you know what I been thinking moving to Atlanta might not be such a bad idea. I whispered, Thank you Lord I love you too. Dee are you saying you want to move to Atlanta? Yes, we just need to find work out there; the first thing we need to do is go out there and check it out. Oh my God, I love you Babe I kissed his face and cheeks and his bald head. Thank you, thank you, thank you. And that was all I needed to hear. Ring, ring hey Anthony what's up its Sherry. Hey Sherry so did you make up your mind about coming to Georgia. I did and I definitely want to come down. Is that interview still available?

It sure is she wants to meet you. She wants to know when you will be able to come to Atlanta for the interview. Hey Anthony I will call you back tonight. Ok but don't wait too long, I don't know how long the position is going to be available. I will call you tonight. Anthony thanks so much!! Dee wasn't even in the door good Babe I yelled OMG we are going to Atlanta, I have a job interview set up at some big hospital out there. I told you about Anthony he spoke to his Manager and she is interested in interviewing me for a counseling position. Do you know what this means? Once I have the job we can leave, I can take care of the bills until you find work. Can you take off a

A FIRE WITHIN

couple of days from work so we can fly out there this week? I already got a couple of days off from Samaritan. Slow down Babe, slow down I know you are excited but let me talk to my job and get back to you. When Dee, can you call them now. Sherry, everyone is gone for the day Babe, I will talk to them tomorrow ok let me call Anthony and let him know something. Ring, ring hello, Hey Anthony it's Sherry we will be in Atlanta by the end of the week let your Manager know I am very interested in interviewing for the counseling position. I will call you when I get to Atlanta. After I got the address to the hospital where Anthony worked I located a Hotel nearby. The next day Dee spoke to his Employer and he was able to get a couple of days off. I booked our flights and in a couple of days we were going to be on our way to Atlanta. Cocoa listen I got to tell you something, you will not believe what is going on. Oh Lord, what is going on Sherry? Girl Dee and I are thinking about moving to Atlanta, I already spoke to Aus and everything. I have a job interview set up for Monday. WHAT? Cracking up laughing I said I know girl, it sounds crazy but I'm serious. Sherry you are thinking about moving to Atlanta?

Yes, girl you should see the apartments out there I went on line and found some places the rent is so cheap and the apartments are absolutely beautiful. Cocoa you know I have looked everywhere in N.Y and these run down places are charging an arm and a leg and I refuse to pay all that money for some hole in the wall. Not when I can have an apartment with a swimming pool, tennis courts, washer, dryer and dishwashing machine. And all of the apartments out there ALLOW PETS I screamed. And sis the best part is the apartments are as low as $700.00, $800.00 a month or whatever you could afford. I gotta go at least check it out. I have to. Atlanta, you and Dorian I hear that. You know our cousins are out there too. Who? Neece and her husband, Charles and his wife. You should call them and see where they live in Atlanta.

You know I will girl I am so excited I am about to burst. Um, Um, Um Sherry going to Atlanta. You know I want the best for you but I can't even think about you leaving N.Y. I know but let me go check it out first and I will call you when we get down there Friday. FRIDAY! This Friday? Yes girl we have a flight for Friday I told you I have a job interview already setup. We are going to check out some apartments while we are out there. Well I guess there ain't nothing to say, give me a hug, I love you Sherry call when you get there. I love you too gotta go; I'll see you when we get back.

Passengers for Flight 193 leaving New York at 3:40 pm scheduled to arrive in Atlanta, GA at 5:30 pm please board at Gate C-2. Oh my God Dee that's us come on let's go. Can you believe it we are on our way to Atlanta. Alright, alright take it easy girl. You grab that small bag, I'll take these. Come on Dee I practically ran and left him. Sitting on the plane we had our food and each other we were good. Right before the plane took off, I released my Prayer, Father I release your Angels to cover this plane and form a hedge of protection around us and bring us to our comings and goings safe and sound in Jesus Name, Amen. I was so excited I was about to burst and we hadn't even taken off the ground from N.Y yet. Not even two hours later I heard Welcome to Atlanta, GA the time now is 5:24 pm please fasten your seatbelts were are approaching landing. Dee look at how beautiful it is. I was sitting by the window seat and looking out and all I saw was beautiful greenery. It was so pretty I was in love already. I almost pushed the people in front of us out of the way, Dee was back there grabbing our luggage by the time he came off the plane I was already at the escalator. Hartsfield Jackson Airport wow Babe we are in Atlanta. As we headed outside the nice, clean Airport I called my Uncle Aus to see if he was outside. Ring, ring hello, hey unc we are here, are you outside? Yes I'm pulling up by Delta now, you guys already got your luggage? Yes we brought our bags on the plane with us. WE ARE IN THE ATL, I'm screaming like a crazy woman, see you in a minute we are coming out now. I ran outside and that was it I fell in love. My uncle and aunt Pam met us at the Airplane, he was loaning us his SUV for the week so we could take care of our business. We had a GPS which I was so happy for. So I kissed unc and Auntie and gave him a hug. Dee hugged him and thanked Aus and we headed to our Hotel.

 I had never used a GPS before but once we put the address to the Hotel in there it was amazing it took us straight to the Hotel. It was still early by the time we got there and put our luggage away we took a few minutes to check out our room, it was cool. After a few minutes I grabbed the phone and called Anthony. Hey its Sherry we are here, we are in Atlanta. I told Anthony the Hotel we were staying at which was a nice quiet, cozy place and told him we will catch up later on. He said girl you are serious. Anthony you have no idea. I hear that and I like that, a girl with determination. Laughing I said, you ain't seen nothing yet. Come on Babe grab that GPS let's go check out the place. I put on my heels, grabbed my pocketbook and ran out the door behind Dee. Once outside I had a feeling like I haven't had in a long, long time. It was so peaceful and quiet. And pretty just like in my Vision and I took a deep breath and let out years and years of built up feelings. Driving on the roads the first thing I noticed was how clean everywhere is. It was completely different from N.Y. Everything was different in Atlanta the stores, the houses, the gas stations, even the people were different. Everywhere we went the people seemed so nice. Hello, goodnight, people actually greeted us and they were complete strangers. By the time we got back to our Hotel I knew I was in love but to see Dee loving it too I was in complete heaven. And I knew I had to nail that job interview because there was no going back from there. Cocoa I LOVE IT here, I don't think I ever want to come back to N.Y She just laughed and laughed on the phone girl you are so crazy. I'm serious Cocoa we are moving to Atlanta I miss you Cocoa what are you doing, anyway? You know me I doing my thing. I am knee deep in my Tee's, I have an event coming up in a couple of weeks, so I am just getting ready.

A FIRE WITHIN

Listen, I might let you and Ramel bring my line down to Georgia. You know I am thinking about expanding Colet-Tee's, so ya'll get ready. Cocoa, actually I was speaking to this lady down here, she has her own clothing store and I told her all about your line. She wanted to see some of your phrases so I gave her a couple of the phrases that I could remember, tell me the one's I'm missing: 1) A real man does not love a million women, he loves one woman in a million ways, 2) Mommy Does Not Spell Maid, 3) Prayer Works, 4) I Am Blessed, 5) It is, what it is, 6) Me, Myself And, I, and You, If You Act Right, 7) I Am Who I Am, Your Approval Isn't Needed, 8) Woman Up, 9) OMG, 10) Don't Judge Me, 11) I Am Queen of my Castle. Wow is that it? I know I am missing some right? Laughing, girl you remembered all of those. Of course I do. You did good but you forgot 12) Seriously, 13) Independent Women, We Are Doing It For Ourselves, 14) I Love Me and just a couple more. Girl, for real I am so proud of what you are doing with your Colet-Tees (tee-shirts). God gave you that Vision and look how far he is blessing you with it. I told Ms. Lee to go on to your www.colettees.com website and I gave her your email address; colettees@gmail.com. So look out for her she said she definitely wants to order a few of your tees. She liked the fact that you designed your shirts, yourself. And that you were inspired to create a line of tee-shirts for ladies and young girls because you were so tired of seeing all of the negativity these young girls (and ladies) are wearing on their tee-shirts.

And she loves all the pretty colors your tees come in, because she said these are the hardest colors to find nice tee-shirts in. I think she wants to order that beautiful burnt orange, gold and olive green. I told her you have all colors and sizes, so listen out for her. And I gave her some of your business cards too. Send me some more, I am running out. Ms. Lee said she's going to pass them out in her store. Look, Cocoa just let me know when you want to send some of your tees down to Georgia, I know a couple of people who will buy some right now. Ok, I'll let you know Sherry, love you. I gotta go I'll call you again later.

That weekend I called my cousin got her address and told her we would be there later on. Dee and I got our GPS 45 minutes later we were in a place called Fulton County at Neece and her husband Kev's house. When we got to their block driving down her road I couldn't believe my eyes. I had never seen anything so beautiful in my whole life. And by the time we pulled into her TWO CAR driveway and I noticed she even had a garage there was nothing else to be said. As a matter of fact I had to bend down and touch the ground to make sure it was real that's how clean everything was. My God Dee look at this it is so pretty. The only thing I can say is when I walked inside that house I never wanted to leave. Ring, ding-dong even the bell sounds awesome. As I looked through the huge glass door I saw my cuz coming with a huge smile on her face. And when she opened that door all I said was I LOVE YOUR HOUSE. We hugged, kissed, laughed, ate and hung out for a while but unfortunately we had to leave. But I told her right then trust me we will be back. Driving back to our Hotel Dee and I had some of the best laughs ever. We felt at home in Georgia, it was a feeling that I can't explain other than to say I don't want to leave here Babe, I don't want to go back to N.Y. I know Sherry so just pray that you get that job. Babe you already know that is a done deal.

The next day we went and had breakfast and checked out a few places. We only had one more day and I didn't want to get crazy so we went to Al's beautiful home where we talked for a while. He told me about WS Hospital and told me what he does there after hearing that it was a Drug Court Program I wanted that job so bad. I knew even before I went to that interview that job was mine. I Claimed it. Sunday night Dee and I had a heart to heart and I asked him if he was ready to make this Power Move. Yes Babe I am and that was all I needed to hear. I kissed Dee and silently said my favorite Prayer's.

As a little girl I can remember every Sunday ma and daddy dragging us along to Church with them Ramel, Cocoa and I we took the long drive to Manhattan. Some Sundays we liked going to Church but in the winter time when it was freezing cold outside the last thing we wanted to do was get up out of our warm cozy bed and go to Church. But ma didn't care if it was a blizzard outside she was going and so were we. The three of us would sit in the huge Church and instead of listening to the Pastor preach; all three of us would be sneaking and talking or playing with each other. We would hear Shhh, a hundred times before Pastor's Sermon was over. After Church they would take us to our cousin's house to hang out with them and for us that was the best part of the day. We got to play Monopoly and eat dinner while ma and daddy chatted with uncle Gladston by the time we got home we were happy. That went on week after week for years. And on the very rare occasions that ma and daddy couldn't take us to Church which was maybe two times in ten years our aunt Leila would take us.

We loved going with her because she would take us out after Church for some fun. Back then it was different we had to go even though many days we preferred to stay home and play. We grew up in Church and I have always known the Lord. As we got older Ma stopped forcing us to go to Church especially since we would find ways to get out of going. While I was out there on drugs I always knew my Heavenly Father had his Angels covering me because they have saved me more than once. By the time I left Pride-Site I hadn't been to a Church since those days when ma and daddy took us but in 2004 a life changing event happened to me. It started one day when I saw this Pastor on television the more I listened to him the more I became drawn to his teachings. Every chance I got I found myself watching his broadcast then something started happening. Not a day would go by when I didn't watch his Sermons' One day I found out that not only is the Pastor on TV he also has a

Mega Church right there in N.Y.C. I couldn't believe it the day came when I told myself I am going to his Church. My family all thought I had really lost it but I went all by myself. That was the day my life changed forever. I found myself going to this huge Church every week until one day it happened. I have been there many times to hear the Benediction and I would always get a funny feeling in the Spirit when the Pastor said come on down if you know the Lord is speaking to you forget about what everyone else is doing come on down we have people that want to Pray with you. I knew he was speaking directly to me that day and the next thing I knew I found myself getting up out of my balcony seat and started walking past hundreds of people and I got to his stage I bent down on my knees and that day I got Saved. It was an awesome feeling. God is so awesome. I became a member of the Mega Church and attended faithfully. This teacher had the gift in teaching Spiritual Principles and he taught me how to speak Gods Word, how to confess Gods Word over my situations. He taught me that Gods Word has Scriptures for every situation that I would ever face and I just needed to find the Scripture and apply it to my situation. I have never stopped confessing God's Word over my situations since then. He preached that we must meditate on God's Word day and night until it is in my heart, until I know it without looking in the Bible. It was one of the greatest gifts I have ever received and it is how I live my life today.

So on the morning of my job interview I grabbed Dee's hands just like we have done a thousand times before and I released my Faith Prayer. Father I Come to You In The Name of Jesus I confess Matthew 18:19 you said, Where There Are Two or More In Agreement about Anything and Everything There You Are in the Midst of them and what so ever we ask, it will come to pass and be done for them as it is in Alignment with the WORD of the Father. And in Philippians 4:19 you said that You Shall Supply All of Our Needs According to Your Glorious Riches in Christ Jesus.

As I released my Angels to go before me to prepare my way and I put on my Armor which is the Word of God I knew that job was mine. Dee and I walked out of our Hotel room he drove me to my interview and by the time we came back an hour or so later I had my job. I met with one of the nicest, ladies I have ever met in my life and by the time I left there I was hired at WS Hospital as a Substance Abuse Counselor at their Drug Treatment Court Program. Back outside I ran to my Babe I hugged him so hard. Dee I told you we are moving to Atlanta, GA. He just smiled and held me tight.

Our flight was leaving Georgia the next day and with one of our job situations taken care of now we had to find a place to live quick. That afternoon Neece, Dee and I drove around all day looking for our apartment. We went from place to place looking at the apartments that I had found from my search. But we quickly realized that you get what you pay for. First of all the apartments that I found were cheap, too cheap. As we started pulling up to these neighborhoods it was evident that they were not going to work. I realized hey not all areas are beautiful in Georgia some of these apartments were worse than in N.Y. Dee laughed. I can spot a drug area a mile away so needless to say those apartments weren't going to work. After a while Neece just drove right past one or two of the locations refusing to even get out of the car I was cracking up. It didn't take long to figure out we had a problem. With one more day before our flight back to N.Y we were desperate to find something. Ya'll why are we stressing it is only June we still have plenty of time to find a place so we decided instead of rushing around we will just go back to N.Y. and continue our apartment search there. At least now we had a better idea of where not to look. And whenever we found something we liked Neece could go check it out for us and tell us what she thought. Cuz thanks so much for everything we will be in contact, love you we gave each-other hugs and kisses. Can you believe it the next time we see you guys we will be living in Georgia. I know I can't wait. Neece left and Dee and I drove to get dinner we were feeling so relieved that we could take our time and find the best place for us. Ok Dee so now all we have to do is go back to N.Y. and start packing. We looked at each-other and laughed because we both knew that was a whole other challenge. The good news is my start date is October 23 so we have a couple of months. We laughed and talked all the way back to the Hotel.

Back at the hotel I heard my cell phone ringing Mr. Anthony I guess by now you heard the good news ha? Well, well, well seems you aced the interview Congratulations Sherry looks like you are going to be working at WS. Anthony thank you so much yes I am the interview went very well. Mrs. Ritchie seems like a wonderful lady so calm and peaceful. Yea Mrs. Ritchie has been a blessing to me. Listen so what are your plans now she said you start in October right? Yes, we are heading back to N.Y to start packing but we will definitely see you in a couple of months, I will be in contact with you before that time and again thanks Anthony. Don't worry about it as a matter of fact now I can dump some of my work on you he laughs. Oh so you got jokes too, ha!! Alright, tell Dee I can't wait for ya'll to get back to Georgia, I will, ok talk to you later. And again Congratulations, Welcome aboard.

CHAPTER 26

"LIFE AFTER"

Back in New York, I started feeling sad as I always do whenever I have to say goodbye. Once again it was a bittersweet time for me because even though I fell in love with Georgia and couldn't wait to get back there to start our new life, I was so sad because I was leaving the only place that I had called home, my whole life. I love New York I always have and I always will, but it has become too unaffordable to live there especially if you ever dreamt of becoming a home owner. I refused to continue paying $1,200 or more a month for a studio apartment, when I could use that money one day to pay a mortgage. Anyway we looked at it, it was time to go. But just thinking about leaving in a few months was difficult for Dee and I. But when I thought about leaving my family in N.Y., well let's just say that was something that I could never do on my own strength, which for me was just another confirmation that I am walking in Destiny towards the plan that God has for my life, for our lives. But it was going to be another one of the hardest things I would ever have to do.

Dee and I had gotten a gift from my uncle Aus. Remember him he's the one who lives in Georgia. Not too long ago he came up to N.Y. for a visit, and he said he had something for us, it was a car. Aus said, ya'll can have the car, we already have two cars so we aren't using it. He signed the title over to us and we were so grateful. Little did we know at that time that we would definitely need a vehicle, but by the time we left Georgia, we definitely knew for sure we would need a car down there to get around. It wasn't anything fancy but Dee and I loved it, in fact I named her Harmony. I didn't even know how to drive at the time so Dee drove us everywhere. But I promised myself I would have my driving license before we left New York, so over the next couple of weeks I started taking lessons. I had my license before we left, I was ecstatic. Now I was driving all over the place too.

Right after we got back to N.Y., I went to check out my family. Cocoa what's up girl? Hey girl, I see you and Dee are back in town ha? Yes, we are back and I can't believe it girl but we are moving to Georgia in just a couple of months. I know I can't believe it either, Congratulations on the job. So ya'll are really going huh? Thanks! Yes we are definitely outta here by August it is so crazy but I can't wait to get back down there. Wait until ya'll come to Georgia, you are going to love it too, it is so beautiful. Oh you know we are going to come and check it out as soon as we can. That day Cocoa and I laughed and cried about it but deep inside we both knew it was for the best. We will come back home to visit all the time. Yea, I know but it's not the same thing. Stop crying Sherry because you are going to make me cry too. And that went on for months. Dee told his family and it was the same thing, they were happy for us but sad he was moving all the way to Georgia. It was so sad but so happy at the same time. And over the next several months we started packing. Since it was only June we didn't have to rush, we had until August. Dee and I planned to move the end of August so we could give ourselves enough time to unpack and everything, once we got to Georgia. Eventually we did find our apartment and true enough we had our washer, dryer and dishwashing machine. Of course our apartment complex had a swimming pool and tennis court. But the best part was we got a new little dog, just like I had promised Dee.

One day while we were still in N.Y., we got a call from mama, Dee's mother. Ya'll better come on up here I got the cutest little dog for Sherry. The man said he can only hold her for another hour after that he is going to give her away. Mama knew how hurt I was after we had to take Blue back to the A.S.P.C.A. because she felt the same way. Mama loved Blue too. Every time she came to spend the weekend with us she played with him and took him for walks. So she knew how badly I wanted another dog and ever since I told her we could have a dog in Georgia, she had been looking out for one. So when she called, even though Dee and I was both so tired because we had just come home from work, we jumped in Harmony and flew to the Bronx. I had to at least go see the little baby. The funniest thing happened when we got there, mama was standing outside across the street from her building talking to a man. All I saw next to him was this shopping cart. Sure enough when we pulled up in front of them and got out the car and walked over to where she was, I looked in the cart and what did I see? The cutest little black and white Dalmatian dogs sitting in a box in the cart with their mommy and only one other dog was left. He had already given away all the others. I looked into her eyes and I fell in love. When he took her out she was about the size of my shoe I picked her up, held her, gave him a couple of dollars for himself and that was it. After that we hung out with mama for a while then I smothered her with kisses and thanked her. Dee kissed her and we headed back to the BK with Sheyne. On the drive back home after going through several names we finally agreed on her name. It was Sheyne. I named her Sheyne because her coat was shiny and jet black. She rode in my lap all the way back to BK and by the time we got to the apartment both of us were in love with Sheyne. Back at home Na-Na, our cat looked at Sheyne as if to say, oh Lord not another one. But after a while Na-Na fell in love with her too.

Everything was falling right into place and I felt so good. I had a job waiting for me in Georgia and I knew it was only a matter of time before Dee got his job too. We had a beautiful apartment waiting for us. We had our dog back and our cat Na-Na. And we had Harmony, our car. It wasn't a whole lot but it was ours. And we were very grateful for all of it.

By the middle of August 2007 we had packed everything that we were taking to Georgia, which wasn't much. Babe we are not taking any of this stuff with us because everything we get as far as furniture is going to be brand new. What you talking about girl? Yes Dee we want a fresh new start so we can't take any of this old stuff with us. Don't worry we are going to have everything we need when we get there. The only thing we are not leaving of course, is our $2,000 Poster King and Queen Canopy Bed in Cherry Wood Finish. It is the most beautiful bed I have ever seen in my life. I first saw it just a couple of months earlier, sitting there in the store window (and waiting for me to see it). I was actually on a bus on my way home from work at Samaritan when I first saw it. I was not about to get off the bus that day but that same weekend I asked Dee to take me back to the store. I had to go check it out. As soon as we walked in the store I saw it. It was huge and I fell in love. Dee I am coming back for this bed, I have to have it. And a couple of months later after we saved all that money, we did go back for it. Dee knows by now whenever I get my Visions I confess them over and over and they always come to pass. So he doesn't even argue with me anymore, he just says, go for it Babe. I had made all of the arrangements, I found a moving man, and he does long distance moving. He even transports cars. His moving jobs are from N.Y. to Georgia he said it usually takes two days to deliver property to Georgia. So three days before we were leaving, Oscar came to the apartment, we paid him half the money and he packed up our car on his gigantic flat bed, along with several other people's cars that were already on there. He had his moving truck and two guys and they put the rest of our stuff in the truck and I trusted them with all of our property, including our $2,000+ bed. He assured us that he would see us in Georgia by the time we landed. We gave him the address to our new apartment in Georgia and the joke was of course Dee told him yo, man don't let me have to come hunt you down, if for nothing else, that bedroom set, because the last thing I want to do is hear her mouth whining for the rest of our lives about the man who stole our bedroom set. I was cracking up, I said forget about the car ha! I wasn't worried because I had already done my research on him and I prayed. I knew our stuff was going to be fine.

We made flight arrangements on Air Tran for two adults and two pets because I definitely wasn't driving fourteen hours to go to Georgia or anywhere else. A week or so before the flight we had to take Sheyne and Na-Na for their shots because they only allowed pets on the plane with verification that they are up to date on their shots. Of course their airfare cost just as much as Dee and my tickets. But I didn't care, we were taking both of them with us, no matter what. We were told that they would ride under the plane with the other pets and at first I was let's just say, not really comfortable with that. But Dee said, Babe where do you want them to ride on the plane with us? And of course after we finished laughing, I didn't even bother to say a word because he knew what the answer was going to be. But we had their carrying cases and their soft little blankees, so I felt they would be ok for the two hour ride. By now Sheyne was a little bigger, she was definitely bigger than the cat. Not long after we got her, we took her to the Veterinarians and that's when we found out that she is mixed with Boxer. All I could say was thank God she has the Dalmatian face, because I was always scared of Boxer dogs. Their faces look so mean.

Everyone at Samaritan was so happy for Dee and I and as soon as I got back from Georgia, I ran into Jacqueline's office. As I sat down I had the biggest smile on my face and all she said was I told you. I started cracking up. I gave her such a big hug, thank you girl. I never would have known about Georgia if it weren't for you. Jacqueline I fell in love, it is so beautiful and peaceful down there. I know girl I told you. Sherry, I really wished I could have found a job when I was there because I never would have left. And Congratulations Sherry I heard you got that job. So you're going to be working with Anthony? Thanks, yes I got the job and I think I am really going to love it there. It's a Drug Court Program, you know that's my Passion working with the Substance Abuse population! See that's why I have to get my degree too. I'm going back to school too. So get ready because I will be back to Georgia Sherry, just give me a few years. I hear that, well here is my number, call me anytime. I got so much love and support from my Samaritan Village family. All of the staff wished me well. Sherry this is such a huge thing you're doing. Girl I hope everything works out for you and Dee in Georgia. The clients at Samaritan have always been very encouraging to me. Over the years, during many of the groups sessions, I shared my personal experiences to uplift, encourage and motivate them to never give up on their dreams. And all I constantly hear from each of them is, Ms. Sherry how's that book coming? Please, you gotta finish your book. I can't wait to read "A Fire Within". Please call the Counselors and let them know when you are finished "A Fire Within" so we can order it. And when you become a big celebrity on the Oprah show, don't forget us, give us shout out. Ok, ok I will let everyone know when I become famous and anyway you guys will see me on the Red Carpet and I'd just laugh. Because it was so amazing to me that they saw my Vision too. Now I'm still working my way up to the whole Oprah thing but the Vision of birthing "A Fire Within" oh, that's happening now. My last day at Samaritan, they were crying, I was in tears, we were all a mess. Ms. Sherry, Ms. Sherry wait don't go nowhere, I got something for you. I'll be right back. What? What are you talking about? I'm looking out my office door as the client ran up the stairs. Standing in my office, I was talking with my Manager saying goodbye. Well this is it young lady, I know you are going to be such a blessing in Georgia. Just keep on doing what you're doing and keep in touch, you hear me. I definitely will keep in touch. Thank you for everything, I will never forget all of you. It was wonderful working here the past two years. I have learned so much valuable information from everyone. I was hugging my Manager when all of a sudden the client burst in the office. Here, I got this for you, it was a book. I looked at my Manager because we were not allowed to accept gifts from clients. He looked at me and said go ahead take it, it's a gift. When I looked at the Title of the book I melted, "Your Scars are Beautiful to God; Finding Peace and Purpose in the Hurts of your Past". And I knew right then and there, I'm walking in my Destiny. God speaks to us in many ways, through people, books and music. I shook the client's hand and thanked them from the bottom of my heart. I wasn't even sure if the client knew what the book meant to me. And little did I know that book would change the course of my entire life. I put it in my purse and I left Samaritan Village that day, and that part of my journey was completed and over. Two days later at the airport Cocoa and I cried our eyes out, along with my nieces and Dee with tears in even his eyes. Ok Babe, come on ya'll can call in a little while, we gotta go catch this plane. I hugged everyone, kissed them again and ran crying to my new life in Georgia. Life after achieving some of the most incredible triumphs, going through the devastating losses, and the sudden misfortunes was good because even after all that I had been through, I'm still standing, and I'm getting stronger and better every day. I have an even clearer Vision. I had come to the end of a season in my life. And God still has a plan.

CHAPTER 27

"BEYOND MY SCARS"

October 2007, it had been eighteen years since the fire and I was so happy with our life in Georgia. Our apartment is so refreshing, everything is so clean and pretty. Oscar delivered all of our property just like he said, including my $2,000 + bed and our car. And just like I said all of our furniture is brand new. Dee and I love to sit on our balcony and grill and just chill. Sheyne and Na-Na have so much space to just run all around and Dee loves taking Sheyne by the lake in the complex and of course Sheyne loves it. I speak to everyone back home all the time and Cocoa at least two or three times a day. I have even more good news, Shainne gave birth to a baby boy and she named him Shane. Shane is our little Angel. I don't know who he looks like, his father or his mother. I guess he looks like both of them. Big Mikale, lil Mikale and Myasia are in love with Shane and so are we. They made a power move too, they are living in Florida now and they love it. The kids go swimming and Shainne gets to see all those beautiful Palm Trees. So we call each other all the time. Cocoa, Quan and my nieces, they are coming to Georgia next summer to visit. So it's all good.

I was so happy when I started my new job in Atlanta. Dee has a job interview coming up and it sounds like he is getting the job. But still I wasn't really at peace. For the past eighteen years I had been living in bondage to my scars. I was definitely in a much better place than the days when I was anxious even just riding the train. I had to ride the train and bus to work every day so I didn't have a choice about that.

But then I had to forgive. Forgiving those who hurt me was one of the most difficult aspects of my healing process but I believed that if I didn't forgive I wouldn't be free to find the beauty and purpose in the scars of my past. The wounds wouldn't have been able to heal. Forgiveness has nothing to do with whether or not the person who hurt us deserves to be forgiven. Forgiveness is not saying that what the person did or didn't do was right. It is simply saying that we are taking the person off our hook and placing them on God's hook. We are cutting them loose from our backs and giving the burden to God. We are no longer allowing them to hold us captive by holding a grudge. As long as we do not forgive, we are held in satan's trap. It is the number one avenue by which he controls his prey. God gave me the Grace to forgive whoever it was that attempted to kill J and I. I heard in my Spirit to forgive and God said I will not ask you to do something without giving you the Grace to do it, so I did.

But I still was not at peace with my scars. In eighteen years I had never been outside in short sleeve shirts or dresses. I still wore bangs trying to hide my face as much as I could. I didn't think I would ever get over it.

We were so happy when Dee got his first job working at CNN as their Chef. Something miraculous happened. Remember Mina, my mother, well she moved to Georgia too. Right after Dee and I got back to N.Y., after telling everyone how much we loved Georgia, Mina came down for a visit. Sure-nuff she got the Georgia bug too. Shockingly she gave up the beautiful Islands of St. Thomas years earlier and had lived with Ma and Daddy which was perfect because she got to help them out so much. And after that she just ended up staying there. But when she visited Georgia and stayed with her brother Aus and aunt Pam, that was it. The next thing we knew she was packing her things and so the Uhaul truck brought her things and ours. After Dee and I moved to Georgia we started looking for an apartment Mina. We ended up finding her a beautiful two bedroom apartment. Of course it has all the same amenities like ours and it was only a ten to fifteen minute drive from our place. Mina was blessed to get a job. She's working at the Department for the Aging, life was good.

I had my Dee, my mother, my uncle and cousins and we were meeting new people every day. It seems like our whole family will end up living in Georgia one day. We started attending the Word of Faith Church Family Worship Cathedral with Bishop Dale. C. Bronner and First Lady Dr. Nina Bronner, his beautiful wife. It was no surprise that we would feel like a part of the Word of Faith family, their Ministry deals with striving to make a difference every day, being a blessing to someone else, and to never give up and always giving back. Word of Faith is a place where you are encouraged, equipped and empowered to serve better, live better, be better and do better. They teach us to learn how to maximize our potential. At the Word of Faith Church we feel loved, valued and appreciated. We love it there. I would recommend if you are reading this book and don't have a Church home please go there at least once, I promise you will not be sorry.

Over the next several weeks something started happening to me. I began to experience something so awesome, a total spiritual Healing. **Psalm 107:2** says; Let the redeemed of the Lord tell their story. Remember that book that the client gave me the last day at Samaritan Village? I never had the time to read it ever since we got to Georgia with unpacking and just getting things in order but mostly I didn't have the chance to read back then because everything happens in divine timing. So one day while I was in our bedroom I saw the book and I was led to begin reading "Your Scars are Beautiful to Go-, Finding Peace and Purpose in the Hurts of your Past", finally. And just like I knew it would, from that very first time when I saw the name of the book, it touched me again, in the inner most place, my spirit. Reading it was so profound and I knew that as sure as I was Sherry, God put that book in my hands and he was speaking in and through me. And after twenty long, painful years of not liking my scars and hiding myself from myself and not wanting to look in the mirror, when I opened this book, that's when I found out that "Scars" tell a story. Scars by their very nature, imply there's a story to tell. They represent a wrinkle in time in which a person's life is changed forever, and they serve as permanent reminders of an incident that, in one way or another, has made a lasting impression on one's life. Each scar represents a moment in time when something happened to us or through us that we will never forget. I have several scars on my body, and each has a story to tell. Some people have very painful scars too, but we cannot see them. You know the ones I'm talking about. We all have them. They are the scars on our hearts and in our souls. The scar of rejection, disappointment or the scar of broken dreams etc. We receive scars in one of two ways: What has been done to us by other people or what has been done through us by our own mistakes and failures. In reading the book I learned that my scars are not something I need to hide or be ashamed of, but rather an invitation to share the healing power of Jesus Christ with a hurting world. For a scar, by its very definition, implies healing (Jaynes, Sharon 2006). This book inspired me because I had never looked at the wounds in my life as potential treasures. But after digging deeper, and after I pushed aside all the dirt, I discovered the jewels that lie beneath the surface. Like sparkling diamonds, glistening rubies, and shimmering emeralds, my scars are beautiful to God. I was on an amazing journey to finding the peace that I so desperately needed and "purpose in the pain of my past" and when I did, it changed the course of my entire life, forever. In no way could I ever compare myself to the Lord, only I thanked God for helping me to get to the point in my own life where I am no longer ashamed to show my scars to a hurting world. In **John 20: 19-20** Jesus said "Peace be with you!" After he said this, he showed them his hands and side. The disciples were overjoyed when they saw the Lord. But they didn't recognize Jesus until he showed them His scars, and this is how others still recognize Him today…when men and women who have experienced the healing of past wounds are not ashamed to show their scars to a hurting world they can find peace, and that is exactly what happened to me. It was an epiphany, a revelation to me and I began to have a shift in my thinking. Jesus didn't have to retain the scars of the crucifixion on His resurrected body. He could have returned without them. After all, He is the one who put new flesh on the hands and feet of lepers. But He chose to keep the scars, because they were precious to Him… Reading the amazing testimony, it ministered to me and I knew God was speaking to me saying, Sherry don't be ashamed of your scars either. Although I told my testimony everywhere I went, I was still ashamed of my scars. But Jehovah Rapha, the God Who Heals, placed his hand on the gaping wounds of my heart and transformed my wounds into beautiful scars. Healing... it's what He does. Telling others about His healing power in my life, is what I do.

1 Peter 1:6-7

Wherein ye greatly rejoice, though now for a season, if need be, ye are in heaviness through manifold temptations: That the trial of your faith, being much more precious than of gold that perisheth, though it be tried with fire, might be found unto praise and honour and glory at the appearing of Jesus Christ:

I learned that there are many purposes for the scars of my/our past. Our understanding of God's character is broadened, our faith is strengthened, our character is matured, our souls are purified, our vision(s) are clarified our passions are enflamed, and our hearts are softened. Of course, with each of those positive qualities a negative one could occur too. For example, our understanding of God could be distorted, our vision(s) clouded, our passions extinguished, and our hearts hardened. After what happened in my life I could have become hard or soft. I couldn't change the past, but I had to determine the effect it would have on my future and I never wanted it to make me bitter and I am so grateful my experiences made me better.

Healing is a process. Healing begins by recognizing that a wound needs to be healed, a painful memory or an aching heart. Healing usually doesn't happen in an instant, but through a process of steps or decisions. Sometimes God heals immediately, sometimes He chooses to send us through a process of healing steps. Either way I have learned that He is more concerned with the process than the finished product.

April 2009, I was sitting in my office at the Drug Court Program and in walks Mrs. Ritchie, the same beautiful soul that had hired me two years earlier. One of the things I love the most about Mrs. Ritchie is that she has an open door policy and we can talk to her about most anything. This day we just happened to be in my office and I said Mrs. G I want to talk to you about something. Sometimes instead of calling her Mrs. Ritchie, I just called her Mrs. G, so I said, Mrs. G you know a lot about my story but there is something you don't know. Ok, do you want to tell me? Of course I do, well I don't think you know that I still have a complex about my scars. Really, no I didn't know that Sherry. Have you noticed that I don't wear short sleeve dresses or shirts? You know, that is really interesting because I never noticed that you don't ever wear short sleeves. I see you walking around here so confident I would have never known that you have a complex about your scars. Yes, I do and in the twenty years since I was in the fire, I have never been outside wearing anything that would really expose my scars. Well, let me ask you Sherry, what's the worst thing that could happen if you wore short sleeves and anyone saw your scars? Well, I'm sure people would stare at my scars. Yes, they probably will, but what else? Well, I'm sure it would gross them out. Yea, probably, and what else? Well, I will be so embarrassed.

Yes, you probably will, and what else? And by the 5th what else, there was nothing else left to "what else" about. And for the first time, it was like a light bulb went off in my head. No one had ever went through that process with me the way Mrs. G did. Mrs. G said Sherry yes, who knows, it's a possibility that all of those things are likely to happen, but so what? No one can change your scars. Do you know what I think hurts you the most Sherry? What hurts me the most Mrs. G? Your ego. I don't think you have gotten past your ego, again a "light bulb" moment, because she was right. I have never gotten over not being one of the prettiest girls in the room anymore. And I have never gotten past not being the one who was in control of situations. And I certainly have never gotten over the fact that I'm no longer that beautiful little girl. Sherry I want you to do something for me, will you do it? What Mrs. G.? What do you want me to do? I would like you to practice right here today at work, by rolling up your sleeves. WHAT? Laughing, oh no Mrs. G, I don't think I can do that. Yes, you can Sherry, go ahead just try. So I rolled up my shirt sleeve, just a little. More she said. Laughing, I rolled them up just a little more, by now they were rolled up to my elbows (which by the way are severely burned). Good she said, now keep them like that until the end of the day and come tell me how it went. Ok? Yes Mrs. G, I will. So I walked around the rest of the afternoon just like that and the funniest thing happened, it was no different. As a matter of fact, once again the people on my caseload who did recognize what I was doing, were cheering me on, and so happy that I did it. And just like at Samaritan Village, all of the staff at the Drug Court Program pretty much knew at least some of my story. As I share it with the staff and clients there all the time. So for them it was such a good thing that I was able to finally do it. But for me it was the first of many huge milestones. That afternoon I hugged Mrs. Ritchie and thanked her because it wasn't half as bad as I thought it would be and I left work that day feeling good.

When I got home from work that night I said to Dee, babe, guess what I am going to do? What's that? I am going to go outside with short sleeves on real soon. I told ya'll already Dee doesn't even get into that stuff with me anymore, he has been going through this with me for so many years already. You are, that's good you, go for it Babe. I keep trying to tell you that you are the only one who can make the choice.

For twenty years I had dreamt of being able to walk into a store and find the prettiest short sleeve shirt and wear it outside. Because I tormented myself every summer, it never mattered how hot it was outside. I would never dream of wearing anything with short sleeves. But a few days after the conversation with Mrs. G, I went into one of my favorite shopping stores and looked for "the shirt". I had already Visualized what it would look like and it was just a plain white dress shirt with "short sleeves" and a collar, simple, nothing fancy. That's all I wanted. When I walked out of that store I had my plain, white, short sleeved dress shirt and when I got home I put it on, looked at myself in the mirror and said, well Sherry this is what it is. Actually it didn't look horrible at all. I had worn short sleeves at home and in front of my family but going outside in one was a whole different ballgame for me. I showed Dee my shirt and he said yes, Babe you should wear it, it looks good on you. It was a process, so over the next couple of days, I hung it in my closet and I had to pray. All I heard was God would not ask you to do anything without giving you the grace to do it. And that was it. The next day I got dressed for work, I put on my pretty new white shirt and black pants, my hair was straight and just as soon as I touched my doorknob to walk outside, satan said, "Sherry, you better grab a jacket just in case". I rebuke you in the Name of Jesus and I opened my door, walked out in the world for the first time in twenty years, wearing my short sleeve, pretty white shirt.

Satan knew that if he could get me to take that jacket with me that more than likely I would have put it on once I got the first funny feeling that someone was watching me outside. And I would have continued to walk in the fear that he had me in the past twenty years. So I walked out my door that morning without any jacket at all. When I got outside, I laughed to myself as I always do when I'm having a moment and I got in my car. I went to work that day with just my pretty white shirt on and no jacket. I have never turned back since that day. Today I am wearing short sleeve dress shirts, and short sleeve tee shirts and short sleeve whatever I want to. And the funniest thing happened when my family came to Georgia, I went to pick them up at the Airport wearing, yes a short sleeve shirt. And as soon as Cocoa saw me, we both cracked up laughing right there in the Airport, hugging each other and making so much noise. I shocked her, because even though I had told her plenty of times talking on phone, seeing me in person actually doing it was completely different. Cocoa, out of everyone knew it was a huge accomplishment, and incredible triumph and unbelievable chance. Wearing short sleeves outside was something neither she or I thought I would ever in a million years be able to do. But I did, and I am SO PROUD of myself. And most of all, I am SO FREE. Yes, people stare at me all the time but God has taken me from that ashamed, embarrassed girl and he has transformed me into a "Confident Woman" today. Not confident in myself, but I am confident in the plan that God has for my life and you know what, there ain't no stopping me now. Oh! I have even taken it a step further, I no longer wear my bangs and I am wearing my hair pushed all the way back in a ponytail, exposing ever scar on my face, hands, arms, legs and everywhere because I am fearfully and marvelously made, and for what I have to do in my life, I fit perfectly. I am right where I need to be. I am walking in the Destiny that God has for me. And today I am no longer "Hiding Behind My Scars" I am living "Beyond My Scars" and the best part of it all is that, this is just the beginning.

Everything was so beautiful in our lives and then in Sept 2011 it happened again. This time our world got rocked so hard once again and we faced another one of the hardest times of our lives.

What I miss most about mama, ya'll remember mama, she's Dee's mother. I miss her laugh so much. Mama had this laugh that would have everyone else laughing too, because it was so funny. And she definitely didn't hold no punches. Mama never took sides, if you were wrong, she told you so. If you were right, she told you so. I don't care who you were. Sometimes I look at Dee and he looks so much like his mother. Mama was his precious jewel. Not a day went by when Dee didn't speak to his mother while living in N.Y. and Georgia. I knew leaving N.Y. and coming to Georgia and Dee leaving his jewel behind, was definitely the hardest thing he ever had to do, besides leaving his two children. And one of the best blessings for Dee moving to Georgia was that we are closer now to his grandfather, Mr. Trume, he lives in Charlotte, N.C. and we finally got the chance to visit him. Over the years, I watched the closeness between Dee and his mother. Mama was probably the strongest and the most intelligent woman I have ever known. But she had tremendous medical issues too and she fought through them all. Mama is the first and only person that I know that beat that cancer so bad, it never came back. Her cancer went into remission years ago and by the grace of God that's where it stayed. Mama will you please sit down and get some rest, I would say. Child please, was her favorite thing to say. Mama would sit down for two seconds and then there she goes right back up again, doing something else. She never, ever stopped. She would put on her African wraps and she was ready to go. Mama loved her family so much and she did everything to make sure they were taken care of. After Ms. Shirl passed, mama took Dee's three little nieces Meka, Shawn and Cheryl and she raised them from the time they were little girls until they became young adults. She was always there for them no matter what. Mama loved the Lord and she would worship the Lord inside, outside, at church or anywhere, she didn't care. Baby girl, make sure you finish our book, don't you let nothing stop you, you hear me? Yes, mama I hear you. I love you mama and just like I promised you, I will take care of your son, always.

> **My tribute to Dee's and my, "Mama"**

How fortunate I am to have known you;
To have been taught what the strength of a woman is, by you;
How gracious I am to have seen such strength in you;
To have watched the fight and triumph in you;
To have seen deliverance every day in you;
To have watched an indestructible faith in you;
How joyful I am to have helped you;
To have been there, able to take care of you;
To have done what you so often have done for me, I was able to do for you;
To have shown what it meant for me to be loved by you;
How glorious, unbelievable and remarkably so;
To have a miracle in its own right, be called to go home;
To have a sensational, inconceivable, irreplaceable soul…
Live in me, the everlasting life of Mama.

Mama, thank you for sharing your son, your family, and your life with me. I will miss our talks we shared.

CHAPTER 28

"A FIRE WITHIN"

As you read in my story, even as a young girl I always had a fire within me. But early on I started to use the fire that was in me in negative ways and began walking in the flesh making my own choices. Once I got off the path that ma and daddy had set before me, which was walking with the Lord, and I got out of the will that God had for my life, I went in the wrong direction, and it nearly cost me my life. I made one bad choice after the next. I just believe that God allows us to go through some things so He can use our trials to be a blessing to others. And I thank God because even when I was at my lowest point, he reached down, lifted me up and He brought me out of the life of destruction that I chose for myself. And, after all that I've been through on my journey now, it blesses me so much because I love the calling that's on my life. Today I'm using my past hurts to be a blessing to others, touching lives everywhere I go. That same drive, determination and fire that I have inside now is being used in a positive way to motivate, encourage and lift up the brokenhearted, from New York City to Georgia. The past several years I have used the gifts that God has given me to empower thousands of men and women, young and old who have substance abuse problems and those people who were broken in their spirits due to pain from life's experiences. I'm using my testimony to encourage them that they too can conquer their demons and rise out of that life of self-destruction to emerge as confident, powerful and successful women and men of God.

As a Motivational Speaker my passion is helping anyone with a broken heart and who wants help, to find peace and purpose in the hurts of their past too. In speaking to so many individuals both throughout my professional career and personally since my own tragedy, I have been targeting those individuals with involvement in the Criminal Justice System, Substance Abuse Programs, in Colleges, Universities and in Hospital settings. I have started my own company called Beyond My Scars (BMS), a Counseling Program for men, women and especially teens dealing with substance abuse issues, in particularly catering to those individuals in need of a spiritual healing.

It's 2012, and I am in a new season in my life, as a matter of fact, we are all in a new season. My family and I are the happiest we have been in quite some time.

God is so awesome, in 2008 He gave us a beautiful five bedroom house and we absolutely love it. Some days I look out our bedroom window and I am amazed. Our backyard reminds me of Central Park in New York, it is huge. When God blesses us he does so amazingly, all of those years ago when I asked him for trees and grass, well now we have at least twenty trees on our property. Our house is on a corner and there is grass going all the way around our house. And, I kept the promise that I made to Dee so many years ago. And now we have two dogs, Sheyne was gotten so big, and we also got another dog his name is Brawny, my troublemaking beautiful, golden Chow. But sadly our Na-Na passed away in June 2012 (RIP, my baby).

In 2010 Dee and I were at Hartsfield Airport to pick up Mina, my mother. She was coming home from her vacation in St. Thomas, when tragedy almost struck again. My car spun out of control and I lost control of the vehicle and when it was over I had totaled my beautiful BMW and the underground tunnel at the airport was demolished, along with five other cars. But God is so awesome because no one got hurt in that horrible accident and the next month he gave me another BMW, even prettier. Dee's Entertainment and Catering business is starting to pick up here in Georgia, he's so happy about that.

And the best blessing of them all, Mina lives right downstairs from us! The house has an in-law suite, she loves it. Remember my brother Ramel, well he is living in Georgia now too and soon he will have his own beautiful home for his family when they come to Georgia. Ramel's three children are all grown up now. Tanique his oldest daughter, gave birth to our little baby girl on July 26th, her name is Chloe. Ty his son, is in college and his youngest girl who just turned seventeen is about to graduate high school. And Cocoa's very happy, her Coletee-Tee's, line of Tee-shirt's which is her business, is blowing up in N.Y. and very soon we are going to expand her line here in Georgia as well. Her oldest daughter Telly, remember my niece who was scared of me after the fire, well she is a college graduate and has a big time job working as the Executive Secretary at her company. Tyani, she's Cocoa's youngest child, I am so proud of her she is in her second year in college and also working hard. I am still waiting for Cocoa and Quan to move to Georgia but as long as I know they are coming, I'm good with that. And Shainne and Mikale they are looking to purchase a home in Florida and their three children are growing up so fast. Lil Mikale and Myasia are in high school. And Shane, well I'll just say he's is going to be our next black President. And everyone else is living their lives happily in N.Y., Georgia and the Virgin Islands. As for me, I am just ecstatic about the release of my book "A FIRE WITHIN" coming out in 2012. I am having a book signing tour in the very near future, so stay tuned and keep in touch on my website for details:

www.sherrygravesafirewithin.com

You know we all have a story to tell, but the most powerful story we can ever tell is what Christ has done for us, how He brought us from death to life! I learned that incredible power is released when we drop the chains of bitterness, fear, and shame to show the world our scars. Because satan knows that our stories are instrumental in his ultimate defeat, he will do anything and everything to convince us to keep the treasures hidden away. But He is calling us to "not" be ashamed of our scars, because it is by those very scars that others will recognize the Savior. He has great purposes in our trials. Trials are not random acts meant to make us miserable or to destroy us. They are meant to refine us and make us strong. I know now that I was saved and set on this journey to share the hope that is within me. I am not saying that I am glad the fire happened but I definitely see Gods hand in the healing process. If that tragedy never occurred, I would probably never have had the passion to minister to other women and men through counseling in substance abuse groups and leading so many of them on their journey to the heart of God. Through my healing journey I have found purpose in my pain.

Today I see my scars and yours as priceless treasures that our Master has entrusted to me and to us. We can choose to invest those treasures in the lives of others, or we can choose to hide them because of fear. I have seen how investing the scars from the past in the lives of others has produced dividends far beyond even my own expectations. One small investment can have resounding effects that continue for generations to come. It is the story of my life. There is power in our scars. Each day I go to work I am investing my scars in other people and touching the lives of people with substance abuse problems, they are looking for a way out and even those people who are depressed, feeling hopeless and they are having suicidal thoughts.

I am no longer ashamed of my scars. I boldly tell my story and women and men see hope displayed before them.

In "Who Holds the Key to Your Heart?" Lysa TerKeurst gives us this assurance:

> *Rest assured, my friend, inside most hearts exits a secret place. Behind a door of hidden thoughts and painful memories brews a hurt so overwhelming, it can't be allowed to surface. The slightest peek inside reveals insecurities better left alone. So the door is locked and secrets are kept even from God. Or are they?*
>
> *The truth is God knows the secrets of your heart and He wants them. The maker of this vast and wonderful universe is waiting for the key to the heart of His greatest creation, you. He wants the key to your heart, your whole heart, especially the hidden parts. When you hold this key, satan will wrestle it from you, unlock your shame, and use it to accuse and condemn you. He loves to keep a person in such a defeated state of mind that he/she becomes totally ineffective for the cause of the Lord. The irony is that the very things you consider shameful can be used by God for His glory.*

While we must accept God's forgiveness and forgive ourselves, we never truly forget. Honestly, I'm glad.. If I forgot the sins and the pain that was attached to them, then I would be more likely to make the same mistakes again. God removes the shame and the penalty, but memory helps us to never go down that path again. Remembering our weakness also helps us to be more compassionate with others when they fall into seductive traps. When I go to work every day and have an assessment to do on someone that has been seen in the hospital a many times before and for the same thing I am much more compassionate towards them because I know how it is to not get it the first, second or third time around. For some people they may have to go through Detox from Alcohol five times or more, before they get it. Unfortunately some people never get it.

What hurts me are my clients that say to me they don't believe in God. They say the churches are filled with people who outwardly look contented and at peace but inwardly are crying out for someone to love them, just as they are. Confused, frustrated, often frightened, guilty, and often unable to communicate even within their own families. But that other people in the church look so happy and contented, that one seldom has the courage to admit his or her own deep needs in front of such a self-sufficient group of people at church. A person named Yaconelli talks about "messy spirituality" as the refusal to pretend, to lie. Or to allow others to believe we are something we are not. He stated we need not hide all that is ugly and repulsive in us. Because Jesus comes not for the super spiritual but for the wobbly and the weak kneed, who know they don't have it all together, and who are not too proud to accept the handout of amazin' grace. I guess what I'm saying is that I agree with Yaconelli. And unfortunately, people are seeking help outside the church, because so few of us are willing to admit we have or have had a problem. I refuse to be anything but authentic, regardless of how messy my life may seem. In order to reveal a scar we must put aside take off the mask, and get real. I learned that the process involves dying to our own selfish pride that convinces us to appear happier, healthier, or holier than we really are. I found out that when we take the seed of our testimony and plant it into the soil of another's wounded heart, it will bring in a harvest of healing for those who need it most, those wounded souls who feel as though they are the only ones who have experienced such failure and pain. And when we reveal the truth that has been hidden like a treasure beneath the soil, there will be some who will scoff and scorn but that's ok, it just means "they missed it". But when we are truly repentant, humbled and broken, we don't mind who knows about our scars because we have nothing to lose. And those who hear our stories or redemption have everything to gain. Brennan Manning wrote, "To live by grace means to acknowledge my whole life story, the light side and the dark". Once I decided to reveal the truth and use the scars of my past to be a blessing to others as I took one believing step after another, I realized that I was not alone, God was right there with me. Yes, I have many, many scars, but I am no longer ashamed. I am free. How precious that God chose to give me this journey of revealing the truth of my scars and using my scars to bring the message of healing to others.

In *When I Lay My Isaac Down*, Carol Kent explains: There is a common ground of understanding, forgiveness, acceptance, and healing when we are authentic with each other. When we tell our real-life stories of what we have encountered on the journey of life, we break down barriers and create safe places to risk revealing the truth. Intimacy in our relationships springs to life when we are no longer hiding behind the mask of denial, embarrassment, guilt or shame. We're just people who have had some good days in life and people who have had some very bad days. We've quit pretending that everything is "fine" and that life is grand. When we share our stories with each other, we find a way of relating without the façade and without the need to impress. We can just be real. And this brings tremendous freedom. Carol further says, I used to wonder how any good could come out of reviewing the details and reliving the pain of an unwanted experience. But I've discovered (so have I) that tremendous power is released when we dare to speak up and communicate our personal stories with honesty and vulnerability. By doing so we remind others that life is an unpredictable journey for all of us. Bad things happen, and the enemy tries to destroy our spirit and or sense of purpose. But if we can remember that we are engaged in a spiritual battle, not with weapons and hatred, but with hope, faith and joy, we affirm our ultimate security in God and our love for Him in the midst of our heartaches. The grace filled reward is that we find ourselves enveloped in steadfast, intimate, extravagant love that continues to move us into the heart of the greatest adventure of all.

> *"I have discovered and released the power of my scars to give hope to the hopeless, encouragement and strength to the weary, and healing to the broken-hearted." We tend to think that our scars hinder our service for God, when it is our very scars that render us able. Through our weakness, He makes us strong. Through our dying, He makes us alive. And through our wounds, He makes us whole. It is in the telling and showing that God's power is released. Many times, before moving into our Promised Land, God will take us full circle. And what has wounded us is often the very thing He uses to take us to our Promised Land of ministry. When we are not ashamed of our scars, God takes us to our own personal Gilgal and leads un into a land flowing with opportunity. For example: An ex-drug addict reaches out to women and men strung out on cocaine and offers freedom". (Jaynes, Sharon, 2006).*

When God brought me full circle and asked, "Are you ready to enter into your Promised Land now?" I responded, definitely. Scars? We've all got them but it's how we view them that will change our hearts. And it's what we choose to do with them that can change the world. Are there beautiful scars in your life that need to be revealed? I wonder what God wants to accomplish through you. I wonder how long He's been waiting for you to remove the covering. Don't be ashamed of your scars, for it is by those very scars that the world will recognize the Savior, the Healer, and Lord. Where ever God leads, I pray that you will not be ashamed of your scars but reveal the truth of God's healing and restoring power in your life (Jaynes, Sharon, 2006)

This is not the end of our journey together my friend, but just the beginning.

Coping Strategies In Times of Need: *Here are a few coping mechanisms that have helped me in "times of need".*

- Daily Prayer.
- Read your Bible, find the Scripture in your Bible and apply them to your situation(s).
- Do not let anyone or anything deter you from your purpose, hold on to your Vision(s) of yourself crossing the finish line, knowing that you have run the race with the bold integrity of who you are.
- Read daily meditations (Joyce Meyer has awesome meditation books).
- Confront fears; the only way to conquer our fears, are to confront them, so instead of running away from them, run to them.
- If you have a substance abuse problem seek help; enroll yourself into a substance abuse treatment program, find a support group for your drug(s) of choice, e.g., Narcotics Anonymous or Alcoholics Anonymous, get yourself a Sponsor. Go to the nearest emergency room if you are in need of detoxification.
- If you are a family member of an addicted person, find a support group for families e.g., Al-Anon.
- When we stop using drugs, we must find something "good" or something "fun" to fill the void, such as a hobby.
- Set goals and develop strategies so that we may be all that God wants us to be and fulfill the plan He has for us.
- Claim your Victory.

Research has shown that while some people seem to come by resilience naturally, these behaviors can also be learned. The following are just a few of the techniques you should focus on in order to foster your own resilience.

1. Build Positive Beliefs in Your Abilities
Research has demonstrated that self-esteem plays an important role in coping with stress and recovering from difficult events. Remind yourself of your strengths and accomplishments. Becoming more confident about your own ability to respond and deal with crisis is a great way to build resilience for the future.

2. Find a Sense of Purpose in Your Life
Finding a sense of purpose can play an important role in recovery. This might involve becoming involved in your community, cultivating your spirituality, or participating in activities that are meaningful to you.

3. Develop a Strong Social Network
Having caring, supportive people around you acts as a protective factor during times of crisis (Jones). It is important to have people you can confide in. While simply talking about a situation with a friend or loved one will not make troubles go away, it allows you to share your feelings, gain support, receive positive feedback, and come up with possible solutions to your problems.

4. Embrace Change
Flexibility is an essential part of resilience. By learning how to be more adaptable, you'll be better equipped to respond when faced with a life crisis. Resilient people often utilize these events as an opportunity to branch out in new directions. While some people may be crushed by abrupt changes, highly resilient individuals are able to adapt and thrive.

5. Be Optimistic
Staying optimistic during dark periods can be difficult, but maintaining a hopeful outlook is an important part of resiliency. Positive thinking does not mean ignoring the problem in order to focus on positive outcomes. It means understanding that setbacks are transient and that you have the skills and abilities to combat the challenges you face. What you are dealing with may be difficult, but it is important to remain hopeful and positive about a brighter future.

6. Nurture Yourself
When you're stressed, it can be all too easy to neglect your own needs. Losing your appetite, ignoring exercise, and not getting enough sleep are all common reactions to a crisis situation. Focus on building your self-nurturance skills, even when you are troubled. Make time for activities that you enjoy. By taking care of your own needs, you can boost your overall health and resilience and be fully ready to face life's challenges.

7. Develop Your Problem Solving Skills
Research suggests that people who are able to come up with solutions to a problem, are better able to cope with problems than those who cannot (Jones). Whenever you encounter a new challenge, make a quick list of some of the potential ways you could solve the problem. Experiment with different strategies and focus on developing a logical way to work through common problems. By practicing your problem solving skills on a regular basis, you will be better prepared to cope when a serious challenge emerges.

8. Establish Goals

Crisis situations are daunting. They may even seem insurmountable. Resilient people are able to view these situations in a realistic way, and then set reasonable goals to deal with the problem. When you find yourself becoming overwhelmed by a situation, take a step back to simply assess what is before you. Brainstorm possible solutions, and then break them down into manageable steps.

9. Take Steps to Solve Problems

Simply waiting for a problem to go away on its own only prolongs the crisis. Instead, start working on resolving the issue immediately. While there may not be any fast or simple solution, you can take steps toward making your situation better and less stressful. Focus on the progress that you have made thus far and plan your next steps, rather than becoming discouraged by the amount of work that still needs to be accomplished.

10. Keep Working on Your Skills

Resilience may take time to build, so do not become discouraged if you still struggle to cope with problematic events. According to Dr. Russ Newman, "research has shown that resilience is not an extraordinary thing but is rather ordinary and can be learned by most anyone" (2002). Psychological resilience does not involve any specific set of behaviors or actions, but can vary dramatically from one person to the next. Focus on practicing some of the common characteristics of resilient people, but also remember to build upon your existing strengths.

Official website for **Sherry Graves**: **www.sherrygravesafirewithin.com**

To book, National and International Author, and Motivational Speaker **Sherry Graves** visit: **www.booksherrygraves.com**

To book Dee for Entertainment or Catering
Email: **deeentertainer4u@aol.com**

To purchase Colet-Tees (tee-shirts) visit her website: **www.colettees.com**
Email-**colettees@gmail.com**

"Love thoughts to the Lord" & Thank you's...

I am eternally grateful to you Father. You didn't have to save me and I know that now. I also know that you were right there with me all along and you still are. And when I cried out to you, you sent your Angel of mercy and saved me and J. Thank you for giving me your Holy Spirit to guide and direct my path. Thank you for using me as a vessel to encourage, motivate and lift up the broken-hearted. Thank you for watching over my family, guiding and protecting us always. I treasure the gifts you have given me, every one of them. I live to give you the Glory, Honor and Praise. I lift you up and magnify you. I worship you Father, because you are so AWESOME. Thank you for doing a work inside me, I know you are not finished with me yet (there's still a whole lot of work you have to do). Ya'll pray for me, lol. To God Be the Glory!!

"To my family"

I love every one of you so much. You never turned your backs on me and when I needed you all the most, you were right there for me.

To Dorian, the love of my life,

Thank you for loving me and for riding the rollercoaster ride with me for so long. Through the many, many ups and downs, the in's and out's, the backwards and forwards, baby we are still standing, loving each other and growing stronger and better all the time. But it has definitely been some ride. Some days we get off the ride and we are swaying back and forth trying to land on solid ground. Other days we grab hold of each other and we hold on tight, so tight. I never dreamed that I would have a man who would love me with my scars yet, you do. You stood by me when I was going through some of the most difficult times in my life and I will always love you for that. You were and you always will be my Champ, standing there right beside me, protecting me. Ty and Tory, I love you both, you accepted me into your father's and your lives and you have loved me since day one. (Ty, kiss my little man). Towana & Sandy love you, for loving me.

To my wonderful mother,

I love that God has put us together for such a time as this. You are my strength, you inspire me to be and to do anything I put my mind too. You give me the courage to spread my wings and fly, and that's right, "ain't no stopping us now". Papa-cito I can't thank you enough for all that you do. I am so happy that mommy has you in her life, love you.

To my brother,

Jamel you are my sanctuary, in you I find all the peace, wisdom and support, to be the best that I can be. You are a wonderful, supportive and loving father to your three beautiful children, and I know you are going to be the best grandfather because you learned from the best (daddy/pops). I treasure you big bro... Never give up on your dreams! Nicola, I am so happy that you are a part of our family, I love you for Jamel. Taniqua I love you too, I am so proud of you and I know you are going to be a wonderful mother for little Klowe. What's up Michael, take care of our girls. Tyref you are every aunt's dream nephew. I love you. Tajah, my little Laila Ali you keep fighting for your rights, but stay outta trouble, love you baby.

To my big sis Colette,

You saved me and I will never, ever forget. When I couldn't be there for myself you had my back. Just like when we were little girls. You, my sis really are my next breadth. I cherish our love for each other (you and me must never part), lol. Seriously though, you bring a smile to my heart, thank you my love. Quan, you have been there for me since day one, I will never forget that. I love you, brother-in-law. Telly, and my Yana, I am so very proud of the young ladies you have become. If I had daughters, you both are the best role models they could ever have.

To my little sis, Shana,

I am so sorry that because of me you had to go through that trauma when you were just a little girl, when you got that horrible phone call the night of the fire. No little girl should ever have to hear what you heard about your sister. You have grown up to be the most loving, caring, little sister I could ever have asked for. Thank you for always being there for me. You are and you will always be our Diamond. You are a phenomenal woman and you are the best mom that I know of, to all three of my beautiful nieces and nephews. I am so very proud of all of them, they are growing up so respectful, caring and well-mannered. Big Mike, you are the best, I thank God for you. Michael, you are growing up into a fine young man, we are so proud of you. Mya (our beauty queen), one day you are going to be famous for your beautiful Art Creations. Never give up on your dreams. And Shane, all I can say is, you are so smart already and your only five. I know you are going to be our next black President so keep on learning all you're a,b,c's and 1,2,3's, love you baby!

To my aunts, uncles & great-uncles,

Uncle Lar, Lar I love you so much. Uncle Darwin whatever you are doing I need to start doing, because for an almost 90 year-old man you don't look a day over 80, keep it up, love you. Aus and Maalik, the two of you are so special to me. Maalik I am so proud of the man that you are. You have come such a long way in your own journey. Thank you for taking care of me when I couldn't take care of myself. Give "lil Mo" my love and tell him he has two blessings, God and his Angel, "his mom" watching over him! Keisha I love you, congrats on the little angel. Aus you have been there for me for as long as I can remember and you still are. Thank you so much for everything, from the bottom of my heart. Aunt Pearl, Rhoda, the girls and my little man, I love you so much. Glo you are priceless, like an emerald. You are the sweetest person and I love you so much. Charles, you have never turned your back on me, thank you unc, love you. Lee, I will never forget, you have taken care of me and us since we were babies. You have always been there. You are truly a blessing in our family, I love you so much. Cito, "LEE, LEE" lol, I am glad that my aunt has you in her life. You are a good guy. To my beautiful aunt Judy, you know how much I love you. I am so grateful that you are in our lives. Thank you for never forgetting my birthday. Ritza, thank you, I have never forgotten how much of yourself you gave when I was in the hospital, I will always love you for that.

To my cousins,

Brina & Xavier I love you both cuz, thank you for reading our Daily Meditations together. Denise and Kev, you guys are my driving force. Kev thanks for all of your wisdom keys, kiss little Ava. And thank you so much for giving me the name for "A Fire Within" (you and Kev). Derek (Sherri and the girls) thank you for always being such a blessing to our family. You guys are the best. Yvette, Adrienne and Audra thank you guys for all of your Prayers. I love you so much, I am so glad your mom has all her girls in her life. Adrienne, kiss my little Melody for me. Rachael and Robin, you both are awesome thank you for being such an inspiration to me. Rosi and Roy, I am so proud of you both. I love you so much!!

To Mark, thank you cuz, for always looking out for me and making sure I am riding "pretty". Karen you know how much I love you, mommy and baby girl. To my ATL "hang-out" cousins, Greg and Naomi, thank you both for all the tips, your support and all the good times, love you!! And to our "Winny", Angels are covering you as we continue to pray for your Supernatural healing, love you so much...

To my girls, Rochelle and Dee-Dee,

Love you so much!

To All of the family in St. Thomas , love you. Tortola British V.I.,

We have our Aunt "Limpy and Vee", Angels watching over us. To Vee's girls, I know your mom is smiling down on her beautiful granddaughter, and the little one, keep your head up, look for the best Star in the sky, when you need your mother.

To Mama & Mr. Hutchy,

You guys are such a blessing in my life, I will Thank God forever for you both. You never turned your backs on me & Josh and I will never, ever forget you. To the rest of my Hutchy family, I love you so much. Valerie you and I did it together, thank you for helping me get through Pride-Site, love you sis.

Tributes to all of my family that have gone to be with the Lord!! Hey, (fam) they are watching over us... and a special thanks to everyone. I am so proud that we are all honoring Ma's legacy and taking care of each other. She is definitely smiling down on each one of us!! Never forget.

To everyone that was instrumental in my life in any capacity,

Thank you so much. Just so you know, I couldn't mentioned everyone's name in my story, but I want you to know that you hold a very special place in my heart.

To the wonderful staff at Pride-Site 2-The Educational Alliance,
Located at 25 Avenue D, New York, New York 10009
212 780-5475 Ext. 308 For men and women.
Pride-Site 1-371 East 10th Street, New York, New York 10009
212 533-2470 Ext. 212

I couldn't have done it without all of you making my life a living hell (lol), and loving us at the same time. Mr. Carl Feinman (my Social Worker), if I ever could have had a white father, you know you would have been "that dude". Seriously, I owe it all to you! Thank you for putting up with me. I don't know what I would have done without you there going through it with me, making me laugh. Helping me to be the best Sherry I can be. I would never have pursued a career as a social worker if it weren't for you and I will always love you. Leona, love you so much!

To my Samaritan Village Family,

To the staff Suzette, Jacqueline, John, Eddie, and everyone else, thank you for everything, and all of your prayers. Even though all the client's that were there in 2005-'07 (better be gone by now), here's the "shout-out" that I promised you. Thanks for encouraging me to finish "A Fire Within". Hope you guys get a chance to read it one day! Mosby, you have been such an inspiration. You keep on doing your thing and being a blessing to everyone whose life you touch.

To the Drug Treatment Court Program,

Gloria, I can't thank you enough for being such a blessing to me and my family. You were so much more than my employer, you are a great woman and friend. Tom, "old man" you are the best. You encouraged me when you didn't even know it. Your ability to keep it together during the most difficult challenges amazes me. I'm praying for our lil man, as always. Marlene, hope your knee is doing good, you are the best. To everyone at DTCP, Tee & Alisha love you. Thank you guys so much for always being there for me. Just like I promised here's the "shout-out" to all of the wonderful clients who encouraged me to finish "A Fire Within", blessings to all of you. To the clients who graduated, congratulations and keep taking it "One Day at a Time" and those of you who graduated and relapsed you have the tools to succeed, use them. Get back in treatment and get the help you know you still need.

To my WellStar Family,

To everyone in Pod 1, 2 and especially POD 3, Love you all. Steve you have been a tremendous blessing in my life, I will never forget you! Larry "Big Poppa" you are truly a good guy. I love you for all of our conversations, thank you for motivating me. Give our girl a big hug for me. "Angels are covering her always". Scott (N.Y is in the house), from day one that I walked into the E.R., you were my Night in Shining Armor. Thank you so much for just being real. I love you!! To all of the girls & guys in all of WS E.R.'s. there are way too many for me to write, just know that I love all of our late night laughs. To all of my fellow Assessors & Therapists, you guys have made working at WS such a pleasure. Thanks for welcoming me aboard.

To my "big sis" Linda G. in the CC,

You have no idea how much our late night prayers, readings & laughter mean to me. I have learned so much from watching & listening to you. Thanks from the bottom of my heart!

To LaShawn, my friend,

We were both working that night when we first met at WS Kennestone Hospital and from the very first time we talked, I knew God had put you in my life for a divine purpose. You are an awesome woman of God and I am so glad to have you in my life. Love you!!

To my Peachford Family,

Thank you so much for welcoming me aboard!

To Dr. Jones and Professor Myricks,

Thank you from the bottom of my heart. You both have been there for me on numerous occasions. Whenever I call you are there. I love you for it!!

To JoAnn

Thank you for being a wonderful neighbor and friend! We appreciate you so much and so does Shadow!

Laura Darling,

I want to say thank you from the bottom of my heart. Thank you so much for thinking about me, when you were in the Spotlight. You have no idea how grateful I am for what you have done to help me. Connecting me with this awesome Woman of God is such a blessing to me and I can't thank you enough. Who would have thought God would use a little, crazy (lol), Jewish girl from Queens, to be such a tremendous blessing in my life.

And to the awesome Ms. Lady Rhonda Knight...

We were put together by a Divine Appointment and I don't take it for granted. God uses people to be a blessing in our lives and you have absolutely blessed me with your gift to motivate and lift people up. Thank you so much for publishing my baby, "A Fire Within". Thank you for all of our conversations throughout the process and most of all, thank you for seeing my Vision. We are both Survivors, and I thank God, He saved us both and brought us together for a purpose so that we can tell our story and be a blessing to others. Love you!!

Note from the Publisher... It has been my absolute pleasure in meeting you and working with you on your vision and baby. You are on your way to your destiny and purpose, young lady. God has a master plan for you, and He knew before the foundation of the earth, that you would accept the calling. I want you to soar high above the clouds, where you can see everything God wants to reveal to you. See yourself as that eagle pictured on your dedication page, strong, focused, determined, but yet carefree and trusting in its journey.

You've known since you were a child, that you are special, and that's how God sees you too and so do I Sherry, my new friend for life... Humbly embrace it

He is blessing you in this season, reap your harvest. **Jeremiah 29:11**,
"For I know the thoughts that I think toward you, saith the LORD, thoughts of peace, and not of evil, to give you an expected end" (KJV).

Love you too Sherry and Laura, kisses, I love you too!

Love Letters from My Family

To the love of my life; from your Babe, Dorian…

Phenomenal Woman

Pretty women wonder where my secret lies.
I'm not cute or built to suit a fashion model's size
But when I start to tell them,
They think I'm telling lies.
I say,
It's in the reach of my arms
The span of my hips,
The stride of my step,
The curl of my lips.
I'm a woman
Phenomenally.
Phenomenal woman,
That's Sherry.

She walks into a room
Just as cool as she pleases,
And to a man,
The fellows stand or
Fall down on their knees.
Then they swarm around her,
A hive of honey bees.
I say,
It's the fire in her eyes,
And the flash of her teeth,

A FIRE WITHIN

The swing in her waist,
And the joy in her feet.
She's a woman
Phenomenally.
Phenomenal woman,
That's Sherry.

Men themselves have wondered
What they see in her.
They try so much
But they can't touch
Her inner mystery.
When she tries to show them
They say they still can't see.
She says,
It's in the arch of my back,
The sun of my smile,
The rise of my breasts,
The grace of my style.
She's a woman

Phenomenally.
Phenomenal woman,
That's Sherry.

Now you understand
Just why her head's not bowed.
She don't shout or jump about
Or have to talk real loud.
When you hear her passing
It ought to make you proud.
She says,
It's in the click of my heels,
The bend of my hair,
the palm of my hand,
The need of my care,
'Cause I'm a woman
Phenomenally.
Phenomenal woman,
That's my Sherry.

Maya Angelou wrote it, especially for my Babe

A Mother's Prayer

Receive the blessing that is the "Fire Within"

1 Corinthians 3:13-16

Every man's work shall be made manifest; for the day shall declare it, because it shall be revealed by fire; and the fire shall try every man's work of what sort it is. If any man's work abide which he hath built thereupon, he shall receive a reward. If any man's work shall be burned, he shall suffer loss, but he himself shall be saved, yet as by fire...Know ye not that ye are the temple of God, and that the Spirit of God dwelleth in you?

"I went through fire and through the water, but God brought me out into a wealthy place"

I am Sherry Graves mother... I remember the day I got the call that my child was in a fire and it was critical. I screamed the scream that only a mother can, hearing that one of her children had been hurt and in such a way. I was in the Caribbean at the time and when I got that call, I didn't waste any time in getting a plane out of there to get to New York to be with Sherry and the family. I Thank God for a family like ours. They were there for her before I got there. From grandparents, brother, sisters, cousins, all the family was there, praying and keeping the vigil.

When I got to New York and went to the hospital and saw my Sherry, the burns were extensive, and the doctors were doing all they could to save her life. After she was stable, they started the grafting of her skin from various parts of her body, to cover the areas that were burned. That started the life giving efforts to save and preserve my daughter's body. For some reason when I saw the bandages and the burns on her body, I feared like every one feared the worse, but I hoped for the best, knowing that only God could bring her out of this. I trusted that he would do a good work in her. I believed she would recover and get healed. We never lost faith. There was so much love around her from her family and friends, even the Doctors, Nurses and staff, she had to get better. By the Grace of God she did recover, with the family by her side and her will to live.

She remembers those times, especially her grandfather who took her to all her appointments after getting out of the hospital, and waited with her no matter how long it took for her Rehabilitation. It surprised her that he did that for her, but like he said why wouldn't he do it for her. Her grandmother was also a blessing during her ordeal. I give thanks our family who stood by Sherry during those times, giving her encouragement, being there for her, praying for her, uplifting her spirit, helping to make her every bit whole. Yes God is truly good, and so are those we know and love. We especially give God the Glory.

As time went by Sherry got better. Her scars were there to remind her of the days when she walked outside of God's will for her life, when she was doing her thing which led her into the way of the world, but the Lord had greater plans for her life. I have seen her go from a recluse who hid behind shirts with high collars and long sleeves to hide her scares from the world, to someone who now see with the eyes of Spirit, who is not afraid to show her scars. It has not been easy, there were time of stress, painful reminders, and regression, but Sherry's faith only got stronger. She had the help of her relationships, which were and are a source of strength and encouragement. She started going to church, which helped renew her resolve to get better inside and out. Going back to school, then college has been one of the gifts that God has given her for her trials, and trust that he was there for her and now she is on the road to being, and doing what is her God given purpose in life. There is now a source of freedom to say, "I know you see my scars, but God sees my heart." I see my child now walking in the Spirit. Her scars have become second nature to her and has become a blessing, so much so that she has written this book of her trials to triumphs. She has become a blessing to me, and to so many other people whose lives she has touched through counseling, prayer and her giving nature.

In recent times Sherry and I have had conversations about what happen that night. We have spoken about the fire, how she thinks it happen, and what happened at that time. She remembers the circumstance surrounding what happened, but what she remembers most of all is while the fire was raging around them, calling out for help, and feeling the presence of a covering her, keeping her from death. The firemen seem led to where she was huddling under a window, and came to where she was at the right time. We know and believe that could only have been God keeping her safe. The Holy Spirit surrounded her with protection, and Jesus' love keeping her for such a time as this to tell her story, and be a blessing to the world. She was not in the fire by herself, her boyfriend Josh was also in this horrific fire. They later married, he died years later, but Thank God Sherry has survived to tell their story. Through the depression and the pain she has come forth as pure gold. The memories are no less hurtful, that someone would be so hateful to do such a thing, but God has a way of making all things right. In **Isaiah 43: 18-19**, "Remember ye not the former things, neither consider the things of old. Behold I will do a new thing; now it shall spring forth; shall ye not know it? I will even make a way in the wilderness, and rivers in the desert."

It is not by chance that Sherry is alive to telling this victorious story about her life experience. It is supposed to be a blessing, a praise report of what God can do even in a very bad situation. God kept her and Josh safe during the fire. The Lord protected and bought her out to tell this remarkable redemption story of how we can all go from the pit to the palace; from drugs and other substance abuse, to healing of our minds, bodies, and souls; to be faithful even in times of adversity. Through writing her experiences and letting the world know that with God all things are possible, Sherry has brought this into fruition. We thank God for the knowledge and his will and wisdom to uplift us in all circumstances and all situations. Sherry has always said God wanted her to tell about her experiences, to use it to be a blessing and inspire others. There are many out there who are going through similar situations, or worse. They need help, a word of encouragement, an example of what not to do, whether it is drugs, substance abuse of any kind, bad relationships, horrors that we know not of are being done to others every day. We can only hope and pray they have the will and the way to get out in time, and not be caught up into the world's way of living, becoming victims, whether through violence, hatred, or lack of knowledge. This is word to the wise, make that change that might save your life, become a victor, not a victim.

Sherry started out as a beautiful child, got caught up in worldly things, but has become a beautiful spiritual woman, on the journey of life. She is anointed, and appointed to tell her story, a story filled with ups and downs. "Now we see in a mirror darkly, but then we shall see face to face" as the Lord's word says. Her scars has only helped to show the world that beauty comes from within, when you have the beauty of Spirit, peace in your soul, and love in your heart for God and believe in his word. To paraphrase our Pastor, Bishop Dale C. Bronner of Word of Faith here in Austell, GA., "When you realize why God put you here, you passionately know your purpose. Whatever gives light must endure burning. Dare to believe God even in the face of adversity. Out of pain comes purpose."

This book I believe is pleasing in God's sight. It's a journey, her own red sea experience that has bought her to her promise land. Open your minds, hearts and spirit to God's grace and love through the experience of a woman whose scars are a blessing to the world. Now Sherry is experiencing a different kind of fire, the fresh "Fire Within" to bless, heal and deliver other people, through the gifts and talents the Lord has given her. Sherry doesn't hesitate to give a prayer or a word of encouragement to others, to help build up lives and work to be a positive example to all whose lives she touches. She is truly a prayer warrior. I am proud of all my children, I am proud to be the mother of Sherry Graves. Like Sherry likes to say, "Our God is SO awesome." He truly is awesome, forgiving, loving and worthy to be praised. Through God's Grace receive the blessing that is the "Fire Within".

"Let the words of my mouth, and the meditation of my heart
Be acceptable in thy sight O Lord, my strength and my redeemer".
Ps. 19:14

Love letter to my sister from Jamel...

When a sister is more than a sister, when she is a friend, an advisor, and a source of pride... My sister is a blessing. I thank God for you Sherry. I thank God for all the love and support you have shown me. I remember the night you helped to change my life forever. I called you and I talked to you about all the stuff that was going on with me at that time in my life, living in New York. And I remember the words you said to me that sparked the transformation in my life you said, "Just come to Georgia, and I got you". And ever since you said those words to me, my life has been blessed in so many ways. So, I would like to let the world know that you are more than just my little sister, you are an example of what it means to be a Woman of God. And I am so proud to call you MY sister...

Love you always, Jamel!!

Love letter to my sis, from Colette...

My sister, my friend, my confidant, I am so proud of you. I look at you and see a strong, motivated, determined, caring person and I admire your soul and your spirit. It's amazing for me to see all that you have accomplished. I have seen the worse and the best of this entire journey of yours. One of our biggest moments was taking you hand in hand to Pride-Site, that was the first step to the rest of your life. I watched as you struggled with your burns and I struggled with you. At that time you could not see past your scars, but even though you could not see past them, I did. I watched you slowly come out of what I like to call your "scar shell". I remember the day when you embraced them. And after all the pain you have lived with all of these years now, you have learned how to use your situation to become the woman you are. Today, I can see so far beyond your burns, it's as if they are not even there, you are so beautiful. You have overcome so many obstacles and I have watched in awe the way you have turned your life around in such a profound way. You continue to amaze me Sherry, I have seen you go from a drug abuser, to almost losing your life in the fire, to a college graduate, to a Substance Abuse Social Worker and now to an Author but most of all you are my sister. You inspire me. Words could barely describe my feelings about you. This book is such a huge accomplishment for you Sherry. I am proud of you girl!

I love you……your Sis

Love letter to my sister Sherry, from your younger sister Shana...

When my sister Sherry called me and asked me to write something about a day I wish had never even occurred I was so happy to do it for her. But I didn't know that writing the letter would bring back all of those feelings that I had inside me the day I got that horrible, horrible phone call, but it did. I can't believe that after all of these years, it still traumatizes me. Just having to remember the day now as I am writing, I am feeling the anxiety and remembering how scary the whole thing was. Even now I can only remember certain parts of what happened. I was only 13 years old at the time, but the one thing that I will never forget was that I was home alone, everyone was at work. And when I answered that telephone call and the person said, Sherry was in a fire and she died. When they said that my sister was in a fire and she died, then they just hung up the phone like that. I can't even begin to explain what it felt like. It was my sister's boyfriend at the time that called. I almost felt as if I had stopped breathing. I remember grabbing on to the wall and crying and I couldn't stop. And right after that, he calls back and I can hear a lot of noise and people in the background and I heard my sister scream out my name, her voice sounded scratchy and hoarse and all I could think was, "Thank God, she's alive". I don't even remember hanging up the phone. All I could do is sit at the top of the stairs, waiting for someone, anyone to come home, crying and praying. And when my sister Colette finally came home, I only felt a slight relief even then. After my sister came home from the hospital, she had to deal with her recovery which I think is something that she is still doing day by day. But she goes through it with God and she does it so gracefully. She is my **shero**!! Thank you God for allowing my sister to be a survivor and for her to be able to help people by speaking to them about what she's been through.

"10 Jewels for my Readers" to help you get through...

Women are a precious gift from God to the world. We are creative, sensitive, compassionate, intelligent and talented.

Jewel #1-

"A Confident Woman" by Joyce Meyer

What is confidence? I believe confidence is all about being positive concerning what you can do and not worrying over what you can't do. A confident person is open to learning, because she knows that her confidence allows her to walk through life's doorways, eager to discover what waits on the other side. She knows that every new unknown is a change to learn more about herself and unleash her abilities.

Confident people do not concentrate on their weaknesses; they develop and maximize their strengths. So, what are your strengths?

Jewel #2-

Take a day to heal from the lies you've told yourself and the ones that have been told to you.

There comes a time when we have to pause to listen to what we are telling ourselves. "I'm so stupid", "I'm broke", "I don't know how", "I can't take it anymore...". Yet in the midst of our dishonest chatter, we are making great strides, accomplishing many tasks, overcoming seemingly insurmountable odds. We can't see it because we keep lying to ourselves. We lie because we've been lied to. "You're no good", "You can't do it", "You'll never make it" or "How do you think you're gonna do that...". We can't think because there are so many lies running loose in our minds. The only way to eradicate a lie is with the truth. We must not only speak the truth, we must think in truth. The truth is, we start from a place where success is born, in the mind's eye of the Most High. The truth is that no one has ever made a true deal with the Master and lost.

The truth springs forth from my mind...Maya Angelou

STOP!

Jewel #3-

Most of us know exactly what it is that creates the pain, confusion, stagnation and disruption in our lives. Whether it is a habit, behavior, relationship or fear, we know. Unfortunately, we seem powerless to stop whatever it is. Sometimes we believe we don't have the discipline or willpower to stop. The behavior becomes so habitual we do it without thinking. Other times we know exactly what it is and what we do, but we simply keep doing it anyway. We are the only ones responsible for what goes on in our lives. We can make excuses and blame others, but we are responsible to and for ourselves. When we find something or someone creating in our lives that which we do not want, we must muster the courage and strength to stop it.

Today I use my power to stop what is no longer good to me…

Iyanla Vanzant

Jewel #4-

Everything that happens to us, and every choice we make, is a reflection of what we believe about ourselves. We cannot draw to ourselves more than we believe we are worth. The things we believe and say about ourselves come back to us in many ways. Self-motivation comes from self-knowledge. We must inspire ourselves by believing we have the power to accomplish everything we set out to do. We must put faith in our ability to use mind and spirit and picture our lives the way we want them to be. We must use inner strength and the power of our being to tear down the walls, break through the barriers and move through the obstacles with ease. Our bodies have been freed. Now we must train our minds to believe it.

Iyanla Vanzant

Jewel #5-

Everyone has something they are ashamed of, afraid of or that they feel guilty about. Each of us in our own way will devise a neat little method of handling it. Some of us deny. Some of us blame. Some of us do a combination of both. Undoubtedly the day will come when we will be forced to examine that which we have tucked away. We can willingly begin the process of examination by telling the truth to ourselves about ourselves.

We all have the right to make mistakes. Our fault is being righteous about it. When we fail to admit our faults, the faults become what everyone can see. When we refuse to admit what we have done in the past, we block our path to the future. No matter how terrible we think we are, how bad we believe we have been, how low we think we have fallen, we can clean out our minds and begin again.

Iyanla Vanzant

Jewel #6-

A minister once said, "On the seventh day God rested". He said, "It is good and very good." Then we come along and try to improve on perfection. One of the most damaging habits is trying to be who and what we are not. We expend so much energy trying to fix who we are, we rarely get to really know ourselves. If we truly realized how precious the gift of life is, we would not waste a moment trying to improve it. If we really understood how precious we are to the gift of life, we would not waste time trying to

fix ourselves. It's not about what we look like or what we have. It's not about fixing our face, body or lives. It's about taking what we have and doing as much as we can with it. It's about learning and growing. When we are willing to learn what we don't know and use our experiences, our perfection will begin to show.

Iyanla Vanzant

Jewel #7-

The most difficult things to face in life are the things you do not like about yourself. Not your ears, legs, hair or those habits and abilities you feel are not up to par. It is the ugly little things you know about yourself that need a good long look. You recognize it when you see it in others, but you make excuses for yourself. You may go to any length to cover a shortcoming, while you quickly point out the ills of another. Since the very thing you want to hide is the thing that shows itself, you need to be able to say, "I know that and I'm working on it!" It takes a loving heart, a willing mind and a sensitive spirit to get to the core of the self. But when you do, you can root out the seeds of ugliness.

Iyanla Vanzant

Jewel #8-

When you concern yourself with doing only what others "think" you can do, you lay the floor of your prison. When you conform your activities based on what others might say, you put the bars around your prison. When you allow what others have done or are doing to determine what you can do, you build the roof of your prison. When you allow fear, competition or greed to guide your actions, you lock yourself up and throw away the key. It is our concern over what others say, do and think about us that imprisons our mind, body and spirit.

What other people think about me is not my concern.

Iyanla Vanzant

Jewel #9-

There are times when we feel bad about ourselves, what we've done and what we are facing. In these moments we may even believe we deserve to be punished, because we are "bad" or have done bad things. There are times when we feel so low, we convince ourselves that we don't matter and neither does anything or anyone else. That is when we usually start to think about God. Is there such a thing? Does God really care? Maybe if we had gone to God before, we wouldn't be where we are now. No matter. We're here, so let's go. This is a prime opportunity to make a new start, begin again and move on. The key is to remember that no matter where we've been, what we've done or how awful we feel right now, the One we may be running from knows exactly where we are. He has placed a light of peace in our hearts. A Prayer will flip the switch.

In our deepest hour of need the Creator asks for no credentials:

Iyanla Vanzant

Jewel #10-

We all get to a point where we feel confused and indecisive. We can't seem to figure out what we want or what to do. We want everything, but nothing brings satisfaction. Our spirit is restless because the mind is racing. It may not be that we don't know, it is probably that we are afraid to ask. We may feel as if we are running to something, but actually we are running away. In those times we need to sit down, get still and evaluate just what it is we want. We must do this quietly, honestly and often, if necessary. We are human beings, blessed with the power of reason. We have, at all times, the right and the power to figure out what we want. Once that's done, we must have the courage to ask for it. If we let the color of our skin, the gender we express or the ways of the world limit us, we will forever be denied. We owe it to ourselves to choose a way and ask for it. Once we ask, we can rest.

Iyanla Vanzant

> I offer these jewels to assist in the redevelopment of your minds, bodies and spirits. Use these jewels to dig up the secrets so that they can be put to use. You can use these jewels to accomplish a goal: stress-free, peace-filled living. You must be willing to accept that stress is the result of unfinished business. Stress will not go away until you decide it no longer has a place in your life. Obstacles and challenges will not stop until your perception of them changes. Difficulties and disappointments may not cease, yet you can see them in a different light, with a new sense of knowing; everything in life is purposeful.

Buried deep in the earth are precious diamonds. In order to get them, however, we must dig and dig deep. Once we get to the foundation rock, we must apply pressure to shape and mold the diamond. It is not the digging, it is the pressure that makes diamonds. Softness is what marshmallows are made of. Soft, sweet, easy to squish under pressure and no good for anybody. You are being challenged to decide what you want to be, a diamond or a marshmallow, wait, I think I see a **sparkle** in your eye! The pressure is on, the healing has begun! May the glow from the sparkle in your eye bring light to all the world.

Iyanla Vanzant

CHAPTER 29

"THE STRAIGHT FACTS ABOUT DRUGS"

"I believe that increased understanding of the basics of addiction will empower people to make informed choices in their own lives".

What is Drug Addiction?

Drug addiction is a complex, and often chronic, brain disease. It is characterized by compulsive drug craving, seeking and use that can persist even in the face of devastating life consequences. It is considered a brain disease because drugs change the brain, they change its structure and how it works. Addiction results largely from brain changes that stem from prolonged drug use. Changes that involve multiple brain circuits, including those responsible for governing self-control and other behaviors (NIDA, 2012). Drug addiction is treatable, often with medications (for some addictions) combined with behavioral therapies. However, relapse is common and can happen even after long periods of abstinence, underscoring the need for long-term support and care. Relapse does not signify treatment failure, but rather should prompt treatment re-engagement or modification.

Abuse and addiction to alcohol, nicotine, and illegal substances cost Americans upwards of half a trillion dollars a year, considering their combined medical, economic, criminal, and social impact. Every year, abuse of illicit drugs and alcohol contributes to the death of more than 100,000 Americans, while tobacco is linked to an estimated 440,000 deaths per year.

Drugs, Brains, and Behavior: The Science of Addiction-

An Article from the National Institute on Drug Abuse (NIDA), (2012)
Drugs and the Brain

Introducing the Human Brain:

The human brain is the most complex organ in the body. This three pound mass of gray and white matter sits at the center of all human activity. You need it to drive a car, to enjoy a meal, to breathe, to create an artistic masterpiece, and to enjoy everyday activities. In brief, the brain regulates your basic body functions; enables you to interpret and respond to everything you experience; and shapes your thoughts, emotions, and behavior.

The brain is made up of many parts that all work together as a team. Different parts of the brain are responsible for coordinating and performing specific functions. Drugs can alter important brain areas that are necessary for life-sustaining functions and can drive the compulsive drug abuse that marks addiction. Brain areas affected by drug abuse:

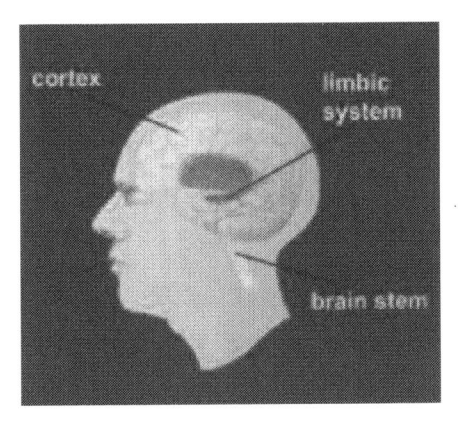

- **The brain stem** controls basic functions critical to life, such as heart rate, breathing, and sleeping.
- **The limbic system** contains the brain's reward circuit - it links together a number of brain structures that control and regulate our ability to feel pleasure. Feeling pleasure motivates us to repeat behaviors such as eating - actions that are critical to our existence. The limbic system is activated when we perform these activities - and also by drugs of abuse. In addition, the limbic system is responsible for our perception of other emotions, both positive and negative, which explains the mood-altering properties of many drugs.
- **The cerebral cortex** is divided into areas that control specific functions. Different areas process information from our senses, enabling us to see, feel, hear, and taste. The front part of the cortex, the frontal cortex or forebrain, is the thinking center of the brain; it powers our ability to think, plan, solve problems, and make decisions.

How does the brain communicate?

The brain is a communications center consisting of billions of neurons, or nerve cells. Networks of neurons pass messages back and forth to different structures within the brain, the spinal column, and the peripheral nervous system. These nerve networks coordinate and regulate everything we feel, think, and do (NIDA,2012).

- **Neuron to Neuron**
  Each nerve cell in the brain sends and receives messages in the form of electrical impulses. Once a cell receives and processes a message, it sends it on to other neurons.
- **Neurotransmitters - The Brain's Chemical Messengers**
  The messages are carried between neurons by chemicals called neurotransmitters. (They transmit messages between neurons.)
- **Receptors - The Brain's Chemical Receivers**
  The neurotransmitter attaches to a specialized site on the receiving cell called a receptor. A neurotransmitter and its receptor operate like a "key and lock," an exquisitely specific mechanism that ensures that each receptor will forward the appropriate message only after interacting with the right kind of neurotransmitter.
- **Transporters - The Brain's Chemical Recyclers**
  Located on the cell that releases the neurotransmitter, transporters recycle these neurotransmitters (i.e., bringing them back into the cell that released them), thereby shutting off the signal between neurons.

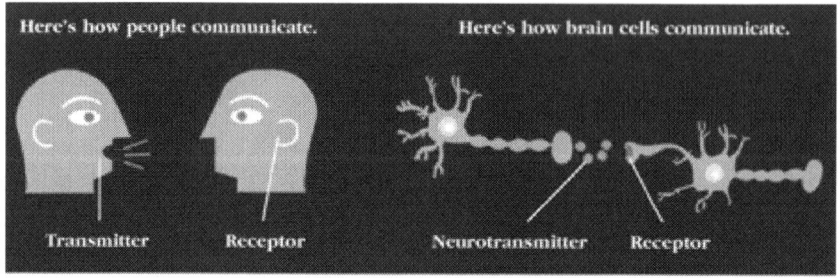

Here's how people communicate. | Here's how brain cells communicate.
Transmitter | Receptor | Neurotransmitter | Receptor

Concept courtesy: B.K. Madras

To send a message a brain cell releases a chemical (neurotransmitter) into the space separating two cells called the synapse. The neurotransmitter crosses the synapse and attaches to proteins (receptors) on the receiving brain cell. This causes changes in the receiving brain cell and the message is delivered.

Most drugs of abuse target the brain's reward system by flooding the circuit with dopamine.

How do drugs work in the brain?

Drugs are chemicals. They work in the brain by tapping into the brain's communication system and interfering with the way nerve cells normally send, receive, and process information. Some drugs, such as marijuana and heroin, can activate neurons because their chemical structure mimics that of a natural neurotransmitter. This similarity in structure "fools" receptors and allows the drugs to lock onto and activate the nerve cells. Although these drugs mimic brain chemicals, they don't activate nerve cells in the same way as a natural neurotransmitter, and they lead to abnormal messages being transmitted through the network.

Other drugs, such as amphetamine or cocaine, can cause the nerve cells to release abnormally large amounts of natural neurotransmitters or prevent the normal recycling of these brain chemicals. This disruption produces a greatly amplified message, ultimately disrupting communication channels. The difference in effect can be described as the difference between someone whispering into your ear and someone shouting into a microphone.

How do drugs work in the brain to produce pleasure?

Most drugs of abuse directly or indirectly target the brain's reward system by flooding the circuit with dopamine. Dopamine is a neurotransmitter present in regions of the brain that regulate movement, emotion, cognition, motivation, and feelings of pleasure. The overstimulation of this system, which rewards our natural behaviors, produces the euphoric effects sought by people who abuse drugs and teaches them to repeat the behavior.

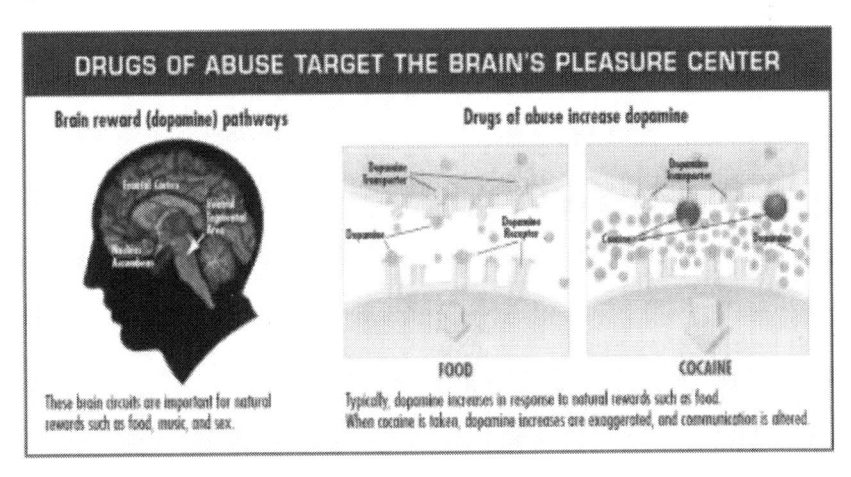

Why do people take drugs?

In general, people begin taking drugs for a variety of reasons:

- **To feel good.** Most abused drugs produce intense feelings of pleasure. This initial sensation of euphoria is followed by other effects, which differ with the type of drug used. For example, with stimulants such as cocaine, the "high" is followed by feelings of power, self-confidence, and increased energy. In contrast, the euphoria caused by opiates such as heroin is followed by feelings of relaxation and satisfaction.
- **To feel better.** Some people who suffer from social anxiety, stress-related disorders, and depression begin abusing drugs in an attempt to lessen feelings of distress. Stress can play a major role in beginning drug use, continuing drug abuse, or relapse in patients recovering from addiction.
- **To do better.** The increasing pressure that some individuals feel to chemically enhance or improve their athletic or cognitive performance can similarly play a role in initial experimentation and continued drug abuse.
- **Curiosity and "because others are doing it."** In this respect adolescents are particularly vulnerable because of the strong influence of peer pressure; they are more likely, for example, to engage in "thrilling" and "daring" behaviors.

If taking drugs makes people feel good or better, what's the problem?

At first, people may perceive what seem to be positive effects with drug use. They also may believe that they can control their use; however, drugs can quickly take over their lives. Consider how a social drinker can become intoxicated, put himself behind a wheel and quickly turn a pleasurable activity into a tragedy for him and others. Over time, if drug use continues, pleasurable activities become less pleasurable, and drug abuse becomes necessary for abusers to simply feel "normal."

Drug abusers reach a point where they seek and take drugs, despite the tremendous problems caused for themselves and their loved ones. Some individuals may start to feel the need to take higher or more frequent doses, even in the early stages of their drug use.

References
The National Institute on Drug Abuse (NIDA) the Science of Drug Abuse & Addiction, (2012).

A FIRE WITHIN

People of all ages suffer the harmful consequences of drug abuse and addiction.

- **Babies** exposed to legal and illegal drugs in the womb may be born premature and underweight. This drug exposure can slow the child's intellectual development and affect behavior later in life.
- **Adolescents** who abuse drugs often act out, do poorly academically, and drop out of school. They are at risk of unplanned pregnancies, violence, and infectious diseases.
- **Adults** who abuse drugs often have problems thinking clearly, remembering, and paying attention. They often develop poor social behaviors as a result of their drug abuse, and their work performance and personal relationships suffer.
- **Parents'** drug abuse often means chaotic, stress-filled Holmes and child abuse and neglect. Such conditions harm the well-being and development of children in the home and may set the stage for drug abuse in the next generation.

Signs That Someone May Have a Drug or Alcohol Problem

Diagnosis is important in general because it helps doctors to know how to treat a problem. The diagnosis of a substance use problem (abuse or dependence) is important because it helps justify getting an addicted person into treatment. Getting an addict to the point where a substance abuse or dependence diagnosis can be made is often a difficult task. People with drug and alcohol problems are often secretive about their use, or blind to the idea that a problem exists. It is helpful then to have a list of behaviors that one can look for that, when present, may suggest that someone has a substance use problem.

Behaviors to look for include:

- A repeating failure to meet social, occupational or familial duties;
- Repeated lateness or absence
- Poor work performance
- Neglect of children
- Bizarre or lame excuses for social, occupational or family failures
- Borrowing (or stealing) money without good reasons
- Uncharacteristic mood or personality changes

Physical signs may include:

- Puncture marks, or long thin lines along the arms or legs (IV drug use such as heroin)
- Skin Infections
- Nose and throat problems (snorted drugs such as cocaine)
- Bloody nose
- Coughing
- Loss of the sense of smell
- Drowsiness, or loss of coordination (depressant drugs such as alcohol)
- 'Pinned' (tiny constricted) pupils in the eye (secondary to opioid abuse)
- Eye movement disturbances
- Red or bloodshot eyes (secondary to smoking marijuana)
- Drug-related smells on clothing (drugs that are smoked)
- Drug-related paraphernalia (pipes, 'works', pill bottles, small plastic or vials, lighters, etc.)

Medical signs (only apparent upon formal testing) may include:

- Positive findings of drug related metabolic (break-down) byproducts in the urine, blood, hair
- Hypertension (High Blood Pressure) may point to alcoholism
- Elevated levels of the liver enzyme 'delta-glutamic transferase' (GGT) may point to alcoholism)
- Enlarged red blood cells (may point to alcoholism)

References:

The National Institute on Drug Abuse (NIDA) The Science of Drug Abuse & Addiction, (2012).

What is Substance Dependence?

Substance dependence, commonly called **drug addiction** is defined as a drug user's compulsive need to use controlled substances in order to function normally. When such substances are unobtainable, the user suffers from substance withdrawal.

Substance Dependence:

According to the DSM-IV- The essential feature of Substance Dependence is a cluster of cognitive, behavioral, and physiological symptoms indicating that the individual continues use of the substance despite significant substance-related problems. There is a pattern of repeated self-administration that can result in tolerance, withdrawal, and compulsive drug-taking behavior. A diagnosis of Substance Dependence can be applied to every class of substances except caffeine. The symptoms of Dependence are similar across the various categories of substances, but for certain classes some symptoms are less salient, and in a few instances not all symptoms apply (e.g., withdrawal symptoms are not specified for Hallucinogen Dependence). Although not specifically listed as a criterion item, "craving" (a strong subjective drive to use the substance) is likely to be experienced by most (if not all) individuals with Substance Dependence.

Criteria for Substance Dependence

A maladaptive pattern of substance use, leading to clinically significant impairment or distress, as manifested by three (or more) of the following, occurring at any time in the same 12-month period:

(1) tolerance, as defined by either of the following:

  (a) a need for markedly increased amounts of the substance to achieve intoxication or desired effect

  (b) markedly diminished effect with continued use of the same amount of the substance

(2) withdrawal, as manifested by either of the following:

  (a) the characteristic withdrawal syndrome for the substance (refer to Criteria A and B of the criteria sets for Withdrawal from the specific substances)

  (b) the same (or a closely related) substance is taken to relieve or avoid withdrawal symptoms

(3) the substance is often taken in larger amounts or over a longer period than was intended (e.g., continuing to drink until severely intoxication despite having set a limit of only one drink).

(4) there is a persistent desire or unsuccessful efforts to cut down or control substance use. Often there have been many unsuccessful efforts to decrease or discontinue use.

(5) a great deal of time is spent in activities necessary to obtain the substance (e.g., visiting multiple doctors or driving long distances), use the substance (e.g., chain-smoking), or recover from its effects. In some instances of Substance Dependence, virtually all of the person's daily activities revolve around the substance.

(6) important social, occupational, or recreational activities are given up or reduced because of substance use. The individual may withdraw from family activities and hobbies in order to use the substance in private or to spend more time with substance-abusing friends.

(7) the substance use is continued despite knowledge of having a persistent or recurrent physical or psychological problem that is likely to have been caused or exacerbated by the substance (e.g., current cocaine use despite recognition of cocaine-induced depression, or continued drinking despite recognition that an ulcer was made worse by alcohol consumption).

What is Substance Abuse?

Substance abuse can be defined as a pattern of harmful use of any substance for mood-altering purposes. Medline's medical encyclopedia defines drug abuse as "the use of illicit drugs or the abuse of prescription or over-the-counter drugs for purposes other than those for which they are indicated or in a manner or in quantities other than directed

Substance Abuse:

According to the DSM-IV- the essential feature of Substance Abuse is a maladaptive pattern of substance use manifested by recurrent and significant adverse consequences related to the repeated use of substances. In order for an Abuse criterion to be met, the substance-related problem must have occurred repeatedly during the same 12-month period or been persistent.

Criteria for Substance Abuse

A. A maladaptive pattern of substance use leading to clinically significant impairment or distress, as manifested by one (or more) of the following, occurring within a 12-month period:

   (1) recurrent substance use resulting in a failure to fulfill major role obligations at work, school, or home (e.g., repeated absences or poor work performance related to substance use; substance-related absences, suspensions, or expulsions from school; neglect of children or household)

   (2) recurrent substance use in situations in which it is physically hazardous (e.g., driving an automobile or operating a machine when impaired by substance use)

   (3) recurrent substance-related legal problems (e.g., arrests for substance-related disorderly conduct)

   (4) continued substance use despite having persistent or recurrent social or interpersonal problems caused or exacerbated by the effects of the substance (e.g., arguments with spouse about consequences of intoxication, physical fights)

B. The symptoms have never met the criteria for Substance Dependence for this class of substance.

Substance-Induced Disorders:

<u>Substance Intoxication:</u>

Substance Intoxication is often associated with Substance Abuse or Dependence. The most common changes involve disturbances of perception, wakefulness, attention, thinking, judgment, psychomotor behavior, and interpersonal behavior. The maladaptive nature of a substance-induced change in behavior depends on the social and environmental context. The maladaptive behavior generally places the individual at significant risk for adverse effects (e.g., accidents, general medical complications, disruption in social and family relationships, vocational or financial difficulties, legal problems). Signs and symptoms of intoxication may sometimes persist for hours or days beyond the time when the substance is detectable in body fluids.

Criteria for Substance Intoxication:

A. The development of a reversible substance-specific syndrome due to recent ingestion of (or exposure to) a substance.

B. Clinically significant maladaptive behavioral or psychological changes that are due to the effect of the substance on the central nervous system (e.g., belligerence, mood lability, cognitive impairment, impaired judgment, impaired social or occupational functioning) and develop during or shortly after use of the substance.

C. The symptoms are not due to a general medical condition and are not better accounted for by another mental disorder.

Substance Withdrawal:

The essential feature of Substance Withdrawal is the development of substance-specific maladaptive behavioral change, with physiological and cognitive concomitants.

Criteria for Substance Withdrawal:

A. The development of a substance-specific syndrome that is due to the cessation of (or reduction in) heavy and prolonged substance use.

B. The substance-specific syndrome causes clinically significant distress or impairment in social, occupational, or other important areas of functioning.

C. The symptoms are not due to a general medical condition and are not better accounted for by another mental disorder.

Tolerance:

Is the need for greatly increased amounts of the substance to achieve intoxication (or the desired effect) or a markedly diminished effect with continued use of the same amount of the substance. The degree to which tolerance develops varies greatly across substances.

Withdrawal:

Is a maladaptive behavioral change, with physiological and cognitive concomitants, that occurs when blood or tissue concentrations of a substance decline in an individual who had maintained prolonged heavy use of substances. After developing unpleasant withdrawal symptoms, the person is likely to take the substance throughout the day beginning soon after awakening.

References:

Diagnostic and Statistical Manual of Mental Disorders, Fourth Edition, Text Revision (pgs. 191-202, 2000).

Cocaine-Use Disorders

Drug Class: Stimulants

Street Names: coke, blow, snow, rock (cocaine).

Cocaine is a powerfully addictive central nervous system stimulant that is snorted, injected, or smoked. Crack is cocaine hydrochloride powder that has been processed to form a rock crystal that is then usually smoked.

Cocaine Dependence

Cocaine has extremely potent euphoric effects, and individuals exposed to it can develop dependence after using the drug for very short periods of time. An early sign of Cocaine Dependence is when the individual finds it increasingly difficult to resist using cocaine whenever it is available. Because of its short half-life of about 30-50 minutes, there is a need for frequent dosing to maintain a "high". Persons with Cocaine Dependence can spend extremely large amounts of money on the drug within a very short period of time. As a result, the person using the substance may become involved in theft, prostitution, or drug dealing. Important responsibilities such as work or child care may be grossly neglected to obtain or use cocaine.

Cocaine users can experience mental or physical complications of chronic use such as paranoid ideations, aggressive behavior, anxiety, depression, and weight loss are common. Regardless of the route of administration, tolerance occurs with repeated use. Withdrawal symptoms, particularly hypersomnia, increased appetite, and dysphoric mood, can be seen and are likely to enhance craving and the likelihood of relapse.

Cocaine Abuse

The intensity and frequency of cocaine administration is less in Cocaine Abuse as compared with dependence. Episodes of problematic use, neglect of responsibilities, and interpersonal conflict often occur around paydays or special occasions, resulting in a pattern of brief periods (hours to a few days) of high-dose use followed by much longer periods (weeks to months) of occasional, non-problematic use or abstinence. Legal difficulties may result from possession or use of the drug.

Cocaine Intoxication

The essential feature of Cocaine Intoxication is the presence of clinically significant maladaptive behavioral or psychological changes that develop during, or shortly after, use of cocaine. Cocaine Intoxication usually begins with a "high" feeling and includes one or more of the following: euphoria with enhanced vigor, gregariousness, hyperactivity, restlessness, hypervigilance, interpersonal sensitivity, talkativeness, anxiety, tension, alertness, grandiosity, stereotyped and repetitive behavior, anger, and impaired judgment, and in the case of chronic intoxication, affective blunting with fatigue or sadness and social withdrawal. These behavioral and psychological changes are accompanied by two or more of the following signs and symptoms that develop during or shortly after cocaine use: tachycardia or bradycardia, pupillary dilation; elevated or lower blood pressure; perspiration or chills; nausea or vomiting; evidence of weight loss; psychomotor agitation or retardation; muscular weakness, respiratory depression, chest pain, or cardiac arrhythmias; and confusion, seizures, dyskinesias, dystonias, or coma. Intoxication, either acute or chronic, is often associated with impaired social or occupational functioning. Severe intoxication can lead to convulsions, cardiac arrhythmias, hyperpyrexia, and death.

Cocaine Withdrawal

The essential feature of Cocaine Withdrawal is the presence of a characteristic withdrawal syndrome that develops within a few hours after the cessation of (or reduction in) cocaine use that has been heavy and prolonged. The withdrawal syndrome is characterized by the development of dysphoric mood accompanied by two or more of the following physiological changes: fatigue, vivid and unpleasant dreams, insomnia or hypersomnia, increased appetite, and psychomotor retardation or agitation. These symptoms cause clinically significant distress or impairment in social, occupational, or other important areas of functioning.

References

Diagnostic and Statistical Manual of Mental Disorders, Fourth Edition, Text Revision (pgs. 191-202, 2000).

Did you know that "Drugs Don't Discriminate"?

Specific Culture, Age, and Gender Features

Cocaine use affects all race, socioeconomic, age, and gender groups in the United States. Although the current cocaine epidemic started in the 1970's among more affluent individuals, it has shifted to include lower socioeconomic groups living in large metropolitan areas. Rural areas that previously had been spared the problems associated with illicit drug use have also been affected. Males are more commonly affected than females, with a male-to-female ratio of 1.5-2.0:1.

Prevalence

As with most drugs, the prevalence of cocaine use in the United States has fluctuated greatly over the years. After a peak in the 1970's the proportion of the population who have used cocaine in any of its forms gradually decreased until the early 1990s, after which the pace of diminution continued but at a slower rate of decline. A 1996 national survey of drug use reported that 10% of the population had ever used cocaine, with 2% of the population reporting lifetime use, 0.6% reporting use in the prior year, and 0.3% reporting use in the prior month. Individuals between ages 26 and 34 years reported the highest rates of lifetime use (21% for cocaine and 4% for crack) was 18-to 25-year-olds.

The Buzz: Cocaine causes a sense of energy, alertness, talkativeness, and well-being that users find pleasurable. At the same time, the user experiences signs of sympathetic nervous system stimulation, including increased heart rate and blood pressure and dilation of the bronchioles (breathing tubes) in the lungs. This drug also causes a stimulation of purposeful movement that is the reason for its description as a psychomotor stimulant. When injected or smoked, this drug causes an intense feeling of euphoria.

Overdoses and Other Bad Effects:

There are three kinds of dangers with stimulants. First and most important, at high doses death can result. High-dose cocaine use can lead to seizures, sudden cardiac death, stroke, or failure of breathing. The second kind of danger is psychiatric. With repeated use of high doses of stimulants over days to weeks, a psychotic state of hostility and paranoia can emerge that cannot be distinguished from paranoid schizophrenia. Finally, profound addiction can develop to any stimulant.

Dangerous Combinations with Other Drugs:

Stimulants can be dangerous when taken with over-the-counter cold remedies that contain decongestants because the effects of the two can combine to raise blood pressure to a dangerous level. Cocaine is also dangerous with anything that would affect the heart rhythm, such as medication taken for certain heart diseases, because these drugs would act in an addictive way with the effects of cocaine on the heart.

What Stimulants Do To the Body/Effects

They increase blood pressure and heart rate, constrict (narrow) blood vessels, dilate the bronchioles (breathing tubes), increase blood sugar. The effects on the heart can be so excessive that they may result in a disordered heartbeat or, eventually, failure of the cardiovascular system. Most of the stimulants also increase body temperature, which presents a real problem. Cocaine causes a sense of energy, alertness, talkativeness, and well-being that users find pleasurable. When injected or smoked, this drug causes an intense feeling of euphoria.

Effects of Long-Term Use of Stimulants

Snorting cocaine can cause ulcers in the lining of the nose from inadequate blood supply, while smoked cocaine can cause bleeding in the lungs as small blood vessels burst. Stomach ulcers or damage to the intestines can occur with long-term oral or even intranasal use. Heart problems are fairly common. Long-term stimulant use seems to accelerate the development of fatty plaques that block blood vessels and may cause direct damage to the heart muscle from lack of oxygen.

References

The Straight Facts About The Most Used And Abused Drugs, (JUST SAY NO) Cynthia Kuhn, Ph.D., Scott Swartzwelder, Ph. D., and Wilkie Wilson, Ph. D., of the Duke University Medical Center (p. 210, 211, 212, 218, 219, 2003)

Diagnostic and Statistical Manual of Mental Disorders, Fourth Edition, Text Revision (pgs. 241, 242, 243, 244, 245, 248, 249, 2000).

Prevention:

For the purpose of this reading prevention relates to actions taken to minimize and eliminate drug abuse. Prevention includes establishing those conditions in society that enhance the opportunities for individuals, families, and communities to achieve positive fulfillment.

Valuable Information that every parent, "Needs to know"

Preventing Drug Abuse among Children and Adolescents- *Early Signs of Risk That May Predict Later Drug Abuse*

Some signs of risk can be seen as early as infancy or early childhood, such as aggressive behavior, lack of self-control, or difficult temperament. As the child gets older, interactions with family, at school, and within the community can affect that child's risk for later drug abuse.

Children's earliest interactions occur in the family; sometimes family situations heighten a child's risk for later drug abuse, for example, when there is:

- a lack of attachment and nurturing by parents or caregivers;
- ineffective parenting; and
- a caregiver who abuses drugs.

But families can provide protection from later drug abuse when there is:

- a strong bond between children and parents;
- parental involvement in the child's life; and
- clear limits and consistent enforcement of discipline.

Parents did you know?

Association with drug-abusing peers is often the most immediate risk for exposing adolescents to drug abuse and delinquent behavior. Other factors such as drug availability and beliefs that drug abuse is generally tolerated are risks that can influence young people to start abusing drugs.

Statistics and Trends

In 2009, 4.8 million Americans age 12 and older had abused cocaine in any form and 1.0 million had abused crack at least once in the year prior to being surveyed. The NIDA-funded 2010 Monitoring the Future Study showed that 1.6 % of 8th graders, 2.2% of 10th graders, and 2.9% of 12th graders had abused cocaine in any form and 1.0% of 8th graders, 1.0% of 10th graders, and 1.4% of 12th graders had abused crack at least once in the year prior to being surveyed.

References

The National Institute on Drug Abuse (NIDA) the Science of Drug Abuse & Addiction, (2012).

NIDA. Source: Monitoring the Future, (Mar 2010).

Lists substances of abuse, including tobacco, alcohol, illicit and prescription drugs, listing their common and street names, how they are generally administered, and their potentially harmful health effects.

Revised: March 2011

Author: National Institute on Drug Abuse

Lists substances of abuse, including tobacco, alcohol, illicit and prescription drugs, listing their common and street names, how they are generally administered, and their potentially harmful health effects.

Tobacco

Category & Name	Examples of Commercial & Street Names	DEA Schedule	How Administered*
Nicotine	Found in cigarettes, cigars, bidis, and smokeless tobacco (snuff, spit tobacco, chew)	Not scheduled	Smoked, snorted, chewed

Acute Effects - Increased blood pressure and heart rate

Health Risks - Chronic lung disease; cardiovascular disease; stroke; cancers of the mouth, pharynx, larynx, esophagus, stomach, pancreas, cervix, kidney, bladder, and acute myeloid leukemia; adverse pregnancy outcomes; addiction

Alcohol

Category & Name	Examples of Commercial & Street Names	DEA Schedule	How Administered*
Alcohol (ethyl alcohol)	Found in liquor, beer, and wine	Not scheduled	Swallowed

Acute Effects - In low doses, euphoria, mild stimulation, relaxation, lowered inhibitions. In higher doses, drowsiness, slurred speech, nausea, emotional volatility, loss of coordination, visual distortions, impaired memory, sexual dysfunction, loss of consciousness

Health Risks - Increased risk of injuries, violence, fetal damage (in pregnant women); depression; neurologic deficits; hypertension; liver and heart disease; addiction; fatal overdose

Cannabinoids

Category & Name	Examples of Commercial & Street Names	DEA Schedule	How Administered*
Marijuana	Blunt, dope, ganja, grass, herb, joint, bud, Mary Jane, pot, reefer, green, trees, smoke, sinsemilla, skunk, weed	Schedule I drugs have a high potential for abuse. They require greater storage security and have a quota on manufacturing, among other restrictions. Schedule I drugs are available for research only and have no approved medical use.	Smoked, swallowed
Hashish	Boom, gangster, hash, hash oil, hemp	Schedule I drugs have a high potential for abuse. They require greater storage security and have a quota on manufacturing, among other restrictions. Schedule I drugs are available for research only and have no approved medical use.	Smoked, swallowed

Acute Effects - Euphoria; relaxation; slowed reaction time; distorted sensory perception; impaired balance and coordination; increased heart rate and appetite; impaired learning, memory; anxiety; panic attacks; psychosis

Health Risks - Cough, frequent respiratory infections; possible mental health decline; addiction

Opioids Category & Name	Examples of Commercial & Street Names	DEA Schedule	How Administered*
Heroin	*Diacetylmorphine*: smack, horse, brown sugar, dope, H, junk, skag, skunk, white horse, China white; cheese (with OTC cold medicine and antihistamine)	Schedule I drugs have a high potential for abuse. They require greater storage security and have a quota on manufacturing, among other restrictions. Schedule I drugs are available for research only and have no approved medical use. Schedule II drugs have a high potential for abuse. They require greater storage security and have a quota on manufacturing, among other restrictions. Schedule II drugs are available only by prescription (unrefillable) and require a form for ordering. Schedule III drugs are available by prescription, may have five refills in 6 months, and may be ordered orally. Some Schedule V drugs are available over the counter.	Injected, smoked, snorted
Opium	*Laudanum, paregoric*: big O, black stuff, block, gum, hop		Swallowed, smoked

Acute Effects - Euphoria; drowsiness; impaired coordination; dizziness; confusion; nausea; sedation; feeling of heaviness in the body; slowed or arrested breathing

Health Risks - Constipation; endocarditis; hepatitis; HIV; addiction; fatal overdose

Stimulants

Category & Name	Examples of Commercial & Street Names	DEA Schedule	How Administered*
Cocaine	*Cocaine hydrochloride*: blow, bump, C, candy, Charlie, coke, crack, flake, rock, snow, toot	Schedule II drugs have a high potential for abuse. They require greater storage security and have a quota on manufacturing, among other restrictions. Schedule II drugs are available only by prescription (unrefillable) and require a form for ordering.	snorted, smoked, injected
Amphetamine	*Biphetamine, Dexedrine*: bennies, black beauties, crosses, hearts, LA turnaround, speed, truck drivers, uppers	Schedule II drugs have a high potential for abuse. They require greater storage security and have a quota on manufacturing, among other restrictions.	swallowed, snorted, smoked, injected

Stimulants

Category & Name	Examples of Commercial & Street Names	DEA Schedule	How Administered*
Methamphetamine	*Desoxyn*: meth, ice, crank, chalk, crystal, fire, glass, go fast, speed	Schedule II drugs are available only by prescription (unrefillable) and require a form for ordering. Schedule II drugs have a high potential for abuse. They require greater storage security and have a quota on manufacturing, among other restrictions. Schedule II drugs are available only by prescription (unrefillable) and require a form for ordering.	swallowed, snorted, smoked, injected

Acute Effects - Increased heart rate, blood pressure, body temperature, metabolism; feelings of exhilaration; increased energy, mental alertness; tremors; reduced appetite; irritability; anxiety; panic; paranoia; violent behavior; psychosis

Health Risks - Weight loss, insomnia; cardiac or cardiovascular complications; stroke; seizures; addiction

Cocaine also causes – Nasal damage from snorting

Methamphetamine also causes – Severe dental problems

Club Drugs

Category & Name	Examples of Commercial & Street Names	DEA Schedule	How Administered*
MDMA (methylenedioxy-methamphetamine)	Ecstasy, Adam, clarity, Eve, lover's speed, peace, uppers	Schedule I drugs have a high potential for abuse. They require greater storage security and have a quota on manu-facturing, among other restrictions. Schedule I drugs are available for research only and have no approved medical use.	swallowed, snorted, injected
Flunitrazepam**	*Rohypnol*: forget-me pill, Mexican Valium, R2, roach, Roche, roofies, roofinol, rope, rophies	Schedule IV drugs are available by prescription, may have five refills in 6 months, and may be ordered orally.	swallowed, snorted

Club Drugs

Category & Name	Examples of Commercial & Street Names	DEA Schedule	How Administered*
GHB**	*Gamma-hydroxybutyrate*: G, Georgia home boy, grievous bodily harm, liquid ecstasy, soap, scoop, goop, liquid X	Schedule I drugs have a high potential for abuse. They require greater storage security and have a quota on manufacturing, among other restrictions. Schedule I drugs are available for research only and have no approved medical use.	swallowed

Acute Effects, for MDMA - Mild hallucinogenic effects; increased tactile sensitivity; empathic feelings; lowered inhibition; anxiety; chills; sweating; teeth clenching; muscle cramping

Also, for Flunitrazepam - Sedation; muscle relaxation; confusion; memory loss; dizziness; impaired coordination

Also, for GHB - Drowsiness; nausea; headache; disorientation; loss of coordination; memory loss, unconsciousness; seizures; coma

Health Risks, for MDMA - Sleep disturbances; depression; impaired memory; hyperthermia; addiction

Also, for Flunitrazepam – Addiction

Dissociative Drugs

Category & Name	Examples of Commercial & Street Names	DEA Schedule	How Administered*
Ketamine	*Ketalar SV:* cat Valium, K, Special K, vitamin K	Schedule III drugs are available by prescription, may have five refills in 6 months, and may be ordered orally.	injected, snorted, smoked
PCP and analogs	*Phencyclidine:* angel dust, boat, hog, love boat, peace pill	Schedule I & II drugs have a high potential for abuse. They require greater storage security & have a quota on manufacturing. Schedule I drugs are available for research only & have no approved medical use; Schedule II drugs are only by prescription.	swallowed, smoked, injected
Salvia divinorum	Salvia, Shepherdess's Herb, Maria Pastora, magic mint, Sally-D	Not Scheduled	chewed, swallowed, smoked

Dissociative Drugs

Category & Name	Examples of Commercial & Street Names	DEA Schedule	How Administered*
Dextromethorphan (DXM)	Found in some cough and cold medications: Robotripping, Robo, Triple C	Not Scheduled	swallowed

Acute Effects - Feelings of being separate from one's body and environment; impaired motor function

Also, for ketamine - Analgesia; impaired memory; delirium; respiratory depression and arrest; death

Also, for PCP and analogs - Analgesia; psychosis; aggression; violence; slurred speech; loss of coordination; hallucinations

Also, for DXM - Euphoria; slurred speech; confusion; dizziness; distorted visual perceptions

Health Risks - Anxiety; tremors; numbness; memory loss; nausea

Hallucinogens

Category & Name	Examples of Commercial & Street Names	DEA Schedule	How Administered*
LSD	*Lysergic acid diethylamide:* acid, blotter, cubes, microdot yellow sunshine, blue heaven	Schedule I drugs have a high potential for abuse. They require greater storage security and have a quota on manufacturing,	swallowed, absorbed through mouth tissues

Hallucinogens

Category & Name	Examples of Commercial & Street Names	DEA Schedule	How Administered*
Mescaline	Buttons, cactus, mesc, peyote	among other restrictions. Schedule I drugs are available for research only and have no approved medical use. Schedule I drugs have a high potential for abuse. They require greater storage security and have a quota on manufacturing, among other restrictions. Schedule I drugs are available for research only and have no approved medical use.	swallowed, smoked
Psilocybin	Magic mushrooms, purple passion, shrooms, little smoke	Schedule I drugs have a high potential for abuse. They require greater storage security and have a quota on manufacturing, among other restrictions. Schedule I drugs are available for research only and have no approved medical use.	swallowed

Acute Effects - Altered states of perception and feeling; hallucinations; nausea

Also, for LSD - Increased body temperature, heart rate, blood pressure; loss of appetite; sweating; sleeplessness; numbness, dizziness, weakness, tremors; impulsive behavior; rapid shifts in emotion

Also, for Mescaline - Increased body temperature, heart rate, blood pressure; loss of appetite; sweating; sleeplessness; numbness, dizziness, weakness, tremors; impulsive behavior; rapid shifts in emotion

Also, for Psilocybin - Nervousness; paranoia; panic

Health Risks, for LSD - Flashbacks, Hallucinogen Persisting Perception Disorder

Other Compounds

Category & Name	Examples of Commercial & Street Names	DEA Schedule	How Administered*
Anabolic steroids	*Anadrol, Oxandrin, Durabolin, Depo-Testosterone, Equipoise*: roids, juice, gym candy, pumpers	Schedule III drugs are available by prescription, may have five refills in 6 months, and may be ordered orally.	Injected, swallowed, applied to skin
Inhalants	*Solvents (paint thinners, gasoline, glues); gases (butane, propane, aerosol propellants, nitrous oxide); nitrites (isoamyl, isobutyl, cyclohexyl)*:	Not scheduled	Inhaled through nose or mouth

Other Compounds Category & Name	Examples of Commercial & Street Names	DEA Schedule	How Administered*
	laughing gas, poppers, snappers, whippets		

Acute Effects, for Anabolic steroids - No intoxication effects

Also, for Inhalants (varies by chemical) - Stimulation; loss of inhibition; headache; nausea or vomiting; slurred speech; loss of motor coordination; wheezing

Health Risks, for Anabolic steroids - Hypertension; blood clotting and cholesterol changes; liver cysts; hostility and aggression; acne; in adolescents—premature stoppage of growth; in males—prostate cancer, reduced sperm production, shrunken testicles, breast enlargement; in females—menstrual irregularities, development of beard and other masculine characteristics

Also, for Inhalants - Cramps; muscle weakness; depression; memory impairment; damage to cardiovascular and nervous systems; unconsciousness; sudden death

Prescription Medications Category & Name	Examples of Commercial & Street Names	DEA Schedule	How Administered*
CNS Depressants Stimulants Opioid Pain Relievers	For more information on prescription medications, please visit the Commonly Abused Prescription Drug Chart		

Notes

Some of the health risks are directly related to the route of drug administration. For example, injection drug use can increase the risk of infection through needle contamination with staphylococci, HIV, hepatitis, and other organisms.
**Associated with sexual assaults.*

Principles of Drug Addiction Treatment

More than three decades of scientific research show that treatment can help drug-addicted individuals stop drug use, avoid relapse and successfully recover their lives. Based on this research, 13 fundamental principles that characterize effective drug abuse treatment have been developed. These principles are detailed in *NIDA's Principles of Drug Addiction Treatment: A Research-Based Guide*.

Reference

The National Institute on Drug Abuse (NIDA) the Science of Drug Abuse & Addiction, (2012).

Treatment

Through treatment that is tailored to individual needs, patients can learn to control their condition and live normal, productive lives. Like people with diabetes or heart disease, people in treatment for drug addiction learn behavioral changes. Behavioral therapies can include counseling, psychotherapy, support groups, family therapy. Treatment medications offer help in suppressing the withdrawal syndrome and drug craving and in blocking the effects of drugs.

In general, the more treatment given, the better the results. Many patients require other services as well, such as medical and mental health services and HIV prevention services. Patients who stay in treatment longer than 3 months usually have better outcomes than those who stay less time. Over the last 25 years, studies have shown that treatment works to reduce drug intake and crimes committed by drug-dependent people. Researchers also have found that drug abusers who have been through treatment are more likely to have jobs.

The ultimate goal of all drug abuse treatment is to enable the patient to achieve lasting abstinence, but the immediate goals are to reduce drug use, improve the patient's ability to function, and minimize the medical and social complications of drug abuse.

Therapeutic Communities

What is a Therapeutic Community?

Therapeutic communities are highly structured programs in which patients stay at a residence, typically for 6 to 12 months. Patients in TC's include those with relatively long histories of drug dependence, involvement in serious criminal activities, and impaired social functioning (APA, 2005). The focus of the TC is on the re-socialization of the patient to a drug-free, crime-free lifestyle.

Therapeutic communities (TCs), treats individuals who are severely dependent on any illicitly obtained drug or combination of drugs and whose social adjustment to conventional family and occupational responsibilities is severely compromised as a result of drug seeking. As of the 1980's, cocaine dependence has overtaken heroin dependence in the TC population.

The Traditional TC

Traditional TC's-(drug-free residential programs for substance abuse) are similar in planned duration of stay (15-24 months), structure, staffing pattern, perspective, and rehabilitative regime, although they differ in size (30-600 beds) and patient demography. Some of the staff may be composed of TC-trained clinicians and other human service professionals. Primary clinical staff are usually former substance-abusing individuals who themselves were rehabilitated in TC programs. Other staff consists of professionals providing, medical, mental health, vocational, educational, family counseling, fiscal, administrative, and legal services. TC's accommodate a broad spectrum of drug-abusing patients. TC'S treat patients with drug problems of varying severity, different lifestyles, and various social, economic and ethnic/cultural backgrounds.

The principal aim of the TC is a global-change in lifestyle: abstinence from illicit substances, elimination of antisocial activity, development of employability and pro0social attitudes and values. The rehabilitative approach requires multidimensional influence and training, which for most can only occur in a 24-hour residential setting. TC's coordinates a comprehensive offering of interventions and services in a single treatment setting. Vocational counseling, work therapy, recreation, group and individual therapy, educational, medical, family, legal and social services all occur within the TC.

The primary "therapist" and teacher in the TC is the community itself, consisting of peers and staff who role model successful personal change. Staff members also serve as rational authorities and guides in the recovery process. The community as a whole provides a crucial 24-hour context for continued learning in which individual changes in conduct, attitudes and emotions are monitored and mutually reinforced in the daily regime. The TC approach to rehabilitation is based on an explicit perspective of the drug abuse disorder, the patient, the recovery process and healthy living. It is this perspective that shapes its organization structure, staffing and treatment process.

View of the Disorder

Drug abuse is viewed as a disorder of the whole person, affecting some or all areas of functioning. Cognitive and behavioral problems appear, as do mood disturbances. Thinking may be unrealistic or disorganized; values are confused, nonexistent or antisocial. Frequently there are deficits in verbal, reading, writing and marketable skills. Rehabilitation focuses on maintaining a drug-free existence.

View of Recovery

In the TC's view of recovery, the aim of rehabilitation is global, involving both a change in lifestyle and personal identity. The primary psychological goal is to change the negative patterns of behavior, thinking and feeling that predispose drug use; the main social goal is to develop the skills, attitudes and values of a responsible drug-free lifestyle.

Self-help and mutual self-help

Treatment is not provided but rather made available to the individual in the TC environment, its staff and peers, the daily regime of work, groups, meetings, seminars and recreation. However, the effectiveness of these elements depends on the individual who must constantly and fully engage in the treatment process. Self-help recovery means that the individual makes the main contribution to the change process. Mutual self-help emphasizes the fact that the main messages of recovery, personal growth and "right living" are mediated by peers through confrontation and sharing in groups; by example as role models; and as supportive, encouraging friends in daily interactions.

Contact and Referral

Patients voluntarily contact TCs through several sources: self-referral, social agencies, treatment providers and active recruitment by the program. Approximately 30% of all admissions to TCs are under some form of legal pressure, parole, probation, or another court-mandated disposition.

TC Structure

The daily operation of the community itself is the task of the residents, working together under staff supervision. The broad range of resident job assignments illustrates the extent of the self-help process (e.g., cooking, cleaning, kitchen service, minor repair) serving as apprentices, running all departments and conducting house meetings and peer-encounter groups. The TC is managed by staff who monitor and evaluate patient status, supervise resident groups, assign and supervise resident job functions and oversee house operations. Clinically, the staff conduct therapeutic groups (other than peer encounters), provide individual counseling, organize social and recreational projects and confer with significant others. They decide matters of resident status, discipline, promotion, transfers, discharges, furloughs and treatment planning.

The new patient enters a setting of upward mobility. The resident job functions are arranged in a hierarchy, according to seniority, clinical progress and productivity. Job assignments begin with the most menial tasks (e.g., mopping the floor) and lead vertically to levels of coordination and management. Patients can come in as patients and leave as staff.

Privileges

In the TC, privileges are explicit rewards that reinforce the value of achievement. Privileges are accorded by overall clinical progress in the program. Displays of inappropriate behavior or negative attitude can result in loss of privileges, which can be regained by demonstrated improvement.

Privileges acquire importance because they are earned through investment of time, energy, self-modification, risk of failure and disappointment. The earning process establishes the value of privileges and gives them potency as social reinforcements.

Because privilege is equivalent to status in the vertical social system of the TC, loss of even small privileges is a status setback this is particularly painful for individuals who have struggled to raise their low self-esteem. Also, because substance-abusing patients often cannot distinguish between privilege and entitlement, the privilege system in the TC teaches that productive participation or membership in a family or community is based on an earning process. Privileges provide explicit feedback in the learning process. They are tangible rewards that are contingent on individual change. This concrete feature of privilege is particularly suitable for those with histories of performance failure or incompletion.

The Change Process

Rehabilitation and recovery in the TC/Residential Program unfold as a developmental process occurring in a social learning setting. Values, conduct, emotions and cognitive understanding (insight) must be integrated toward the goals of a new life-style and a positive personal-social identity. Achievement of the goals of the process reflects the individual's relationship to the community and acceptance of its teachings.

TCs Success Rates

Positive concrete results of Therapeutic Communities are well documented-due to lengthy treatment time frames (one year or more) and ongoing maintained with former members. Therapeutic communities consistently report 70 to 80 percent success rates, as measured by indicators like former members' abilities to hold down jobs, secure adequate housing or remain drug-free.

Effectiveness of the TC approach-Success rates
Substantial improvements noted on (NIDA, 2001):
Drug use (reduced from 40-60%)
Criminality (decreased arrest rates of up to 40%)
Employment (gains of up to 40% after completing treatment)

References

The American Psychiatric Press. Textbook of Substance Abuse Treatment. 2005.

What is Relapse Prevention?

Relapse prevention is a cognitive-behavioral treatment that combines behavioral skill-training procedures with cognitive intervention techniques to assist individuals in maintaining desired behavioral change. **Relapse prevention** (RP) is a type of coping-focused psychotherapy or psycho-education that strives to teach drug or alcohol dependent persons coping skills to help them avoid relapsing back to using drugs and/or alcohol. Goals of a relapse prevention program include: 1) teaching coping skills to allow the recovering person to "identify, anticipate, avoid and/or cope" with high risk situations (for relapse), 2) to help recovering persons learn how to keep a single 'lapse' from turning into a multiple 'relapse' situation, and 3) to help the recovering person feel as though he or she is really capable of controlling his or her own behavior.

Multiple skills are taught in a relapse prevention class. Such skills include:

- Learning to discriminate a 'lapse' from a 'relapse'
- Learning to identify stressful situations and objects ("people, places and things") in the environment that can trigger relapse
- Once a stressful situation, person, place or thing is identified, learning coping skills which help people to avoid or defuse that situation, person, place or thing so that it doesn't trigger relapse
- To learn how to identify, plan and participate in positive and fulfilling sober activities that can fill in time formerly devoted to using drugs or alcohol, or fill in blank spots in the addict's schedule (which would otherwise be filled with cravings and stress)
- To learn how to identify and change unhealthy habits for healthier ones

Reference

The National Institute on Drug Abuse (NIDA) the Science of Drug Abuse & Addiction, (2012).

"Some Tools to Use"

Intensive Outpatient Drug Addiction Rehab Programs typically occur in a private therapeutic environment, with a group of clients who are working on a similar focus. The typical number of therapeutic sessions is 3 times per week totaling 9-12 hours per week. Intensive Outpatient is a step-down program used as aftercare upon completion of a residential addiction rehab program.

Outpatient Drug Addiction Rehab programs include a variety of approaches for clients who seek therapeutic **interventions** in a private therapy setting. **Outpatient addiction treatment** allows a client to maintain their typical daily schedule while seeking therapeutic assistance in resolving interpersonal conflicts and **addiction treatment**. The typical duration of a therapeutic session is 1 hour per week. A primary format for outpatient therapy is individual, group, or family therapy. Outpatient therapy is typically ineffective during the initial stages of treatment and is more effective as an after care plan, once **residential treatment** is completed.

What is Detoxification?

Detoxification refers to the process whereby an individual who is physically dependent on a drug is taken off that drug either abruptly or gradually while managing the symptoms of withdrawal. There are several options in the use of medications to aid in detoxification. It is often the first step in a drug treatment program and should be followed by treatment with a behavioral-based therapy and/or a medication, if available. Detox alone with no follow-up is not treatment

1) the drug on which the individual is dependent,
2) other drugs that produce cross tolerance
3) medications to provide symptomatic relief, or
4) drugs that affect the mechanisms by which withdrawal is expressed
   Settings for detoxification can include inpatient, residential or outpatient programs.

Goals of Detoxification

1) Ridding the body of the acute physiological dependence associated with the chronic daily use of narcotics.
2) Diminishing or eliminating the pain and discomfort that can occur during withdrawal.
3) Providing a safe and humane treatment to help the individual over the initial hurdle of stopping narcotic use.
4) Providing a situation conducive to a more long-range commitment to treatment and making appropriate referrals to these other treatment modalities.
5) Treating any medical problems discovered or making appropriate referrals.
6) Beginning the process of educating the patient around issues related to health and relapse prevention, and exploring issues such as family, vocational and legal problems that may need referral.

Referrals

The National Institute on Drug Abuse (NIDA) the Science of Drug Abuse & Addiction, (2012).

There are valuable referrals provided on pgs 159 on where you can go for Inpatient, Outpatient or Detoxification Services....

"Suicide Prevention"

"I have worked in hospital settings for over five years now. It is so heart-breaking when I think about the hundreds of people I have met that presented to the Emergency Room with suicidal thoughts or after having a suicide attempt. The good news is that I have also helped so many people by using these valuable lifesaving tools listed below. If you or someone you know are having thoughts to hurt yourself call 911 immediately or go to the nearest emergency room, there are trained professionals there just waiting to help".

What Can I Do to help Someone Who May Be Suicidal

Take it seriously.

Myth: *The people who talk about it don't do it.* Studies have found that more than 75% of all completed suicides did things in the few weeks or months prior to their deaths to indicate to others that they were in deep despair. Anyone expressing suicidal feelings needs immediate attention.

Myth: *Anyone who tries to kill himself has got to be crazy.* Perhaps 10% of all suicidal people are psychotic or have delusional beliefs about reality. Most suicidal people suffer from the recognized mental illness of depression; but many depressed people adequately manage their daily affairs. The absence of craziness does not mean the absence of suicide risk.

Those problems weren't enough to commit suicide over, is often said by people who knew a completed suicide. You cannot assume that because you feel something is not worth being suicidal about, that the person you are with feels the same way. It is not how bad the problem is, but how badly it's hurting the person who has it.

Remember: suicidal behavior is a cry for help.

Myth: *If a someone is going to kill himself, nothing can stop him.* The fact that a person is still alive is sufficient proof that part of him wants to remain alive. The suicidal person is ambivalent -- part of him wants to live and part of him wants not so much death as he wants the pain to end. It is the part that wants to live that tells another I feel suicidal. If a suicidal person turns to you it is likely that he believes that you are more caring, more informed about coping with misfortune, and more willing to protect his confidentiality. No matter how negative the manner and content of his talk, he is doing a positive thing and has a positive view of you.

Be willing to give and get help sooner rather than later.

Suicide prevention is not a last minute activity. All textbooks on depression say it should be reached as soon as possible. Unfortunately, suicidal people are afraid that trying to get help may bring them more pain: being told they are stupid, foolish, sinful, or manipulative; rejection; punishment; suspension from school or job; written records of their condition; or involuntary commitment. You need to do everything you can to reduce pain, rather than increase or prolong it. Constructively involving yourself on the side of life as early as possible will reduce the risk of suicide.

Listen.

Give the person every opportunity to unburden his troubles and ventilate his feelings. You don't need to say much and there are no magic words. If you are concerned, your voice and manner will show it. Give him relief from being alone with his pain; let him know you are glad he turned to you. Patience, sympathy, acceptance. Avoid arguments and advice giving.

ASK: Are you having thoughts of suicide?

Myth: *Talking about it may give someone the idea.* People already have the idea; suicide is constantly in the news media. If you ask a despairing person this question you are doing a good thing for them: you are showing him that you care about him, that you take him seriously, and that you are willing to let him share his pain with you. You are giving him further opportunity to discharge pent up and painful feelings. If the person is having thoughts of suicide, find out how far along his ideation has progressed.

If the person is acutely suicidal, do not leave him alone.

If the means are present, try to get rid of them. Detoxify the home.

Urge professional help.

Persistence and patience may be needed to seek, engage and continue with as many options as possible. In any referral situation, let the person know you care and want to maintain contact.

No secrets.

It is the part of the person that is afraid of more pain that says "Don't tell anyone". It is the part that wants to stay alive that tells you about it. Respond to that part of the person and persistently seek out a mature and compassionate person with whom you can review the situation. (You can get outside help and still protect the person from pain causing breaches of privacy.) Do not try to go it alone. Get help for the person and for yourself. Distributing the anxieties and responsibilities of suicide prevention makes it easier and much more effective.

From crisis to recovery.

Most people have suicidal thoughts or feelings at some point in their lives; yet less than 2% of all deaths are suicides. Nearly all suicidal people suffer from conditions that will pass with time or with the assistance of a recovery program. There are hundreds of modest steps we can take to improve our response to the suicidal and to make it easier for them to seek help. Taking these modest steps can save many lives and reduce a great deal of human suffering.

WARNING SIGNS

Conditions associated with increased risk of suicide

- Death or terminal illness of relative or friend.
- Divorce, separation, broken relationship, stress on family.
- Loss of health (real or imaginary).
- Loss of job, home, money, status, self-esteem, personal security.
- Alcohol or drug abuse.
- Depression. In the young depression may be masked by hyperactivity or acting out behavior. In the elderly it may be incorrectly attributed to the natural effects of aging. Depression that seems to quickly disappear for no apparent reason is cause for concern. The early stages of recovery from depression can be a high risk period. Recent studies have associated anxiety disorders with increased risk for attempted suicide.

Suicide Risk Factors

- Having attempted suicide previously or having family members or friends who have attempted suicide.
- Having a family history of physical or sexual abuse.

- Talking or writing about death, dying, or suicide, especially when these actions are out of the ordinary for the person.
- Making comments like "It would be better if I wasn't here" or "I want out".
- Acting reckless or engaging in risky activities that could lead to death, like driving through red lights-seemingly without thinking.
- Losing interest in things one used to care about.
- Putting affairs in order, typing up lose ends changing a will.
- Looking for ways to kill oneself by seeking access to firearms, pills. Or other means.
- Increasing alcohol or drug use.
- Withdrawing from friends, family and society.
- Experiencing dramatic mood swings.

This resource is hosted by WellStar Health System.

Emotional and behavioral changes associated with suicide

- Overwhelming Pain: pain that threatens to exceed the person's pain coping capacities. Suicidal feelings are often the result of longstanding problems that have been exacerbated by recent precipitating events. The precipitating factors may be new pain or the loss of pain coping resources.
- Hopelessness: the feeling that the pain will continue or get worse; things will never get better.
- Powerlessness: the feeling that one's resources for reducing pain are exhausted.
- Feelings of worthlessness, shame, guilt, self-hatred, no one cares. Fears of losing control, harming self or others.
- Personality becomes sad, withdrawn, tired, apathetic, anxious, irritable, or prone to angry outbursts.
- Declining performance in school, work, or other activities. (Occasionally the reverse: someone who volunteers for extra duties because they need to fill up their time.)
- Social isolation; or association with a group that has different moral standards than those of the family.
- Declining interest in sex, friends, or activities previously enjoyed.
- Neglect of personal welfare, deteriorating physical appearance.
- Alterations in either direction in sleeping or eating habits.
- (Particularly in the elderly) Self-starvation, dietary mismanagement, disobeying medical instructions.

- Difficult times: holidays, anniversaries, and the first week after discharge from a hospital; just before and after diagnosis of a major illness; just before and during disciplinary proceedings. Undocumented status adds to the stress of a crisis.

Suicidal Behavior

- Previous suicide attempts, mini-attempts.
- Explicit statements of suicidal ideation or feelings.
- Development of suicidal plan, acquiring the means, rehearsal behavior, setting a time for the attempt.
- Self-inflicted injuries, such as cuts, burns, or head banging.
- Reckless behavior. (Besides suicide, other leading causes of death among young people in New York City are homicide, accidents, drug overdose, and AIDS.) Unexplained accidents among children and the elderly.
- Making out a will or giving away favorite possessions.
- Inappropriately saying goodbye.
- Verbal behavior that is ambiguous or indirect: I'm going away on a real long trip., You won't have to worry about me anymore., I want to go to sleep and never wake up., I'm so depressed, I just can't go on., Does God punish suicides?, Voices are telling me to do bad things., requests for euthanasia information, inappropriate joking, stories or essays on morbid themes.

Crisis intervention hotlines that accept calls from the suicidal, or anyone who wishes to discuss a problem, are available 24/7 please call for advice. At (770) 732-3789, a mental health professional will be able to help. You may also use the resources below, alternately:

- Call the Behavioral Health Link of Georgia Crisis Hotline at 1-(800)-715-4225.
- Call the toll-free, 24-hour hotline of the National Suicide Prevention Lifeline at 1-(800)-237-8255 to be connected to a trained counselor at a suicide crisis center nearest you if you live out of the state of Georgia.

This resource is hosted by mental health information at Psych Central.

"Tools to Use"

Psychiatric Services:

Peachford Behavioral Health Systems
2151 Peachford Road
Atlanta GA 30338
Phone: (770) 455-3200
Hotline: (770) 455-3200x2302

Peachford Hospital

Since 1973, Peachford Hospital has been one of the premiere providers of mental health and chemical dependency treatment to Atlanta and the Southeast. We offer a safe and nurturing environment for children, adolescents, adults and senior adults to find hope and healing from emotional, psychiatric and addictive diseases. The Peachford Hospital system includes a 246-bed inpatient acute-care facility, partial-hospitalization and intensive outpatient programs.

Adult Services

Today, alcohol and drug dependencies are recognized as life-threatening diseases and Peachford's philosophy regards them as treatable medical illnesses. Emphasis is placed on learning relapse prevention skills. Discharge meetings are held with family and, if appropriate, employers to strengthen patients on their road to recovery.

Adult Acute Inpatient

The acute inpatient program treats adults in an intensive therapeutic structure, providing medical and psychiatric stabilization and 24-hour nursing care for patients experiencing critical symptoms. It offers a comprehensive treatment approach to stabilizing acute psychiatric and addictive disease problems in adults of all ages.

Patients in crisis will find a safe and structured environment that offers compassion and hope. A multi-disciplinary treatment team including physicians, nurses, activities therapists and social individualized treatment plan is initiated with a special emphasis placed on medication management, as well as individual, group and family therapy.

The ultimate goal of treatment is to stabilize the immediate crisis and to enable the patient to return to the community with skills to promote personal and emotional development, relationship building and independence. Interventions are designed to provide patients with practical tools to manage their symptoms improve their coping abilities and solve their problems. A primary focus of treatment is placed on relapse prevention and education.

In order to reduce the need for future hospitalization, discharge planning is seen as a priority. Staff works towards identifying and coordinating community resource support and aftercare services to assist each patient in meeting their goals. Whenever possible, and clinically appropriate, a patient's family is engaged in the therapeutic process. Family or social support involvement is seen as being a critical issue in the area of relapse prevention.

Adult Partial Hospitalization

This program is appropriate for patients who have mild to moderate mental or emotional disorders who require coordinated, intensive, comprehensive, and multi-disciplinary treatment. PHP is appropriate for patients who are able to maintain themselves in the community at a minimum to moderate level of functioning and those who present no immediate threat to themselves or others. PHP also is beneficial for patients who are making a transition from inpatient care back into the community or can be a supplement to the recovery process for patients who have failed to respond adequately to standard weekly outpatient therapy.
The average length of stay varies between 1 to 3 weeks. Programming includes four group therapy sessions with a short wrap-up session. Group therapy is the primary mode of treatment, and patients in PHP will have two individual sessions per week with their assigned psychiatrist. PHP starts at 9:00am and concludes at 3:00pm Sunday thru Saturday (7 days per week). Lunch is provided as part of the program.

Adult Intensive Outpatient

This program is frequently (but not always) a step down level of care for patients who have been in the Partial Hospitalization Program (PHP). IOP is appropriate for patients who are at a lower risk and no longer require the full day programming that is part of PHP. Hours of operation for IOP are 9:00am to 12:45 pm Sunday thru Saturday (7 days per week). Patients are not followed by a psychiatrist at this level of care.

Adult Dual PHP Services

The Dual Diagnosis program (either at the PHP or IOP level) is designed to meet the needs of adults who have both primary psychiatric disorders and substance abuse problems. The program is based on the 12-step program model and relapse prevention model. The PHP and IOP continuum of care at Peachford offers immediate access to a structured environment and offers assistance in beginning recovery or maintaining recovery.

Adult psychiatric Services

The Psychiatric Program (either at the PHP or IOP level) is designed to meet the needs of adults who have primary psychiatric disorders. The program provides groups that address a variety of problems that may interfere with a person's ability to function at work or home. Mental health conditions are characterized by alterations in thinking, mood, or behavior and associated with distress and impaired functioning. Early intervention is needed many times before it becomes potentially life threatening. The treatment at Peachford Hospital can help a patient function at a higher level in daily living.

When Outpatient Therapy is deemed to be the most effective course of treatment, Peachford provides a variety of outpatient services as well as a referral network to area health professionals.

Adult Treatment Components

Treatment for each adult is administered by a multi-disciplinary team of mental health professionals led by a psychiatrist. Team members may include:

- Psychiatrists
- Internal Medicine Physician
- Nurses
- Social Workers
- Case Managers
- Activity Therapists
- Substance Abuse Counselors

The treatment process begins with a comprehensive evaluation to help diagnose any underlying medical or biochemical origins of disease. An individualized plan of care is written to meet the special needs of each patient.

Therapeutic components may include:

- Individual therapy
- Family therapy
- Group therapy
- Drug/alcohol education
- Recreational therapy
- Activity therapy
- Medication education

Adult Psychiatric Services

For adults, psychiatric, emotional and substance abuse problems can affect careers, marriages and relationships. Peachford offers a confidential, caring environment that promotes crisis resolution, positive self-awareness, social skills, and personal growth. The Program is equipped to address a multitude of psychiatric illnesses including depressive disorders, bi-polar illnesses, anxiety disorders and chronic mental illness. Individuals experiencing severe behavioral disturbance or an inability to function my also benefit from treatment. Care is provided on an inpatient, partial hospitalization and intensive outpatient basis.

PROBLEMS WE ADDRESS

- Suicidal feelings/thoughts
- Extreme anger and/or dangerous behavior
- Anxiety/panic attacks
- Schizophrenia
- Depression
- Hallucinations/delusional thinking
- Phobias
- Manic depressive disorder
- Physical/sexual abuse
- Co-dependency

Adult Addictive Disease Services

The Addictive Disorders/Dual Diagnosis Program is designed to treat individuals with alcohol or drug related problems and psychiatric issues. When addictive behavior and mental illness create problems that prohibit the patient and family from functioning, Peachford Hospital provides a comprehensive program to assist in stabilizing the situation.

A 12-step recovery program provides a framework to treating the addictive process while a multidisciplinary treatment approach is utilized to address any mental health concerns. The treatment team that includes psychiatrists addictionists, social workers, registered nurses, certified substance abuse counselors and activity therapists. This approach optimizes success by bringing a diversity of perspectives to the forefront of treatment.

Treatment includes a combination of individual, group and family therapies facilitated by qualified professionals. The treatment team focus is on helping the patient recognize his or her behavior patterns and developing healthier ways of relating to and coping with stress. Group therapy facilitates the sharing of feelings and experiences with others who have similar problems. Pertinent issues related to addictive disorders such as shame, grief, anger, control and trust are comprehensively addressed.

Emphasis is placed on education, addressing all aspects of the addictive process, including the disease concept, family issues, and relapse prevention strategies. The treatment program incorporates a strong emphasis on discharge planning and aftercare.

Forms of Payment Accepted:

Self-payment, Medicare, Private health insurance, Military insurance.

"**Tools to Use**"
WellStar Behavioral Health
3950 Austell Road
Austell GA, 30106
770 732-6580
770-732-6580

•Outpatient Counseling Services offers adult services including, Outpatient Counseling Groups, Intensive Outpatient Programs, Partial Hospitalization Programs, Workshops & Seminars, and Professional Development.
Phone:770-732-6960

WellStar Behavioral Health Resource Team responds to psychiatric emergencies in all four WellStar Emergency Departments - Cobb, Douglas, Kennestone, and Paulding. Licensed Mental Health Professionals complete comprehensive, face to face, Mental Health Assessments in our Emergency Departments. WellStar's Behavioral Health Call Center also has Licensed Mental Health Professionals available 24 hours, 7 days a week to answer crisis calls and provide telephonic guidance. Therapists assist with providing referral information, discussing treatment options or provide empathetic listening to assist each individual with their unique needs.
Phone: 770-732-3789 – 24/7 Call Center

Services span:

•Alcoholism, Chemical dependence and other addictions
•Dual diagnosis groups (for people with both psychiatric and addictive disorders)
•Mood Disorders such as Depression and Bipolar Disorder
•Anxiety Disorders such as Panic Disorder, Obsessive Compulsive Disorder and Generalized Anxiety Disorder

- Family and relationship issues
- Work issues
- Age-related issues
- Communication skills
- Psycho education groups
- Trauma, abuse, and post-traumatic stress disorder
- Psychotic Disorders such as Schizophrenia

Other WellStar Medical Stabilization Services: New Vision. Phone:770-739-4670

Adult Inpatient Services

The Behavioral Health Center at WellStar Cobb Hospital provides an intensive therapeutic environment with 24-hour medical care for people struggling from severe depression and other mental illnesses including:

- 24-hour Behavioral Health monitoring and supervision
- Behavioral Health diagnostic assessment and evaluation
- Medication stabilization and management
- Individual and group therapy
- Recreational therapy
- Family therapy
- Patient and family education
- Discharge and aftercare planning

In the event of an emergency, please go to the nearest emergency room. For more information, call 770-732-3789.

Outpatient Counseling Services

Outpatient Counseling Services (OCS) has developed multi-level service options for patients experiencing psychiatric disorders as well as addiction disorders. Participants receive individualized treatment that promotes healthier lifestyle choices, improved relationship dynamics, support, long-term recovery and education.

Partial Hospitalization Program (PHP)

OCS offers behavioral health services to individuals that are experiencing acute symptoms of substance abuse and mental illness, but do not require the 24-hour supervision provided by inpatient psychiatric care. Clients attend

PHP Monday through Friday, from 8:30 a.m. until 12:30 p.m. Alternative schedule maybe available from 11:40 a.m. until 4:00 p.m.

Intensive Outpatient Program (IOP)

OCS offers the intensive outpatient program to meet the needs of individuals whose symptoms are severe, but not acute. While in the IOP patients attend treatment Monday through Friday 8:30 a.m. until 11:30 a.m. Alternative schedule maybe available from 1:00 p.m. until 4:00 p.m. This allows many patients to live at home and maintain a work or school schedule while in treatment.

Outpatient Counseling Services Contact Info:

- Phone: 770-732-6960
- Fax: 770-739-0163
- Address: 3950 Austell Road, Austell, GA 30106

Phone: 770-732-3789 – 24/7 Call Center

Forms of Payment Accepted: Medicaid, Medicare, Private health insurance, Military insurance

"Tools to Use"

Any person's convicted of a DUI in the State of Georgia, or any licensed Georgia driver who gets a DUI in another state must undergo a DUI Clinical Evaluation and, if recommended, complete a Substance Abuse Treatment Program.

Williams DUI & Risk Reduction Schools-
Regina Williams-BS, CAMF, CAC2 * FVIP DUI-Director
1185-B Veterans Memorial Hwy
Mableton, GA 30126

Call for appointment:
Office (770) 944-9946
Fax   (770) 944-9929

Services Provided:
DUI Risk Reduction Course,
Clinical Evaluations, Drug & Alcohol Treatment-
Sherry Graves-DBHDD Clinical Evaluator/Treatment Provider
Court-Ordered Anger Management Classes
Family Violence Intervention Program-FVIP

Risk Reduction Course:
Assessment $82.00
Book $20.00
20 hr. Class $190.00
Total   = $292.00

Risk Reduction Classes are as follows:
Saturday 7am to 4pm
Sunday   7am to 4pm
Monday 6pm to 10pm

What the 9-11 Healing and Remembrance program has to offer:

■A toll-free hotline with mental health support and information regarding 9-11 10th Anniversary events. Also available in Spanish.
Please call 1-(866)-212-0444
■Healing and Remembrance Family Support Centers near commemorative events
We will be populating this page with many resources to support those who are participating in 9-11 10th anniversary events, so please check back often

Volunteering on 9-11-11 is a great way to honor those lost:

The 9-11 Healing and Remembrance Program encourages you to spend the anniversary of 9-11 in the company of others. A great way to be with others, honor those lost and give back to the community, is through volunteering. There are many opportunities available in your local community. A good place to start your search for volunteer opportunities is by visiting 9-11 Day of Service (http://911dayofservice.org/). They have thousands of volunteer opportunity listings including many that are specifically related to 9-11. Their mission "is to honor the victims of 9-11 and those that rose to service in response to the attacks by encouraging all Americans and others throughout the world to pledge to voluntarily perform at least one good deed, or another service activity on 9/11 each year." We encourage you to do the same.

New Vision is a medical stabilization service for adults who are presenting with acute withdrawal symptoms from alcohol or other drugs.

Free, confidential assessments are offered at the Behavioral Health Center at WellStar Cobb Hospital and at Outpatient Counseling Services.
Recommendations and referrals are provided based on each individual's unique situation.
The 24-hour information line is always staffed with caring Behavioral Health professionals to schedule an intake appointment, as well as to provide referrals, information, and supportive direction for those in need.
To schedule an appointment for an assessment call; (770)-739-4670.
Monday-Friday 8:00am until 8:00pm
Saturday and Sunday 8:30am until 5:00pm

Patients who are addicted to opiates "Must" be in withdrawal (generally 24 hours out from last opiate use).

If accepted, patients are admitted to the medical floor of WellStar Cobb Hospital

Average length of stay is 3-4 days
New Vision, accepts traditional Medicare, and most commercial insurance plans

Alcoholics Anonymous:

After Hours Hotline-
You can call (404) 525-3178 anytime day or night to reach volunteers for help or information on A.A meetings and programs. There are over 1,100 A.A meetings each week in Atlanta

Website: You can find AA meetings and much more at http//www.atlantaaa.org/index.php

Drug & Alcohol Addiction

Call 24/7 Hotline Toll Free 866-752-3207

Cocaine Addiction Hotline 1-800 314-8174

Cocaine Anonymous is a fellowship of men and women who share their experience, strength and hope with each other that they may solve their common problem and help others to recover from their addiction. The only requirement for membership is a desire to stop using cocaine and all other mind-altering substances. There are no dues or fees for membership; we are fully self-supporting through our own contributions. We are not allied with any sect, denomination, politics, organization, or institution.

We do not wish to engage in any controversy and we neither endorse nor oppose any causes. Our primary purpose is to stay free from cocaine and all other mind-altering substances, and to help others achieve the same freedom.
We use the Twelve Step Recovery Program, because it has already been proven that the Twelve Step Recovery Program works.

C.A.'s Purpose

C.A. is concerned solely with the personal recovery and continued sobriety of individual drug addicts who turn to our Fellowship for help. We do not engage in the fields of drug addiction research, medical or psychiatric treatment, drug education, or propaganda in any form — although members may participate in such activities as individuals.

Cocaine Anonymous is open to all persons who state a desire to stop using cocaine, including "crack" cocaine, as well as all other mind-altering substances. There are no dues or fees for membership. Our expenses are supported by the voluntary contributions of our members — we respectfully decline all outside contributions. We are not allied with any sect, denomination, politics, organization or institution.

Our program of recovery was adapted from the program developed by Alcoholics Anonymous in 1935. Like AA (with which we are not affiliated), we use the Twelve Step recovery method, which involves service to others as a path towards recovery from addiction. We feel that one addict talking to another can provide a level of mutual understanding and fellowship that is hard to obtain through other methods. The fact that an individual has recovered from their addiction, and is freely passing this experience on to the next person, is a powerful message for someone who is desperately searching for an answer to their own addiction. There emerges a bond among us that transcends all other social boundaries. We hold regular meetings to further this fellowship, and to allow new members to find us and, perhaps, the answers they seek.

Cocaine Anonymous began in Los Angeles in 1982, and has since expanded throughout the United States and Canada, with groups now forming in Europe. Our literature is available in English, French, and Spanish and our first book "Hope, Faith and Courage: Stories from the Fellowship of Cocaine Anonymous" was published in 1994. As of 1996, we estimated our membership at 30,000 members in over 2,000 groups.

Cocaine Anonymous is a Fellowship of, by, and for addicts seeking recovery. Friends and family of addicts should contact Co-Anon Family Groups, a Fellowship dedicated to their much different needs

Get help now and talk to a counselor

Do you or someone you know have a problem with addiction? Get help you right now. Our amazing program has saved thousands of people from the grips of drug and alcohol addiction to regain a life worth living again.

(866)-752-3207 Our counselors are available anytime day or night to assist you with questions you may have about getting help for yourself or your loved one. We have helped people from all across the United States, Canada and Europe to finally get their lives back.

Narcotics Anonymous

Recommended Readings:

Narcotics Anonymous
It Works: How and Why offers detailed discussion of the twelve steps and traditions and is often called the "green and gold" after its cover.
The *Step Working Guides* is a workbook with questions on each step often called the "Flat Book".

Just For Today is a book of daily meditations with quotes from the Basic Text and other NA approved literature including the "Information Pamphlets".

Sponsorship is an in-depth discussion of the role of sponsorship in NA, including the personal experiences of members.

Miracles Happen describes the early years of the NA organization. This book contains many photographs of early literature and meeting places.

"Living Clean-The Journey Continues"

Additional Resources

Rape, Abuse & Incest National Network-**RAINN**
1-(800) 656-HOPE/4673

Al-Anon Hotline
1-(800) 4Al-ANON/2666
Resources

What does the National Institute on Drug Abuse (NIDA) do?

NIDA is a Federal scientific research institute under the National Institutes of Health, U.S. Department of Health and Human Services. NIDA is the largest supporter of the world's research on drug abuse and addiction. NIDA-funded scientific research addresses the most fundamental and essential questions about drug abuse, including tracking emerging drug use trends, understanding how drugs work in the brain and body, developing and testing new drug treatment and prevention approaches, and disseminating findings to the general public and special populations.

How can I receive educational materials regarding drug abuse?

NIDA produces a variety of educational materials for the general public and healthcare providers. NIDA's materials are available via our website, which houses the NIDA Drug PUBS Research Dissemination Center Drugpubs.drugabuse.gov. Multiple featured publications are listed for downloading and for ordering print copies, along with a lookup feature to access materials on particular drugs, for specific audiences, and within the array of NIDA series. The latter includes:

- NIDAMED Resources for Medical and Health Professionals
- NIDA Notes (Research News and Trends)
- Research Reports on Different Drugs of Abuse and Related Topics
- NIDA DrugFacts for Science-Based Facts on Drug Abuse and Addiction
- Topics in Brief on Various Topics Related to Drugs of Abuse
- NIDA Addiction Science & Clinical Practice, NIDA's Peer-Reviewed Journal

References

SAMHSA- Substance Abuse and Mental Health Services Administration
www.SAMHSA.gov
1 (877) 726-4727

SAMHSA Centers

- The Center for Mental Health Services (CMHS) which focuses on the prevention and treatment of mental disorders.| View Org Chart
- The Center for Substance Abuse Prevention (CSAP) which seeks to prevent and reduce the abuse of illegal drugs, alcohol, and tobacco.
- The Center for Substance Abuse Treatment (CSAT) which supports the provision of effective substance abuse treatment and recovery services.
- The Center for Behavioral Health Statistics and Quality (CBHSQ) which has primary responsibility for the collection, analysis and dissemination of behavioral health data. More information about CBHSQ *(formerly known as OASAS)*

ABOUT THE AUTHOR

Sherry Graves- Author, Survivor and Motivational Speaker:

Scars tell a story. In her book entitled "A FIRE WITHIN-Someone Set the Fire and Left us for Dead", Sherry acknowledges how she has found peace and purpose in the hurts of her past. Scars by their very nature, imply there's a story to tell. They represent a wrinkle in time in which a person's life is changed forever, and they serve as permanent reminders of an incident that, in one way or another, has made a lasting impression on one's life. Each scar represents a moment in time when something happened to us or through us, that we will never forget. Sherry says, I have several scars on my body as a fire survivor, and each has a story to tell. Some people have very painful scars too, but we cannot see them. You know the ones I'm talking about, we all have them. They are the scars on our hearts and in our souls, the scars of rejection, disappointments, the scars of years of abuse and broken dreams.

Sherry says, after reading Sharon Jaynes life changing book "Our Scars Are Beautiful to God" she was finally set free from years of living in fear and bondage, hiding myself, from myself and everyone. We receive scars in one of two ways: What has been done to us by other people or what has been done through us by our own mistakes and failures. It was after reading "Our Scars Are Beautiful to God" that I learned that my scars are not something I need to hide or be ashamed of, but rather an invitation to share the healing power of Jesus Christ with a hurting world. For a scar, by its very definition, implies healing (Jaynes, Sharon 2006).

This book inspired me because I had never looked at the wounds in my life as potential treasures. But after digging deeper, and after I pushed aside all the dirt, I discovered the jewels that lie beneath the surface. Like sparkling diamonds, glistening rubies, and shimmering emeralds, my scars are beautiful to God. I was on an amazing journey to finding the peace that I so desperately needed and "purpose in the pain of my past" and when I did, it changed the course of my entire life.

A former drug-addict/dealer, Sherry has been drug free for the past seventeen years. She shares a powerful Testimony of how God SAVED her life and anointed her to use her tragedy to help others. She says, I'm no longer contributing to the problems in our society, today I am an instrumental part to the solutions. I provide Spiritual Healing, Addiction Education and Drug Awareness to hurting people as my way of giving back to God, myself, my family and my community.

In her book entitled- "A FIRE WITHIN" she explains, my story is so much more than just a story about a former drug addict. The beauty in her journey is, now Sherry has emerged as a successful, dynamic and powerful woman and she gives all the Glory to God with a daily prayer of gratitude. She acknowledges that the fire within her is her passion and gifts which she uses to lift God up, and magnify him because she says, He is so great and awesome. In "A Fire Within" she shares her personal experiences of crack addiction and how someone set the fire and left them for dead. Sherry says, in sharing my testimony, I am very transparent giving my readers a close up look in the life of a drug addict. I have not "sugar coated" any of it. This was done intentionally so as to give Hope to those of you who also are caught up using drugs. I share my "Rock Bottom" experiences with my readers to encourage others that no matter how low we go, God will meet us in our lowest places and pick us up, bring us out and set us on higher ground. What was so profound to me was when I found out that after hitting rock bottom, the only place for me to go, was up.

Today Sherry is "Empowering" women and men, young and old who have substance abuse problems and people who are in need of finding healing from the pains of their past and she is encouraging them that they too can conquer their demons and rise out of that life of self-destruction to emerge as confident, powerful and successful women and men of God. In speaking to thousands of individuals, both throughout her professional career and personally since her tragedy, her passions has been targeting individuals with involvement in the Criminal Justice System, Substance Abuse Programs and in Hospital Settings. She has started her own company-Beyond My Scars (BMS), a Counseling Program for men, women and especially teens, dealing with substance abuse issues, physical, sexual and emotional abuse; catering to individuals in need of healing from trauma.

A Prayer Warrior, Sherry prays for herself, her family, friends, even strangers on the street, in supermarket's, hospitals, and jails, everywhere she can. Her gifts and passion in sharing her testimony has been inspirational in making a difference in the lives of others desperately in need of healing.

Since changing her life seventeen years ago, she has earned a Master's degree in Social Work. She is a member of both the National Association of Social Workers (NASW) and the National Association of Professional Women (NAPW). She is also an International Certified Alcohol and Drug Abuse Counselor. Sherry is a Certified DUI Clinical Evaluator and Treatment Provider and is currently employed in the field of Mental Health and has previously worked for the Drug Court Program(s). She has also worked in Residential Substance Abuse Treatment Programs in New York City as a Substance Abuse Counselor, and she worked at the New York City Department for the Aging, Elderly Crime Victims Resource Center.

Sherry stated, I thank God for Bishop Dale C. Bronner at the Word of Faith Church his teachings have been instrumental in my healing journey. Also, a special thanks to the many other Pastor's, and Ministers who have contributed to my growth and bringing me closer to the Lord. I have come into my own, into this new person and I love her very much and that's so awesome.

ADDITIONAL AUTHOR'S INFORMATION

For more information on **Sherry Graves-MSW, CADC**, please visit www.sherrygravesafirewithin.com

To book, National and International Author, and Motivational Speaker, **Sherry Graves** visit: www.booksherrygraves.com

Email: s1graves@msn.com

"A Fire Within" products available at **Rhonda Knight's Bookstore and More:** www.rhondaknight.com and Tee-Shirts are also available through **Colet-Tees** (tee-shirts): www.colettees.com

To purchase Colet-Tees (tee-shirts), visit: **www.colettees.com** or email: **colettees@gmail.com**

To Book Dee for Entertainment or Catering's,
   email: **deeentertainer4u@aol.com**

Laura B. Pagano uses therapeutic hypnotherapy to help people push past their limitations, break difficult habits, gently dissolve emotions from the past and reach goals. Laura is a Licensed Professional Counselor, Licensed Marriage and Family Therapist, Board Certified Coach, Clinical Hypnotherapist DUI Evaluator and Treatment Provider.
Ready to Outsmart Your Limitations? Contact Laura B. Pagano of **Achievement Strategies, Inc.** at: **www.Achieve-Able.com** 770.998-3881. Email:**LauraPagano@bellsouth.net**

Made in the USA
Charleston, SC
07 August 2012